*"Symbols cannot be invented. Like living beings, they grow and they die. They grow when the situation is ripe for them."*

Paul Tillich

*"The coming age is to be seen as the age of stewardship."*

Henryk Skolimowski

# THE STEWARD

*A Biblical Symbol Come of Age*

Revised Edition

DOUGLAS JOHN HALL

WILLIAM B. EERDMANS PUBLISHING COMPANY
GRAND RAPIDS, MICHIGAN

FRIENDSHIP PRESS
NEW YORK

Dedicated to
Keith Ernest Hall

Copyright © 1990 Commission on Stewardship

Published by Wm. B. Eerdmans Publishing Co.
255 Jefferson Ave. S.E., Grand Rapids, MI 49503
and
Friendship Press
475 Riverside Drive, New York, NY 10115

Printed in the United States of America

*Reprinted, March 1994*

**Library of Congress Cataloging-in-Publication Data**

Hall, Douglas John, 1928–
The steward: a biblical symbol come of age / Douglas John Hall. —
Rev. ed.
    p.      cm.
Includes bibliographical references.
Eerdmans ISBN 0-8028-0472-1
Friendship ISBN 0-377-0214-3
1. Stewardship, Christian.   I. Title.
BV772.H179     1989
248'.6 — dc20                   90-32555
                                      CIP

# CONTENTS

# CONTENTS

# Contents

# CONTENTS

# FOREWORD

In a period of mass media and virtually instantaneous communications, the power of the old-fashioned medium of print is sometimes underestimated, even derided. Thus it brings me considerable pleasure to note that Doug Hall has undertaken to revise his ground-breaking work of 1982. The original edition, which went through four printings, was very well received.

More to the point, *The Steward* has exerted strong influence on Christians and churches in North America and other continents about what it means to be a steward. It is no exaggeration to say that it has changed the way that stewardship executives in many denominations understand and carry out their responsibilities.

The power of the book can be illustrated in my own personal journey. In early 1983, when I was director of educational ministries for a region in my denomination, a colleague brought *The Steward* to my attention. Reading it literally changed my life. The realization that my primary *identity* is that of a steward of the gospel of Jesus Christ took a powerful hold on my life. Later that year, I accepted an invitation to become national director of stewardship services for my denomination. Through that position, it was my privilege to become part of the life and work of the Commission on Stewardship of the National Council of Churches of Christ in the U.S.A. In 1987, I became executive director of the Commission, following the retirement of Nordan C. Murphy.

It is my hope that this revised edition of *The Steward* will help many individuals, congregations, and denominations know and celebrate the joy that comes in the realization of our identity as stewards of the mysteries of God.

Thank you, Doug Hall!

*Commission on Stewardship*                    Ronald E. Vallet
*New York, NY*
*Lent 1989*

# PREFACE TO
# THE REVISED EDITION

Someone has said that books are like children: you may have something to do with bringing them into the world, but then they acquire a life of their own, and you can never predict what they will be.

When I wrote the first edition of this book some eight years ago at the request of the Commission on Stewardship of the National Council of Churches, I had no idea that it would enjoy such an expansive life in the world. Of the dozen or so literary "children" I have begotten, this one has to date gone farthest afield. It has also created a good deal of extra work for its "father," who has been summoned here and there to explain his prodigal. Two independent "study guides" have been written to assist those using the book for group study and other purposes, one in England, and one in the United States.[1] And despite its having found its way into many corners of the earth unknown to its author, the book seems still to be in consid-

---

1. J. Phillips Williams, *A Study Guide for Douglas John Hall's The Steward, A Biblical Symbol Come of Age* (New York: Friendship Press, 1985); and *The Steward: A Biblical Symbol for Today,* abridged by Michael Crowther-Green with study guide by Keith Lamdin (Oxford: The Stewardship Adviser, Diocesan Church House, 1985).

erable demand—which is of course the reason for this revision.

This "revised edition" is quite literally that: it has been completely rewritten and reworked from start to finish. A good deal of new material has been added, and references that were clearly dated have been deleted. The present edition also benefits from the input of a great many other persons. Because this book, along with my two subsequent studies of the stewardship motif,[2] has been the occasion for countless discussions with Christians of many denominations in the United States, Canada, and Western Europe, I have discovered in the process not only new insights but also some of the unanswered questions and inadequately based assumptions of the earlier edition. This does not ensure, of course, that the present work is flawless! No work of Christian theology can measure up to its subject—that is a foregone conclusion of the entire enterprise of this "modest science" (Karl Barth). Yet I know that this edition is not only new but also "improved"—thanks to the contributions of many persons, some of whom are named in the text and notes, most of whom are not.

In the course of seven or eight years, the world changes considerably, and a book of theology which tries—as *The Steward* does—to be in dialogue with its worldly context needs, in its revision, to be especially sensitive to change. For this particular subject, one of the most significant events that have occurred since the book's first appearance in 1982 has been the adoption by the World Council of Churches at its Sixth General Assembly (Vancouver, 1983) of the theme, "Justice, Peace, and the Integrity of Creation." I have myself been privileged to be involved in many of the subsequent sessions of the World Council on this JPIC process, around which the whole work of the Council now revolves. I have therefore incorporated a good deal

2. *The Stewardship of Life in the Kingdom of Death,* rev. ed. (Grand Rapids: Eerdmans, 1985); and *Imaging God: Dominion As Stewardship* (Grand Rapids: Eerdmans, 1986).

of this material into the present revision. It was both natural and necessary to do so because the three-pronged theme (justice, peace, and the issues of the environment) was already anticipated by the first edition of *The Steward* (Chapters VI, VII, and VIII), and the dialogue of the ecumenical church on these same themes could only enhance my earlier reflections.

All the same, it has been a delicate and often difficult operation revising this text. I felt that I had to walk a narrow path between extensive change and the retention of the original scheme and approach. If the first edition filled a certain vacuum in this area, as it appears to have done, I did not want to alter the new edition so entirely that it would fail, perhaps, to fulfil the kinds of expectations engendered by its predecessor. So I have kept both the basic thesis of the first edition and the same format, including chapters, headings, and sub-headings, with only minor alterations in the latter. In this way, it should be possible for persons and groups wishing to use the book for study to assume a rudimentary continuity with the first edition, and to use the study guides already in existence.

Finally, I wish to express to the many American, Canadian, European, and other persons who have helped me expand my own understanding of this subject my sincere thanks. Once again, as with all of my other books, I consider this a work of corporate theology. I am grateful to William B. Eerdmans Publishing Company for inviting me to reissue the book in this form, to my colleagues and students for granting me the freedom to do this, and to my wife and children for their customary intellectual and moral support. The book is dedicated to my brother, Keith, a devoted teacher and a very special kind of steward of his time, talents, and treasures.

Notre-Dame-de-Grace            D.J.H.
*Montreal*
*Lent 1989*

# INTRODUCTION

## 1. Hidden Treasures

In the decade following World War II, a famous German bishop, Hanns Lilje, wrote these words:

> To know that with all that we are and all that we have we are God's stewards is the answer to a particularly deep yearning of the time in which we live, namely, the yearning for a *vita nova*, a complete renewal of our life. Here the insights of our American brethren in the faith have, in the perspective of church history, something like the same significance as the lessons which the German Lutheran Reformation has taught us about justification by grace, or the Communion of the Brethren [Brethren of the Common Life] about the unity of God's children.[1]

Bishop Lilje's observation could be considered a kind of text for what follows in this book. While it is far too generous with respect to North American theological and ecclesiastical practice, it does point to a certain potential for depth in our particular experience of the Christian life. Thirty or forty years after

1. Quoted in T. A. Kantonen, *A Theology for Christian Stewardship* (Philadelphia: Muhlenberg Press, 1956), 1.

---

Lilje wrote these words, however, it is still more a matter of potential than of actuality. And if I wanted to say in a word what I hope to accomplish in this revised version of *The Steward: A Biblical Symbol Come of Age*, I think that I could do no better than to wish that the book might contribute to the further actualization of the potentiality that Bishop Lilje's statement implies.

North American Christianity has not been noted for its theological depth or originality. Ours has been a practical faith, more concerned for the ethical side of the Christian life than for the subtleties of theological investigation or doctrinal distinctions. With few exceptions, theological trends have been set for us by European thinkers and schools (now supplemented by Latin American and other forms of liberationism); and our appropriation of the successive waves of theology emanating from the European mother- and fatherlands has usually involved a notorious simplification and sloganization of their complexities. Apparently in their voyage across the Atlantic—not infrequently with a stopover in the British Isles!—the theological systems devised by Germans and other Europeans are habitually reduced to thin facsimilies of themselves, accentuating what is straightforward and portable.

This theological innocence is rightly decried by many sensitive North American Christians today. There is a growing recognition amongst us that morality always presupposes a foundation in reality; that the imperative will not stand by itself but assumes an articulated indicative; that exhortation indulged in too one-sidedly begets, sooner or later, the question "why?" A faith that is not equipped to express the theological principles upon which its moral values and its practical goals are based is a house without foundations. It may stand while there are no serious assaults upon it; but with the winds of doubt and the storms of social unrest, such a faith must either get foundations or fall to the ground. Moreover, dependency upon the foundations laid for other houses (for European or Latin American theological praxis, for instance) will not suffice. Given the realities of religious pluralism and secular skepticism, North

American Christianity today finds itself compelled—where it is alive to the spirit of the times—to develop a theological rationale for its pragmatically orientated religion; and that rationale must grow out of its own experience, its own suffering, and its own hope.[2]

Paradoxically, however, there are points where the very practicality of Christianity on this continent has helped it to retain contact with aspects of the faith lost to the more theoretically sophisticated provinces of Christendom. It befits those who search today for contextual theological expressions of Christianity in North America to pay particular attention to such points.[3] Christian pragmatism will not be despised altogether by those who remember that "by their fruits you shall know them!" Correct theology by no means guarantees that there will be edible, wholesome "fruits!" Similarly, where the fruits, the consequences of faith, are generally wholesome— even though they may be rather spare and underdeveloped—it is always possible that the faith itself contains capacities for depths of wisdom heretofore uncultivated.

Stewardship practice in North American churches, as I shall argue here, has been underdeveloped, and narrowly conceived. But at least it has been present; and it is just this presence that suggested to Hanns Lilje and other, later European Christians that North American Christians have an important

2. "Today Christianity is involved everywhere in a *double confrontation:* with the great world religions on the one hand and with the non-Christian 'secular' humanisms on the other. And today the question is thrust even on the Christian who has hitherto been institutionally sheltered and ideologically immunized in the churches: compared with the world religions and modern humanisms, is Christianity something essentially different, really something special?" Hans Küng, *On Being a Christian,* trans. Edward Quinn (Glasgow: Wm. Collins' Sons and Co., 1978), 23.

One might say of the entire church in North America that it has been, until now, "institutionally sheltered and ideologically immunized." But since World War II the question Küng here identifies has become our question, too.

3. See in this connection my *Thinking the Faith: Christian Theology in a North American Context* (Minneapolis: Augsburg Fortress Publishers, 1989).

gift of insight to contribute to ecumenical Christianity today. For stewardship is one of the givens of North American church life. Every denomination has its division or department of stewardship. Every congregation contains organizational structures to attend to "the stewardship question." The term "stewardship," at least in Protestant circles, is familiar to every parishioner—for many, far too familiar! (But more of that in a moment.)

Anyone acquainted with European Christianity will realize that this constitutes a marked distinction from the churches of our parental culture. With some exceptions, the concept of stewardship is largely unheard of in Europe. Even ministers and professional theologians are perplexed by this idea that, in our ecclesiastical setting, is understood immediately by ordinary churchgoers, as well as by many who have long since given up going to church. Though the term has been (rather recently) translated into European language equivalents, it remains fundamentally a foreign idea. The average German layperson, for example, is wholly baffled by the word *Haushalterschaft*,[4] so that German scholars and administrators who have become interested in the subject very often employ the English word "stewardship" in the attempt to introduce the concept to their contemporaries.[5]

The retention in North American church life of an important biblical metaphor like stewardship does not of course mean that Christians on this continent have been more faithful to their origins than have Christians in Europe and else-

---

4. *Haushalterschaft* is not a particularly good equivalent for "stewardship." As T. A. Kantonen observes, "The German word *Haushalterschaft* . . . retains too faithfully the economic connotation of the *Oikonomia* of classical Greek. Various substitutes have been offered ranging from *Treuhaenderschaft*, trusteeship, to *Liebesdankbarkeit*, gratitude of love. Each of them expresses some important aspect of stewardship but not its full significance. The disposition today is to give up the search for a new word and either to endow *Haushalterschaft* with a richer meaning or simply to use the English word stewardship." Kantonen, *Christian Stewardship*, 4.

5. E.g., Helge Bratgard, *Im Haushalt Gottes: Eine theologische Studie über Grundgedanken und Praxis der Stewardship* (Berlin: Lutherisches Verlagshaus, 1964).

---

where. It is quite simply a consequence of the necessities that were laid upon us by historical providence. Unlike the European parent churches (not all of them, but the most prominent ones), the churches in North America from the outset have had to fend for themselves. We have not been altogether disestablished, of course; for the forms of our societies both in the United States and Canada have favoured Christianity from the beginnings of the European settlement of the continent. Still, by comparison with European forms of Christian establishment, the churches in North America have been independent, separate, and voluntary organizations, whose members have themselves been directly responsible for their maintenance. With few exceptions, therefore, Christian bodies had to develop structures and programs that encouraged the support of their membership and facilitated their stewardship! Not virtue then, but necessity has been the mother of this invention—as in so many of humanity's nobler achievements. The stewardship idea has been perpetuated in our historical experience because it had to be. Still, it has been perpetuated—a treasure hidden in what is undoubtedly a very earthen vessel.

## 2. The Biblical Metaphor Comes of Age

Taking the biblical view of history as normative, however (consider the Joseph narrative, for instance), one could suppose that what people experience as historical necessity not infrequently turns out to be providential. Their relative disestablishment in the New World caused the Christian denominations of this continent to pay attention to what is, after all, a rather prominent biblical metaphor of the life and vocation of the *koinonia*. During the past century or so, the disestablishment ("humiliation")[6] of the church has become an ever more visible phenom-

---

6. See Albert H. van den Heuvel, *The Humiliation of the Church* (London: SCM Press, 1966).

enon in Western societies—dramatically so in those societies that have been taken over by ideologies hostile to Christianity and religion; less conspicuously, but perhaps all the more effectively, in the affluent societies of the First World.[7] Even Western European churches whose economic and legal position vis-à-vis the state seems altogether secure face a highly uncertain future. In West Germany, the state-collected church tax ensures an exceptionally prosperous church (to the extent that the World Council of Churches' budget relies upon West German Protestantism to the tune of 30 percent).[8] But West German churches are sparsely attended, and nothing but convention and inconvenience stand between the continuation of this form of establishment and the advent of a new and (to many) threatening ecclesiastical poverty. Critical voices within the West German church even suggest that the church itself ought to take initiative in cutting the apron strings with the official culture. But this would of course thrust congregations into a degree of self-reliance for which they are on the whole ill prepared. The experience of several centuries of stewardship practice could, if North American Christians became more reflective about the *meaning* of this practice, be of enormous help to Christians throughout the world who have to make the difficult transition from established to non- or disestablished forms of the Chris-

7. The terminology of First, Second, and Third Worlds will be used throughout this study, despite the fact that it is not an entirely satisfactory terminology. It is widely used, and so, in some sense, common coinage; but it should be understood, of course, that (at least for me) these designations are not value categories. Technically, the "First World" refers to the so-called "developed nations"—those in the North Atlantic region, plus other affluent countries such as Japan, Australia, New Zealand, etc. "Second" refers to Warsaw Pact countries and their allies. "Third" refers to the many countries that are *economically* poor compared to First and Second World countries, but it also includes pockets of poverty in these worlds.

A "Fourth" World is sometimes named. It is described in the text, p. 172.

8. Tracy Early, *Simply Sharing: A Personal Survey of How the Ecumenical Movement Shares Its Resources*, Risk Book Series (Geneva: World Council of Churches, 1980), 33.

tian movement. The church on this continent could turn out to have been a kind of pilot project in post-Constantinian Christianity in this respect at least—or a stage on the way.

This, in part, is what Hanns Lilje's statement about the significance of stewardship practice on the part of "our American brethren" implies. As a survivor of Hitler's Germany, Bishop Lilje knew well enough that the church had to move out into a new realm of freedom from the dominant culture if it were ever to make good its calling to be a prophetic voice in God's world. Such freedom could not be had by a church that continued to rely upon established power for its rudimentary support. Stewardship in the North American experience is significant, therefore, not merely as a managerial technique for funding the church's life and work, but as a dimension of a new understanding of the church as such. What North American Christians have to contribute has, for Lilje, a high significance because stewardship practice is in effect the most visible side of a whole alternative image of the church.

The text and context of Lilje's statement indicate, however, that the well-known churchman and theologian was not thinking only of the church when he entertained these thoughts. He writes with the knowledge of a sensitive European at the end of a time of devastation and nihilism; and as such a one he knows, as did many of his contemporaries, that nothing but a new appreciation for the worth and wonder of life could deliver Western humanity from its own self-destructive impulses. Just as Luther's vision of a justifying grace through faith enabled people in an age of anxiety over "eternal guilt and condemnation" (Tillich) to find the courage to go on, so, Lilje is affirming, the sense of being stewards of earth and of life itself could provide a generation of world-weary and apathetic survivors some feeling of purpose.

In the decades that have elapsed since Lilje's provocative statement, his assumptions both about the church and the world have been amply confirmed by events. The church has almost everywhere found itself being edged out of the center of the establishment—though many militant Christians still labor hard to reinstate it![9] As for the world, we know by now that the state of chaos and panic that broke out in two World Wars during the first half of this century, with its accompanying moods of violence on the one hand and apathy on the other, cannot be regarded as unusual. War has been the hallmark of this whole century. It is calculated that the period since 1945, regularly trumpeted by advocates of "peace through strength" to have been an epoch of unprecedented peace, has in reality witnessed no less than 130 wars.[10] Beyond that, we are conscious of living under the shadow of a future catastrophe, whether war or something else, that could put an end to all that our foundational traditions meant by "civilization."

This "future shock" has produced, predictably enough, exaggerated forms of withdrawal from public life and responsibility. In the still affluent world of the North Atlantic nations, human beings seek comfort in the narcissistic cultivation of the private life, leaving the future to forces that are as indifferent to the quality of life as they are "leaderless" (Martin Buber). While minorities in First World societies yearn for "a complete renewal of our life" (Lilje), many of our contemporaries "flee from the wrath to come" by cultivating a programmed indifference to the larger and longer destiny of earth. Kurt Vonnegut, that incognito prophet of American letters, details this social phenomenon better than anyone I know in his 1985 novel, *Galapagos*. Writing from the perspective of an imaginary society one million years from now, he notes that

> There is another human defect which the Law of Natural Selection has yet to remedy: When people of today have full bellies, they are exactly like their ancestors of a million years ago: very slow to acknowledge any awful troubles they may be in. Then is

9. See my *The Future of the Church: Where Are We Headed?* (Toronto: United Church Publishing House, 1989).

10. Carl-Friedrich von Weizsäcker, *Die Zeit drängt: Eine Weltversammlung der Kirchen für Gerechtigkeit, Frieden, und die Bewahrung der Schöpfung* (Munich: Carl Hanser Verlag, 1986), 38.

when they forget to keep a sharp lookout. . . . This was a particularly tragic flaw a million years ago, since the people who were best informed about the state of the planet . . . and rich and powerful enough to slow down all the waste and destruction going on, were by definition well fed. So everything was always just fine as far as they were concerned. For all the computers and measuring instruments and news gatherers and evaluators and memory banks and libraries and expertise on this and that at their disposal, their deaf and blind bellies remained the final judges of how urgent this or that problem, such as the destruction of North America's and Europe's forests by acid rain, say, might really be.[11]

Both those who yearn for renewed commitment to life and (by way of negation!) those who have given up on public life point to the need for a new way of conceiving of human being and vocation. For it is not some external malfunctioning of historical and natural processes by which we are endangered, it is ourselves. As Jürgen Moltmann said about the crisis of the biosphere, "What we call the environmental crisis is not merely a crisis in the natural environment of human beings. It is nothing less than a crisis in human beings themselves."[12] The only adequate response to the great physical and spiritual problems of our historical moment is for the human inhabitants of the planet to acquire, somehow, a new way of imagining themselves. Just in that connection, "the steward" is one of the most provocative as well as historically accessible concepts to contemplate for anyone who cares about the destiny of our civilization.

What is so encouraging—and for Christians of conscience at the same time so humbling—is that the articulation of this concept as a timely image of the human is today being voiced more insistently, and often more imaginatively, by those

11. Kurt Vonnegut, *Galapagos* (New York: Delacorte Press/Seymour Lawrence, 1985), 129.

12. Jürgen Moltmann, *God in Creation: A New Theology of Creation and the Spirit of God*, trans. Margaret Kohl, Gifford Lectures, 1984-1985 (San Francisco: Harper and Row, 1985), xi.

outside the churches and their theological guilds than by Christians themselves. We shall have occasion later to elaborate on this theme, but for the moment we may just notice in passing a movement within an important wing of the scientific community which is being styled "deep ecology" or "ecophilosophy." One of its advocates writes:

> Ecological Humanism offers an authentic alternative to industrial society. It holds that:
>
> (1) **The coming age is to be seen as the age of stewardship:** we are here not to govern and exploit, but to maintain and creatively transform, and to carry on the torch of evolution.
>
> (2) **The world is to be conceived of as a sanctuary:** we belong to certain habitats, which are the source of our culture and our spiritual sustenance. These habitats are the places in which we, like birds, temporarily reside; they are sanctuaries in which people, like rare birds, need to be taken care of. They are sanctuaries also in the religious sense: places in which we are *awed by the world*; but we are also the priests of the sanctuary: we must maintain its sanctity and increase its spirituality.
>
> (3) **Knowledge is to be conceived of as an intermediary between us and the creative forces of evolution,** not as a set of ruthless tools for atomizing nature and the cosmos but as ever more subtle devices for helping us to maintain our spiritual and physical equilibrium and enabling us to attune ourselves to further creative transformations of evolution and of ourselves.[13]

This deployment of the metaphor of stewardship (not to speak of all the other religious language which permeates this statement) rather astonishes and even unsettles some Christians. Here is the world using our language, our term! And this one quotation is only one of countless similar pronouncements coming from strange quarters, especially the so-

---

13. Henryk Skolimowski, *Eco-Philosophy: Designing New Tactics for Living* (London: Marion Boyars, 1981), 54.

called life sciences. We had grown accustomed to scientists who were opposed in principle to all religion. Many of us spent a good deal of time in our high school and college days listening to debates about "science vs. religion." Of course, there are still some vestiges of all that, but they do not predominate. Now we are hearing a different tune altogether. The scientists who are most keen to engage religion are not ready to let religion— notably Christianity—off the hook; but they stage their quarrel with religion along lines very different from those that pertained in the 1940s and 1950s. Their main complaint about Christianity, the dominant religion of the world that gave us modern science and the technological society, is that it went along with the technocratic mentality of the Western world all too uncritically. Indeed, they are saying, it gave to modernity the spiritual wherewithal that it needed for its attack upon the natural world. "Have dominion! Subdue!" The implicit if not explicit criticism of the Christian religion amongst such critics, in short, is that it failed to be prophetic! It was content to undergird, confirm, and conform!

We shall return to this presently, but what is significant for our notice at the moment is that when these same scientific critics of religion cast about for any good that might have come out of Nazareth, they point with uncanny frequency to the concept of stewardship. Here, they tell us, is an image of the human that, if it were pursued with some imagination and seriousness, could offset some of the bad effects of a religion that made too much of humankind's unwarranted superiority to the natural world.

In short, the stewardship tradition, which is rooted in biblical religion and has of necessity been retained in the experience of North American Christianity, has come of age. The ancient metaphor of the tradition of Jerusalem has become a vital contemporary symbol, one that could help a disillusioned and threatened civilization find a *vita nova*, to use Hanns Lilje's apt term—a new life. Both church and society stand in need of precisely such a renovating self-conception. Stewardship refers to a mode of being sorely needed by an ecumenical Christian movement that can no longer count (thank God!) on being the darling of power. That mode of being is even more badly needed by a world that has fallen into the clutches of mindless and inherently destructive forces.

Logically therefore, one could suppose that the Christian church in North America, with several centuries of experience in stewardship praxis, would, under these circumstances, find itself in a position of something like expertise. But in fact we do not and cannot feel such confidence in ourselves. Our practice of stewardship has not, after all, given us the wisdom that we need in order to make the kind of contribution that Lilje and others anticipate from us. What stands in its way?

### 3. The Truncation of the Concept

At this point we must try to be quite honest with ourselves. It is true that stewardship has been retained in our New World Christianity; but it is equally true that it has been retained in a form that scarcely lends itself to the larger meaning and usage we need today. What we have by way of stewardship in our churches is in fact a drastically reduced version of the biblical concept.

It would perhaps be kinder to say that it is a purely functional appropriation of the biblical metaphor. That is, for the majority of churchgoers stewardship signifies a way of thinking about (one could almost say of rationalizing!) the acquisition and management of ecclesiastical monies and properties. Stewardship as means. One tries to inculcate a sense of stewardship in congregations so that the church might get on with its "real" work. The end in relation to which stewardship is means is something spiritual and noble. Often, this end is described as the church's "mission," and mission is contrasted with stewardship. Stewardship is cultivated in the congregational life in order that the mission might be carried on. Stewardship is the material means by which the spiritual end is achieved.

This approach has had very questionable consequences for stewardship theology. It in fact makes it extremely difficult to raise the stewardship metaphor to the level of a holistic symbol within the average congregation. So thoroughly is the term associated with church management and finances; so demeaned is it by the implicitly unfavorable comparison with the spiritual end (mission) for which it is only the means, that it will require a great deal of critical thought and work to bring the stewardship idea to the prominence that its biblical background warrants and the times demand. If, as we have suggested above, the world is today more apt than the church to find the idea of the steward provocative, it is largely, I suspect, because in the churches the metaphor has been relegated to a strictly operational status.

More than that, for many people in and on the edges of the churches stewardship is a word that conjures up very negative feelings. It would not be an exaggeration, I think, even to say that stewardship has a distasteful connotation for the majority of churchfolk, including clergy. It brings to mind the horrors of home visitations, building projects, financial campaigns, and the seemingly incessant harping of the churches for more money. Ministers cringe at the mention of Stewardship Sundays: must they really lower themselves to the status of fundraisers once more? Must they again play the role of a Tetzel?[14]

We should not back away from this aspect of our subject. If it is true that stewardship is held in some kind of disrepute by Christians themselves, then we would be ill-advised to try to redeem it until this reality has been squarely faced. The point was brought home to me forcibly by the testimony of members of the stewardship committee of an Anglican diocese in Canada. They had devised a method for letting

14. Johann Tetzel (1465-1519) was a Dominican monk noted for his persuasiveness as a seller of indulgences at the time of the Reformation. He caused much controversy because of his crass commercialism, and was particularly ridiculed by Luther.

these negative feelings about stewardship surface. In their visitation of parishes, they first distributed blank slips of paper and asked those present to write down the first words that came to their minds when they heard the word "stewardship." The responses obtained in this way astonished even the more skeptical members of the committee. Such words as the following (and some others that I dare not cite in this context!) frequently appeared: "money"; "not again!"; "Oh, no!"; "collection plate"; "dammit!"[15]

The demeaning of stewardship is even built into the organizational structures of many churches. The practice of dividing the work of the congregation into matters handled by the session or elders ("spiritual" items) and, on the other hand, by the board of stewards or its equivalent ("material" matters) has happily been abandoned in favor of unified boards of management in many denominations. Yet the thinking that expressed itself in such divisions has by no means disappeared. Few of us would say so openly, but there is a kind of tacit understanding that those persons appointed to stewardship offices in congregations and denominational headquarters are often rather less than fully spiritual Christians. They are not required to manifest the same seriousness of Christian conviction or theological learning as persons closer to the core, the "real workers." After all, their task is directly associated with the means, not the end. The qualifications we look for in them are not learning or piety but the kinds of talents admired in the business and professional world—which are often frankly despised by the truly spiritual people. They should be good at business, and have a knack for public relations, promotional activities, and the like. Often, such persons are secretly (sometimes not so secretly) scorned. Often they suffer acutely because they know they are scorned.

15. Geo. S. Siudy in an article entitled "Stewardship and Renewal in the Church," reports that one third of the ninety persons he questioned about stewardship ("What is Stewardship?") expressed negative feelings: "The word triggers in me an unbearable sense of duty and guilt. When I hear the word I want to run," said one of these. *Journal of Stewardship* 34 (1981): 7.

Even where it is held in higher esteem, however, stewardship as it is practiced among us seldom rises above this reductionist form. Far from standing for a basic orientation to the world or even a major image of the life and work of the church, stewardship is regarded as a kind of optional ethic for the enthusiastic churchman or -woman. People consider good stewardship something private and vaguely ascetic—the second mile gone by the more zealous church members. Tithing! Or perhaps it is held as a more or less acceptable rhetorical sentiment ("We are stewards of all that we have"). Rarely does one encounter Christians for whom the metaphor represents a kind of summing-up of the meaning of the Christian life. It is just possible that today one would be able to find more people outside the churches who are beginning to think of stewardship in holistic terms than one finds inside of them.

Such a prospect is not a happy one, because as long as stewardship carries negative connotations for churchgoers it is inaccessible for the greater purposes to which it could and should be put today by Christians. More than that, it is even possible that unless it can achieve a more expansive and imaginative significance it will not even serve for very much longer the functional goals that it has been assigned in the past. There is no reason why stewardship should not also have to do with church finances and management. But if it has *only* to do with these material and self-consciously ecclesiastical matters, then it will not even serve such purposes adequately for very much longer.

The reason is clear enough. Significant numbers of persons in generations before ours could be moved by appeals to tithing, giving, and service because it was part of the fabric of their society. It was taken for granted that ministers should be paid salaries, and buildings built and kept up, and organists hired, and missions supported, etc.; and it was therefore assumed that these things had to be paid for by those who believed in them. But none of this is automatic now. There are still exceptions; for the most part, however, if people in or on the periphery of present-day Christian parishes are told that they should give of their time, talents, and treasures, they want to know why. "Shoulds" and "musts" and "oughts" no longer stand alone. There is nothing in the social or ecclesiastical atmosphere to buttress them. Stewardship, even in the congregation and even at the level of basic finances, must from now on find its rationale at the heart of the faith, as an essential aspect of belief: part of the end-purpose, and not merely a means to some ill-defined and nebulous spiritual goal.

## 4. Enlarging Stewardship through Theological Praxis

The preceding critique of the stewardship practices of North American churches should not be read as though its author finds this long history of stewardship, after all, unhelpful or a mere impediment. It is my strong conviction (and it is made stronger by the frequent opportunities I have had in recent years of observing European forms of Christianity which lacked the stewardship tradition) that stewardship constitutes a special and unique charism of North American Christianity. In saying this I do not mean to boast in behalf of the churches of this continent, because it is not as if stewardship is a particular work of ours. It is a gift—a charism—made possible, as I argued earlier, by the very necessities under which we have lived. It is not simply a by-product of our New World inventiveness and enterprise; it is part and parcel of the grace that has been granted us.[16]

The object of these reflections, in that case, is not to make us ashamed of our past by dwelling upon our misuse of the gift, but to discern how we might better use it. It is true that

---

16. I owe this distinction partly to the late W. A. Visser 't Hooft, who, in a World Council of Churches publication, writes: "The word talent suggests an aptitude with which we were born. But a *charisma* [charism] is a gift which belongs to our second nature [i.e., to the 'new birth']." "The Economy of the Charismata and the Ecumenical Movement," in *Empty Hands: An Agenda for the Churches* (Geneva: WCC, 1980), 32.

we have buried this treasure in the financial departments of our churches, and have so domesticated the biblical concept that we have lost sight of its truly radical implications. Yet the intention of this study is not to chastise our institutions for having been unworthy stewards of the stewardship idea itself, but rather to remind us all of the breadth and depth of this ancient piece of wisdom about the human vocation. What we have been harboring in our midst (hiding under our collection plates!) is in fact a pearl of great price. Our task is the elevation and enlarging of the stewardship concept. In its present state, it exists among us as something dormant, almost harmless—a matter of bookkeeping and housekeeping! We have made of this quite revolutionary idea an old shoe that pinches nobody's foot. All the same, it does exist among us, and as a term that is familiar, something of our own, something to build upon.

Of course, building on earlier foundations always involves a bit of tearing down—as Jeremiah well knew when he wrote that God had commissioned him—

> to pluck up and to break down
> to destroy and to overthrow
> to build and to plant. (1:10)

Building upon existing foundations can only be sound and lasting if the infirm aspects of the old foundations are recognized and the rubble set aside. Theology always contains this critical element with regard to the past. For it must not be done simply out of respect for that past, but out of concern for the present and future. The traditions of stewardship that we have inherited are not the best of foundations. They are in many ways problematic. Still, they are better than having no foundations at all. The question is, how shall we benefit from these foundations, using the material that is there at hand, but not simply ignoring the flaws in its construction?

What we are really asking for is a methodology for the study of stewardship. We need a method that does justice to the fact that there has been a long history of stewardship practice among us in the North American churches, and that at the same time enables us to discover the depth of meaning in this ancient biblical metaphor that can both enlarge our comprehension and redirect our practice.

This need has led me to think that we might learn from the approach taken in many circles today, and especially associated with Third World liberation theology.[17] This approach distinguishes between theory-plus-practice, on the one hand, and on the other what is called praxis. The conventional pattern in theology, as in many other disciplines, has been first to enunciate a theory (as in biblical or systematic theology) and then to apply it (ethics, practical theology, etc.). The assumption hidden in this procedure is that thought about reality can occur more authentically and profoundly if it is removed from act, involvement, and practice; that the proper order of things is first knowing and then doing. Praxis thinking challenges this time-honored practice of Western Christianity. It insists that thinking that occurs apart from involved participation regularly entails an ideological taint, and it suggests that far too much theory represents what is in fact a flight from the real world. Praxis is thought emerging in deed and deed evoking thought. To quote from a document which came out of important discussions between North American and Latin American theologians—

> Thinking is not now considered prior or superior to action; rather, it takes place in action. The Christian religion was founded not on a word, but on the Word made Flesh. Faith is no longer simply "applied" or completed in action, but for its very understanding (and this is theology) faith demands that it be discovered in action.
>
> It is necessary to relate Christian theory and historical practice, faith and praxis. Some theologians are talking of a theology defined as critical reflection on historical praxis. Practice refers to any action that applies a particular theory. Praxis is practice as-

17. See in particular Gustavo Gutierrez, "Theology as Critical Reflection on Praxis," in A Theology of Liberation, trans. Sister Caridad Inda and John Eagleson (Maryknoll, N.Y.: Orbis Books, 1973), 6-15.

sociated with a total dynamics of historical vision and social transformation. Through praxis, people enter into their historical
destiny. Since praxis changes the world as well as the actors it becomes the starting point for a clearer vision of God in history.[18]

The pertinence of this distinction for our study of
stewardship will become evident, I think, if the thoughts expressed in our opening paragraphs are brought to mind once
more here. As North American Christians, it was said, we have
not been a theologically original or profound province of the ecumenical church. Our preoccupation has been with the act, the
deed, or the practice of the faith. Combining this with the next
assertion of those opening paragraphs (namely, that sensitive
and thinking Christians on this continent are now conscious of
the shallowness of a pragmatic faith that lacks a theological
foundation), it would be logical to leap to the conclusion, in considering what method we should adopt here, that what is needed
now is a sound theology of stewardship. This is indeed how
many in the churches, including many who have responsibilities for stewardship programs, are expressing our current need.
What is wanted, they affirm, is a sound theoretical basis for the
practice of stewardship—something that would lift it out of the
merely functional and institutional morass and give it the dignity and directedness of the best Christian thinking.

There is certainly much truth in this assumption. It is
even, in a real sense, the implicit direction in which I have been
moving in this Introduction.

But there is a temptation here too, and a very serious one.

18. Sergio Torres and John Eagleson, eds., *Theology in the Americas*
(Maryknoll, N.Y.: Orbis Books, 1976), 435.
There is of course a certain danger in praxis-theology as in every other
theological method. In this case it is that those who are intellectually lazy or
constitutional activists will welcome such an emphasis as a way of avoiding serious theoretical reflection. Against all such, the words of C. F. von Weizsäcker
are to the point: "Anyone neglecting to further his theoretical understanding of
our complex world as much as he can, will in the longrun do more harm than
good in his practical efforts." *The Relevance of Science: Creation and
Cosmogony*, Gifford Lectures, 1959-1960 (London: Collins, 1964), 9.

The danger is pinpointed by the distinction between theory-plus-practice, and praxis. Let me put it this way: It would be quite possible to elaborate a fine theology of stewardship that took no real account of the fact that there had been for some centuries a long experience of stewardship practice in our own midst. That practice has, as we have duly recognized, its real limitations, drawbacks, and impediments. Yet, as we also acknowledged from the outset, it has been the historical vehicle through which a lively image has been at least kept in the stream of dialogue, and in a manner in which this did not happen in the more theoretical forms of the Christian faith in the European settings. Somehow, our current thinking about stewardship has to incorporate and draw upon that experience, that practice. Praxis means that our reflection upon the theological meaning of stewardship should involve not a withdrawal from its practice, but rather a critical reflection on historical practice. A purely theoretical approach to the subject could end by ignoring altogether the lessons that can be learned from our own past, imaginatively and critically revisited.

Accordingly, this present study will consciously attempt to be an exercise in theological praxis. That is, in combining biblical, historical, critical, and constructive theological reflection, it will endeavour to think about stewardship in such a way as to help others to enter into their historical destiny. The charism that we have been carrying about in these imperfect earthen vessels of our ecclesiastical past and present may prove newly potent, if reexamined in the light of its possible future use. It was in anticipation of such a possibility that already in the initial paragraphs of this statement I wrote that theological praxis, as distinct from theory alone, must mean reflecting upon our historical experience with sufficient imagination and spirit to wrest from it its deeper meaning—the meaning that, perhaps, only a future moment could fully evoke.

Elsewhere, I have expressed this through an illustration. Visiting a Canadian farmhouse attic once, I came across a beautiful picture, an antique of the nineteenth century that had been shunted off to the attic by an earlier generation of the family, whose members were presumably ashamed of its old-fashioned lines and theme. The family presently living in the old country mansion either did not know about the picture or else was unaware that, in the meantime, such items were in great demand in fashionable city antique stores. The picture was in fact worth far more now than it had originally cost.

Ideas sometimes suffer a similar fate. Our theological "idea attic" is full, and some of its contents truly are useless, even worthless! But there are others—a few at any rate—that are worth more now than they were originally, because in the meantime things have happened to evoke their great importance and profundity. Stewardship is, in my view, one of these ideas. It has been more or less relegated to the attic (or the basement!) by congregations that have grown ashamed and weary of it. But in the meantime events and attitudes have developed within our world that make it priceless!

To complete the comparison, however, one should conclude that the best Christian thinking in response to those current events and emergent attitudes would surely not now ignore the picture that was shipped off to the attic. Rather such thinking would be a spirited remembering of that picture, dusting it off, refurbishing the frame, bringing it to light—in short, discovering the beauty and appropriateness that was in it all along, waiting for its proper moment to arrive.[19]

## 5. Ordering Our Reflections

We shall try to order our thought in the subsequent sections of this book in such a way as to do justice to these methodological considerations. To begin with, we shall consider the biblical

19. See my booklet, *This World Must Not Be Abandoned!—Stewardship: Its Worldly Meaning,* published by five Canadian denominations: Anglican, Lutheran, Presbyterian, Roman Catholic, and the United Church of Canada, 1981.

background of the stewardship theme—not as an exercise in biblical exegesis alone, but in order to rethink the origins of an idea that has become symbolically viable in our present context. (In terms of the above illustration, we could think of this as the necessary trip to the attic.)

Second, we shall consider the historical evolution of the stewardship idea. What was the fate of this biblical metaphor? What explanation can be found for the fact that it did not flourish in the way that might have been the case? (Why was it hurried off to the attic?)

Having in the first two chapters considered the subject from the perspective of biblical and historical theology, we shall attempt, third, an exercise in critical theology: first (Chapter III) in terms of engaging in a cultural analysis; second (Chapter IV) with a view to identifying the primary religious impediment to a gospel in which stewardship is a major theme. The first part of this exercise in critical theological thought is necessary because without attempting to discern the signs of the times, difficult as that always is, it is impossible to identify the contextual circumstances that have evoked and enriched the old idea. (*Why* has the old picture becomes a valuable antique? What social forces have been at work to create this new assessment of the old reality?) Theology, Karl Barth once quipped, means having the Bible in one hand and the newspaper in the other. Already in reflecting on the biblical background of stewardship we shall have had the newspaper in our other hand; the separation of content in chapters cannot and should not indicate anything more than a matter of convenience—ordering. But in this third chapter we shall have to become more explicit about matters already anticipated in the biblical and historical discussions of the earlier chapters. Hence Chapter III will attempt to delineate the realities inherent in our present context that make stewardship a ripe idea.

The second part of our exercise in critical theology (Chapter IV) is more concerned with the church than with the world. The argument here will seek to identify the underlying reasons why historical Christianity has been hesitant to pick up and use the metaphor of the steward. It is my conviction (to anticipate) that behind this hesitancy there is a much more serious ambiguity—an ambiguity running through the length and breadth of our Christian thinking about the gospel, and about our mission. Only if that deeper hesitancy can be pinpointed (why were we so embarrassed about the old picture as to ship it to the attic?) will it then be possible to evolve a stewardship praxis that is more than a shadow of the biblical metaphor. Critical theology becomes constructive theology at the point where that degree of honesty and self-discovery has been reached.

Accordingly, Chapter V will attempt a constructive theological statement about the meaning of stewardship in our present context. And, since such a statement (according to the methodology we have opted for) could not legitimately be a merely theoretical one, it will be followed directly by three chapters (VI, VII, and VIII) that are attempts to speak quite explicitly to some of the most urgent issues of that context—issues whose destiny could be altered by a stewardship praxis that had become newly aware and obedient.

There is of course no end to the specific problems which such praxis could and should address. Stewardship is a holistic image of human and Christian vocation; it is universally applicable. But in certain areas of our contemporary problem the metaphor of the steward has very direct application. In the first edition of this book, published in 1982, I identified these as (1) the First World / Third World (or North / South) Problem; (2) the Problem of the Human Relation to Nature, and (3) the Problem of War and Peace. It was very gratifying, therefore, when a year later the World Council of Churches (WCC) at its Sixth General Assembly in Vancouver adopted as its overall theme for the next decade: "Justice, Peace and the Integrity of Creation"—precisely the three areas which to me demanded the attention of serious Christians. In the present revision, therefore, I shall draw upon subsequent documents of the WCC relating to these themes. My purpose in these chapters will not be to exhaust the meaning of the concept of stewardship, but to illustrate something of its universal relevance by dwelling explicitly on these overarching issues.

Finally (Chapter IX), I shall attempt something that theologians probably should leave to their betters by trying to answer this question: What does all this have to do with the living of stewardship in congregations, including the management and financing of their work? I do not intend here to work out a theology of Christian bookkeeping! But if it is true (as I have so boldly asserted above) that stewardship has also to do with budgets and investments and the acquisition and use of properties, and with the church's whole mission, then I must show at least in outline what the enlarged view of stewardship might mean for Christian praxis. Such presumptuousness must be risked, for the alternative is another exercise in the kind of Docetism that I have decried above, i.e., the unwarranted division of the Christian life into spiritual and material, the sacred and the secular, or Sunday and everyday.

# CHAPTER I

# BIBLICAL SOURCES
# OF THE SYMBOL

## 1. Introduction: Who Is *Adam*?

We begin with the Bible, not simply out of reverence for its authority, but because the steward concept has its origins in these scriptural writings. I know that certain parallels may be found in other ancient religious and mythic sources;[1] but for our own tradition, the biblical background is the most immediately relevant and necessary. And what is particularly significant in this background is that Scripture's steward metaphor is both a major theme and one which has direct application to the question of human identity and vocation.

This is of course due to the whole manner in which, in these Scriptures, human identity is bound up with God on the one hand, and all the rest of creation on the other. For the biblical way of defining human being is from first to last relational.[2] We are who we are, and as we are perceived, in rela-

---

1. I am indebted for this information to Professor John H. P. Reumann. See his "The Use of 'Oikonomia' and Related Terms in Greek Sources to About A.D. 100, As a Background for Patristic Applications" Ph.D. diss., University of Michigan, 1957.

2. For a systematic development of the relational character of human

tion to the others with whom we live, move, and have our being.

Following this scriptural lead, then, one is not justified in separating humanity off from the others and asking about the character of the human being in isolation. This being has its being—no, receives its being—as it stands in relationship with God and with its own kind and with "otherkind" (i.e., non- or extra-human creatures). The steward is a particularly apt metaphor for humanity because it encapsulates the two sides of human relatedness, the relation to God on the one hand and to the nonhuman creatures of God on the other. The human being is, as God's steward, accountable to God and responsible for its fellow creatures.

The Bible is of course full of metaphoric, as well as more literal and even technical, attempts to capture what the tradition of Jerusalem understands by humanity. From a simple tableau like that of Adam as the namer of the other animals to complex ideas like the Old and New Testaments' concepts of priesthood, one finds these ancient writings preoccupied with the question, "who *is* this creature?" What is the essence of this strange, speaking animal? This is, in a real sense, the Bible's primary question. Or, more precisely, it is an integral part of the primary question of these texts. The other part, from which this question is inseparable, is of course the question about God. The two questions, as Calvin demonstrates at the very outset of his *Institutes of the Christian Religion*,[3] are really two aspects of a single question—which is why Karl Barth insisted that in Christian faith we do not have to do only with theology but with "theoanthropology."[4]

---

being and of all being in biblical thought, see my *Imaging God: Dominion as Stewardship* (Grand Rapids: Eerdmans, 1986).

3. John Calvin, *Institutes of the Christian Religion*, trans. Ford Lewis Battles, rev. ed. (Grand Rapids: Eerdmans, 1975), chap. 1.

4. "Strictly speaking . . . the word 'theology' fails to exhaust the meaning of 'evangelical theology,' for one decisive dimension of the object of theology is not expressed clearly in it. This dimension is the free love of God that evokes the response of free love, his grace *(charis)* that calls for gratitude

---

As the Bible's question, the question about humanity is not an abstract one. It is not the question of either the natural or the social sciences, or of any objective research. The identity and vocation—the *telos* (inner aim)—of humanity is for the writers of these texts an intensely existential inquiry. Always behind the parables, metaphors, images, and theological wrestlings with the nature of this creature there is the Bonhoefferian question, "Who am *I*?" The great concern of the writer of Psalm 8 ("What is the human creature, that thou art mindful of it?") is not the interrogation of a dispassionate observer of human nature. It is the plea of a being who knows that in the universal scheme of things he or she is mediocre and vulnerable indeed; and yet what a great and glorious wonder!

Those who consider that the Bible wants to discuss only the wonder and glory of *God* fail to grasp the primary motivating thrust behind the whole biblical enterprise, including its rather modest attempts to depict God. It is the fact of existence itself that these writers cannot get over. And that does not mean existence in the abstract, but their existence—the existence of Israel, the people that had been no people; the existence of the church—a body that had been nobody; the existence of the world itself—a *creatio ex nihilo* (creation out of nothing) wherein conscious creatures continue to be aware of the "nothing" out of which they and all things were formed.

To be human is above all, for this literature, to "ask about being."[5] It is to be a creature who knows that its being is not self-explanatory but a riddle. It is to feel kinship with the dust as well as with the many beings who do not apparently ask about their being and do not manifest fear of being. Yet this being also knows that it cannot find comfort in its own sheer animality, for it feels within itself a yearning and a potential that makes it

---

(*eucharistia*). 'Theoanthropology' would probably express better what is at stake here." *Evangelical Theology*, trans. Grover Foley (New York: Holt, Rinehart & Winston, 1963), 12.

5. Paul Tillich, *Biblical Religion and the Search for Ultimate Reality* (Chicago: University of Chicago Press, 1955), 11ff.

"restless" (Augustine) and never content with the joys of the body alone.

It is remarkable about these ancient texts that they manifest such deep-seated curiosity about humanity. They are after all religious writings, and we automatically assume that this means that everything is directed towards the eternal. But these writings question this assumption. The truth is (and it is quite astonishing, considering the usual bent of religious literature) that it is not possible to find in these Scriptures of Israel and the church any independent interest in God. There is no speculation, as the Greek philosophers and others have speculated, about deity itself. God's existence or nonexistence, God's perfection or attributes, or God's inner life: this kind of strictly theological preoccupation does not belong to these writings. God appears from the outset—in the very first sentence of Genesis—as Creator. And in the subsequent sagas, poems, and proverbs, and historical and theological reflections of these Scriptures, God is always God in relation to creation; therefore God is Judge, Redeemer, Lord, Saviour, etc. God is the counterpart—the answer to the question that humanity *is*. And it is strictly in keeping with this tradition's inseparability of God and humanity that this answer appears more often in the guise of the questioner: "Where art thou, Adam?" (Gen. 3); "Where were *you* when I laid the foundations of the earth?" (Job 38); "Who do people say . . . who do you say that I am?" (Matt. 16). The question of God's being is immediately transmuted into the question of human being, because the two questions are two parts of a single, larger question.

The Bible knows with great precision and depth the most prominent answers that human beings have given and, with infinite variations on recurring themes, continue to give to the persistent question of their own being, purpose, and destiny. It knows on the one hand the exalted images that Homo sapiens has created for itself: that we are gods, or demigods, or superhumans; that we are in control of our own fates, full of infinite potential for greatness and answerable to no one; that we are first amongst the creatures, or perhaps tragic figures whose unfortunate bondage to the dust and the flesh prevents us from achieving the high destiny of our immortal spirits, etc. It is also aware, on the other hand, of our strange delight in demeaning and degrading ourselves—of the brand of answers to our existential questions that depict us as low, beastial, wormlike, meaningless, or pathetic: humanity as "a useless passion," "a sexual twitch" (Sartre), a "nihilistic thought in the mind of God" (Kafka). The Bible rejects both of these images of the human, both the high and the low, the promethean and the sisyphean. Because its faith is a matter of trust and not adherence to a fixed and inflexible conception of reality, it will not settle for any versions of anthropology, exalted or degraded, in which there can be no surprises, everything having been determined in advance. Against the frequent human attempt to "think more highly of ourselves than we ought" it places the great "I Am" of its Yahweh—and we know again that we are dust. Against the equally frequent human attempts to hide in our frailty and bemoan our finitude, it presents a God who calls us to stand on our feet and be God's covenant partners in the sustaining and enhancing of life.

And so these writings abound in terms, similies, analogies, metaphors, etc., that try to do justice to the great conundrum of human being. And if the reader of these Scriptures does not know beforehand that the only satisfactory answer to the question that "we are" is the presence of this God, this Source who calls us into being and gives us our being daily, and that therefore no final theoretical answer can ever be given to that question—if, I say, the reader does not know this about the Bible's fundamental anthropological presupposition, then such a reader might think that the words and symbols and ideas that these Scriptures use to describe the human condition are terribly confused, even contradictory! For we are one minute "unprofitable servants" and the next "friends" of God. Here we appear "a little lower than the angels," and there beings whose very righteousness is "as filthy rags." Now we are sons and daughters of our heavenly parent, and then—a few pages over—enemies of God, betrayers of God's Anointed, slayers of God's prophets and priests. We are brides; we are harlots. We are lords; we are slaves. We are keepers of earth; we are wastrels and prodigals. We are freedmen and -women; we are prisoners. We are self-righteous boasters, hypocrites; we are little children, innocent and trusting. We are oppressors; we are victims. And all of these things about us are true.

They are of course not all equally true of everyone, everywhere, and at all times, but they are true descriptions both of our potential and actual behaviour. And what this means is that the truth about us can never be set down for good, not even if it is set down dialectically. Because we live, and because that one lives who has called and calls and will call us into being, there must always be this openness, this possibility of accentuation and variation, this unpredictability. Our existing is a process—a dynamic and not a static thing.[6] Therefore the Bible, which wants (as we may say) to bear particular witness to the essential or intended being that is only partly present and distorted in our existing, has to resort to apparently contradictory ideas and images to identify us. And so must theology do this, if it wishes to be true to the Bible and to that transcendent and untranscribable truth to which the biblical writers themselves tried to be true. It must be faithful to the living, the dynamic, the yes-and-no that moves in our life; it must avoid at all costs the ideological defining of humanity which gives the lie to our existing by abstracting certain qualities and potentialities from the whole ongoing reality that we are and are becoming.

In the light of this ongoingness, we may say that the best biblical metaphors for the human condition (and I think the scriptural writers themselves were aware of this) are those in which

6. "Truth, divine truth, then is not the conformity of the mind to a divine message uttered ages ago, but the discernment of present evil judged by this message and the discovery of the redemptive movement in history promised by this message. The norm of theological truth, then, is not drawn from an analogy with classical philosophy; it is drawn rather from its role in the ongoing process of world-building." Gregory Baum in Torres and Eagleson, *Theology in the Americas*, 404.

the dynamic, process-character of life is inherent. This almost invariably means relational metaphors: son/daughter, friend, wife/husband, covenant-partner, servant, or priest, to name a few. All of these terms tell us something about the possibilities and the limitations of human existence. They contain both a yes and a no—but in such a way that they cannot be reduced to a principle, but must be allowed to find ever new ways of relating to each other. They point to what is essential, but without turning it into a program, a theory into which living beings must then be fitted. Friendship, for instance, one of the most important metaphors in this story, contains quite distinctive positive as well as negative connotations; yet there are myriad ways in which friendship may work itself out in real life—as many ways as there are friends!

It is amongst such metaphors that the concept of humanity as the steward should be placed in biblical thought. It at once tells us something about the no and the yes of human identity in relationship: No, Adam and Eve are not masters. Yes, they are types of servants. But no, Adam and Eve are not just slaves, mechanical puppets, or robots. Yes, they are responsible and accountable to others. No, Adam or Eve is not *just* one of the other creatures; but yes, they are also like the others. And so on. Yet, while the metaphor points to something essential in the biblical conception of human nature and destiny, it does not itemize or detail this essence. It could not, without being unfaithful to the character of the metaphor itself. There are countless ways in which stewardship may work itself out in actual day-to-day life. As many ways as there are stewards!

But now we are already anticipating what must be developed more gradually as we consider the specific usages of this metaphor in the Bible.

## 2. The Hebrew Scriptures

The Bible as a whole, New as well as Old Testament, contains some twenty-six direct references to the steward and stewardship. The usage of the term in the Hebrew Scriptures is uniformly technical or literal; that is, it describes an actual office or vocation in society. Nevertheless, it is upon the Old Testament characterization of the office of steward that the more figurative or metaphorical use in the Christian gospels depends.

The steward in the literature of the Old Testament is a servant, but not an ordinary servant who simply takes orders and does the bidding of others. Rather, he (we do not hear of female stewards here, unfortunately, though neither do we hear that such a thing is impossible!) is a rather superior servant, a sort of supervisor or foreman, who must make decisions, give orders, and take charge. "Der Haushalter war eine Sklave, den sein Herr zum Werwalter über Hausgesinde oder sogar über seinen ganzen Besitz einsezte. . . . Sein Amt war eine besondere Vertrauensstellung."[7] That is, the steward is one who has been given the responsibility for the management and service of something belonging to another, and his office presupposes a particular kind of trust on the part of the owner or master.

The latter, to whom the steward is accountable in the Hebraic writings, is usually a royal personage—a king or ruler. Thus in the first usage of the term in the Old Testament (Gen. 43 and 44), the steward in question is a person accountable to Joseph, the Hebrew prisoner who has risen in the court of Egypt to be second only to the Pharoah. Joseph's steward is therefore no mean figure. When the brothers of Joseph address this officer, they speak as to one who bears great authority: "Oh, my lord, we came down the first time to buy food" (43:20ff.). The steward in turn speaks to them as one who enjoys the full confidence of his master Joseph. In fact the whole episode establishes a concept of the office in which the steward is really a full representative or deputy of his master.

A less detailed and intimate, though equally high con-

7. From the article on *Haushalter* in *Biblisch-Theologisches Handworterbuch: Zur Lutherbibel und zu Neuern Uebersetzung* (Göttingen: Vanderhoeck & Ruprecht, 1964), 41.

ception of the steward's work is presented in 1 Chronicles 27 and 28. Here the stewards are named, those who have responsibility for the various properties and aspects of King David's total kingdom (treasuries, vineyards, herds, camels, and flocks), together with the commanders of divisions and leaders of the tribes and the chief counsellors.

A third brief reference to the steward (Dan. 1:11, 16) presupposes a similar degree of significance for the office. In this case, the steward is charged not with properties, but with the care of the young royal Hebrew prisoners of Nebuchadnezzar, and he seems quite at liberty to make immediate decisions respecting them; for when Daniel asks for a radical change in diet the steward complies and, consulting no one, substitutes the desired simple vegetables for the rich royal foods the king had ordered for his prisoners.

This rather lofty conception of the stewardly office is balanced, however, by another dimension that becomes visible in a fourth reference from the sacred texts of Israel: Isa. 22:15-21. In this passage, we learn that however important the steward may be in the scheme of things, he is neither ultimately authoritative nor irreplaceable. He may indeed be a superior servant, as we have seen already, but he is still a servant; and if he forgets this and begins to behave as though he were himself unambiguously in charge (i.e., not accountable) he shall be dealt with most severely. Thus in the passage in question, the prophet is sent to rebuke a certain steward named Shebna—

> Come, go to this steward, to Shebna, who is over the household, and say to him: What have you to do here and whom have you here, that you have hewn here a tomb for yourself, you who hew a tomb on the height, and carve a habitation for yourself in the rock? Behold, the Lord will hurl you away violently, O you strong man. He will seize firm hold on you, and whirl you round and round, and throw you like a ball into a wide land; there you shall die, and there shall be your splendid chariots, you shame of your master's house. I will thrust you from your office, and you will be cast down from your station. In that day I will call my servant

Eliakim the son of Hilkiah, and I will clothe him with your robe, and will bind your girdle on him, and will commit your authority to his hand; and he shall be a father to the inhabitants of Jerusalem. (Vv. 15-21)

As we can easily gather from this reference, the steward concept is here elevated to accomodate the idea that the ruler of God's people is a steward, responsible to the master—that is, to Yahweh. But the passage also tells us a good deal about the qualities that are implied, generally, in the stewardly office. They are such attributes as humbleness of spirit, lack of pretention and ostentation, and parental behaviour towards those for whose welfare the steward has responsibility. In other words, the leap to a more metaphoric usage of the concept has not yet been made; yet the two poles between which the later New Testament usage of stewardship moves have already been established.

One pole—the positive one, if you like—is the close identification of the steward with his master. As we have seen, the steward can be regarded almost as the representative or vicar of the one who has employed him—though he is only a servant, perhaps even technically only a slave or (like Joseph) virtually a prisoner. The other (negative) pole is the insistence that the steward is not, after all, the owner or master. He is strictly accountable to his lord, and he will certainly be deprived of his authority unless he upholds, in his actions and attitudes, the true character and wishes of this other one whom he is allowed and commanded to represent. In establishing these two conditions of stewardship, as we may call them, the Hebrew Bible sets up the two most important points upon which all subsequent discussion of the subject turns.

### 3. The New Testament

The rudimentary picture of the steward as servant manager of something or someone not belonging to himself is also the most obvious meaning of some of the passages referring to steward-ship in the New Testament—for example, Matthew 20:8, Luke 8:3, and John 2:8. In the distinctively Christian writings, how-ever, there is a certain development or evolution in the idea of stewardship. Here it assumes in many places a theological and metaphoric meaning which, while implicit in the Isaiah quota-tion above, now becomes quite explicit in certain key passages.

Thus in Luke 12:42ff., where "steward" and "servant" are used interchangeably, stewardship together with watchful-ness are characteristic marks of Christ's true followers. The "master" referred to here is not an earthly king or lord like the Pharoah, but the risen Christ. The disciples, during their leader's earthly absence, are charged with responsibility for Christ's household. As stewards of this household, the dis-ciples are accountable for those who dwell in it—to see that they are properly fed, and protected from thieves and nocturnal robbers. At the same time, the disciples are warned (in a man-ner very reminiscent of Isa. 22) that stewards who forget their place and begin to assume that they are autonomous, or are at liberty to do as they please with "the servants," will be severely punished:

> But if that servant says to himself, "My master is delayed in com-ing," and begins to beat the manservants and the maidservants, and to eat and drink and get drunk, the master of that servant will come on a day when he does not expect him and at an hour he does not know, and will punish him, and put him with the unfaithful. And that servant who knew his master's will, but did not make ready or act according to his will, shall receive a severe beating. But he who did not know, and did what deserved a beat-ing, shall receive a light beating. (Vv. 45-48)

It is true that the stewards are regarded here—as in the Old Testament—as being a notch higher on the ladder of authority than ordinary manservants and maidservants; but what is from one standpoint their superior authority is from another their greater responsibility. Thus the passage ends with a summary statement that has had great importance for all serious discussion of the meaning of stewardship:

> Every one to whom much is given, of him will much be required; and of him to whom men commit much they will demand the more. (Luke 12:48b)

Behind this simple statement there stands the whole conception of election. Unlike many ancient as well as modern religions and worldviews, the tradition of Jerusalem does not think in terms of an elite—the few amongst the many who will be, or deserve to be, saved. It is true that the concept of election, like that of an elite, assumes the choice of a few amongst the many. But these few are elected, not for their own sake and salvation but in behalf of the many. They are stewards of something—treasures, food, or mysteries—that is intended not simply for themselves but for "all the families of the earth" (as it is so beautifully phrased in the covenant with Abraham, Gen. 12:1ff.). The stewards of God's universal grace are, it is true, given much; but because what they are given is intended for a much wider company, much will be required of them as well. They are a means to something greater, not (as with the idea of an elite) an end in themselves.

In the Pauline and other epistles, the gospels' parabolic treatment of stewardship becomes almost doctrinal. In 1 Corinthians 4:1-2, Paul applies the concept of the steward explicitly to himself as an apostle and implicitly to the church at large. One notes again how this reference is set in a textual context of warning: Christians ought not to act according to the ways of the world, where people try to make names for themselves or form parties around this or that great one—

> Let no one boast of men. For all things are yours, whether Paul or Apollos or Cephas or the world or life or death or the present or the future, all are yours; and you are Christ's; and Christ is God's. (1 Cor. 3:21-23)

This is perhaps the supreme ecumenical/ecological statement of the Bible. We are all bound up with one another. No one can claim or have claimed for her- or himself any independent dignity, authority, or worth. Even Jesus Christ is part of this chain of mutuality. Even the Christ is accountable—he is God's steward. This being so (Paul continues), it follows that "this is how one should regard us [i.e., Paul and his associates—but implicitly the church at large]—as servants of Christ and stewards of the mysteries of God. Moreover, it is required of stewards that they be found trustworthy" (4:2). Here the property for which the Christian stewards have responsibility is not the material effects of a royal household, nor noble prisoners like Daniel and his companions, nor the accoutrements of a feast as in John 2:8, but the mysteries of God: that is, the gospel itself, which is intended for the whole family of humanity, God's household.[8]

This same theological nuance is assigned to the metaphor of the steward in Ephesians. Here, however, the scriptural context adds yet another dimension to the meaning of the steward idea for early Christians. For Paul reminds these Gentile Christians that formerly they were "alienated from the commonwealth of Israel, and strangers to the covenants of promise, having no hope and without God in the world," but that now they have been "brought near" through Christ (Eph. 2:12-13).

> So then you are no longer strangers and sojourners, but you are fellow citizens with the saints and members of the household of God, built upon the foundation of the apostles and prophets, Christ Jesus himself being the cornerstone, in whom the whole structure is joined together and grows into a holy temple in the Lord; in whom you also are built into it for a dwelling place of God in the Spirit. (Eph. 2:19-22)

And just at this juncture the writer finds it meaningful to introduce the stewardship theme:

> For this reason I, Paul, a prisoner for Christ Jesus on behalf of you Gentiles—assuming that you have heard of the stewardship

8. In this connection see Theodore S. Horvath, *Focus on Our Identity as Stewards* (New York: Stewardship Council of the United Church of Christ, 1987), especially "Stewards of the Gospel," 12ff.

of God's grace that was given to me for you, how the mystery was made known to me by revelation, as I have written. (3:1-2)

The new dimension in this important passage is what we may call the dimension of participation. Although the steward of God (or Christ), like the stewards of earthly lords, can claim nothing for him- or herself, that steward is not merely an outsider—hired help, so to speak. Rather, the steward participates in the very "household of God." As such, the steward is called and enable to share "this grace" (v. 8) with others, and to bring them in turn into God's household.

This dialectically offsets the other side of the Bible's discussion of stewardship, i.e., its negative or critical side which repeatedly emphasizes that stewards are only stewards, and warns them therefore not to consider themselves owners or masters. While that warning is certainly sustained by Paul, the Ephesians reference to stewardship accentuates the high meaning of the metaphor: the steward is herself a participant in the very bounty (grace) for whose distribution she has now a mandate. This not only picks up the "positive" connotation of the metaphor as it applies to the office of steward in the Hebrew Scriptures: it adds to it. The steward of the mysteries of God not only represents her sovereign but she shares fully in the grace that these mysteries connote.

A further dimension is added by 1 Peter 4. It would be appropriate for both exegetical and situational purposes to call this the eschatological dimension of the stewardship theme in the New Testament. For here the fundamental assumption is that characteristic, apocalyptic belief of the early church—that the end is near:

> The end of all things is at hand; therefore keep sane and sober for your prayers. Above all hold unfailing your love for one another, since love covers a multitude of sins. Practice hospitality ungrudgingly to one another. As each has received a gift, employ it for one another, as good stewards of God's varied grace: whoever speaks, as one who utters oracles of God; whoever renders service, as one who renders it by the strength which God supplies; in order that

in everything God may be glorified through Jesus Christ. To him belong glory and dominion for ever and ever. Amen. (1 Pet. 4:7-11)

Whatever else the eschatological context of the Christian life implies, one thing that appears prominently in this passage is the way consciousness of the end reinforces the gift character of life. Part of what this means, concretely, is that our human tendency to isolate ourselves and our talents pridefully is reduced. The sense of an ending brings us into a fuller recognition of our own transcience, and of our creaturely solidarity. We are all "in the same boat." And it is God's boat, God's ark. Here the eschatological and the ecclesiastical presuppositions of stewardship are inextricably linked with one another.[9]

## 4. A Linguistic Aside

In a moment, we shall attempt to summarize what we have gleaned from this cursory examination of our theme in the Scriptures of Israel and the church; but before doing so it will

9. The two N.T. references to stewardship to which I have not alluded in the foregoing are Titus 1:7, which insists that "a bishop, as God's steward, must be blameless," and the famous parable of the unjust steward (Luke 16) — perhaps the most difficult parable in the New Testament. One commentator believes that the thrust of this parable is against "the leaders of Israel as stewards of God's property. They should be making friends of those whom they have oppressed, so as to find security when their own present position of worldly privilege collapses with the end of the old order. . . . If they have not discharged their stewardship faithfully, including the use of their usurped privilege for the benefit of those whom they now treat as outcasts, they will not be entrusted with the riches of the Kingdom . . . which belong to Christ and his followers." *Peake's Commentary on the Bible*, ed. Matthew Black (London: Thomas Nelson & Sons, 1962), 836. If this interpretation is accurate, the parable has overtones similar to other passages that we briefly have examined which draw attention to the dangers of stewardship, especially through the misuse of this privileged position for purposes of personal aggrandizement. The parable can also be read in the light of the eschatological dimension treated above. I have refrained from discussing it in the body of my text, however, because it is capable of so many different interpretations, and my discussion here is necessarily circumscribed by the larger purposes of the whole study.

be useful to interject a few remarks concerning the language associated with stewardship in this literature. This is not the place to engage in a complex discussion of linguistic nuances; at the same time the language of stewardship cannot be ignored—and by this I mean not only the original biblical terms but also, and perhaps even particularly, the English term that was employed to render in a meaningful way both the Hebrew and Greek equivalents.

The English word "steward" began to appear in manuscripts in the eleventh century. Originally, the word was not "steward" but *stigweard*, *stig* probably referring to a house or some part of a house or building, and *weard* [later, *ward*] meaning of course "warden" or "keeper."[10] The first meaning offered by the *Oxford English Dictionary* is this: "An official who controls the domestic affairs of a household, supervising the service of his master's table, directing the domestics and regulating household expenditure; a major-domo." The dictionary also notes that the word came to be associated in particular with royal households.

This, then, was the word available to translators of Hebrew and Greek Scriptures into the English language, including the very influential King James Version. All things considered, it was not a bad choice—much better, for instance, than many of the Greek words available to the early Christians who had to translate essential Hebraic ideas into the lingua franca of that epoch, that is, common *(koine)* Greek. *Stigweard* in fact approximated quite accurately both the Hebrew and the Greek terms. In Hebrew, a number of terms were employed to convey the office of steward in the four passages to which I have referred in the previous discussion. The Joseph narrative (Gen. 43 and 44) uses *haish asher al* ("the man who is over") or *asher al bayit* ("who is over a house"). Other terms such as *ben mesheq* (son

10. Kantonen quips that "Since *sti* came to have the meaning which it still retains in *sty*, it would not be amiss to render the literal meaning of steward as sty warden, keeper of swine." But, he continues in a more serious vein, "Already in Middle English . . . it had general reference to anyone who manages the household or property of another." *Christian Stewardship*, 3.

of acquisition—Gen. 15:2), or *sar* (prince, head, chief, or captain—e.g., 1 Chron. 28:1) can also be used.

In the common Greek of the original testamental writings, we seem to be taken even closer to the colors of the English word "steward." Here, although the term *epitropos* is used in Luke 8:3 and Galatians 4:2, the word regularly translated as steward in most English versions of the Bible is *oikonomos;* hence stewardship becomes *oikonomia.* The *oikonomos* has responsibility for planning and administrating (putting into, order, or *nomos*) the affairs of a household *(oikos).* Not only does this suggest that economics *(oikonomia)* is a significant part of Christian stewardship; it means that what we call economics is more than the term regularly connotes in our vocabulary today! Reflecting upon the word picture, we might conclude that stewardship has not only to do with money, budgeting, and finances, but with the whole ordering of our life, our corporate deployment of God's varied grace in the daily life of the world. Beyond that, when one considers that this same *oikonomia* is linguistically close to the term "ecumenical" *(oikumene),* one has a good deal to contemplate on etymological grounds alone.

## 5. Theological Reflections on the Steward Motif in Scripture

Language, however, is not immediately revelatory. The word not only reveals, it also conceals meanings. The idea is larger than the word, even though the word—particularly in the tradition of Jerusalem—is of immense importance (I doubt that Jeremiah could ever have presaged Hamlet's lines: "Words, words, words"!).

To begin to intuit that larger meaning, we may make certain observations. It is instructive to order these observations along systematic lines, and so to discuss the scriptural meaning of the concept from the standpoint of its theological, christological, ecclesiastical, anthropological, and eschatological assumptions. In this way we may begin to sense something of the inclusive character of the metaphor of the steward as it is assumed in biblical literature.

### a. The Theological Dimension

While the first state in the evolution of the steward concept is evidently the simple idea that there should be someone to manage the affairs of another (king, noble, giver of a feast, et al.), the concept easily moves over into a metaphoric meaning.

In the first stage of this transition (as in Isaiah 22), it is natural that the "other" whose affairs the steward is to manage is God. The royal figure by whom the steward is commissioned and to whom this officer is accountable is no longer an earthly king but the eternal sovereign, Yahweh/Elohim.

This simple transfer has very significant implications not only for stewardship in general but also for theology in the restrictive sense of the term (i.e., for our conception of God). What is established here, once and for all, is that ownership, mastery, ultimacy of authority, and sovereignty are attributable to God alone. This is of course no novel idea. It gains its power, indeed, from its entire consistency with other descriptions of the deity in biblical literature: "Thou shalt have no other gods"; "The earth is the Lord's and the fulness thereof." When this idea is combined with its immediate anthropological implications, as it must be, it has a critical theological and ethical connotation: namely, it puts an enormous question mark over all human presumption, not only in relation to material realities (including the alleged possession of properties), but also with respect to more nebulous realities such as authority. As soon as God is pictured as the owner and sovereign of everything in relation to which human beings can be at most stewards, institutions such as the holding of property, the hierarchic distribution of authority, the technocratic mastery of the natural world, and the like are thrown into a critical perspective. It does not require a Marx or a Freud to voice that challenge. It is already contained in this fruitful metaphor and its attendant theological presuppositions.

## b. The Christological Dimension

It has been said that the New Testament's theology of stewardship is first of all a Christology.[11] This seems to me an eminently true and evocative observation—provided one does not neglect the theological assumption referred to above. Jesus Christ is presented in the New Testament not in the role of owner, but as the authentic and preeminent steward: "all are yours; and you are Christ's; and Christ is God's" (1 Cor. 3:22-23).

In a way very reminiscent of the whole servant motif applied to him, Jesus appears here as the steward of "God's varied grace" (1 Pet. 4:10). Jesus in fact defines and fulfils the office of the steward. Because he is a just and faithful steward, unlike the unjust steward of Luke 16, he desires nothing for himself. Because he is obedient to the one he represents,[12] he is not concerned about saving his own life, but lays it down for his friends. He does not think in terms of possession, not even the possession of his own life.

It would in fact be profitable for christological reflection if the office of steward were applied to the Christ in the same way other offices of the Old Testament have been used to interpret his purpose and work. I am referring to the long tradition of contemplating Christ's work as fulfilment of the offices of prophet, priest, and king. While these three offices are prominent in the Hebrew literature, they are not the only offices available for these purposes (for instance, the office of judge, in the tradition of the judges of Israel, has been considerably downplayed). Steward could be a particularly provocative office to consider in this regard. Jesus as chief steward of the mysteries of

11. See Ronald D. Petry, *Partners in Creation: Stewardship for Pastor and People* (Elgin, Ill.: Brethren Press, 1980), chapter 1.

12. See Dorothee Sölle, *Christ the Representative: An Essay in Theology after the "Death of God,"* trans. David Lewis (London: SCM Press, 1967).

God lives in such faithfulness to the stewardly vocation as it is already outlined in Hebraic Scripture and practice, that he becomes the primary model for our stewardship.

He is, however, not only a model or example. That would leave the matter of our being stewards in the realm of commandment and the imitation of Christ, whereas the most basic presupposition of our stewardship is grace. The christological assumption of Christian stewardship is that as those who are (to use Paul's constant expression) "in Christ" we are taken up into his stewardship. It is not that we achieve the stewardly status through our works, our imitation of him. We are graciously brought into a stewarding of God's grace that has already been enacted by God's chief steward.

In other words, Jesus Christ, who is God's, is the initiator and enabler of Christian stewardship: "you are Christ's; and Christ is God's." The christological basis of stewardship means not only that our stewardship is exemplified by Jesus; rather, in keeping with Paul's mystical regard of Christ that is the matrix of so much of the New Testament's stewardship discussion, it is the prior stewardship of Jesus into which, through the Spirit and through faith, we are initiated.

This is very different from a simple exhortation that Christians ought to be good stewards. It is the difference between law (legalistically conceived) and gospel. The law of stewardship, which many know to be true enough, insists that human beings must be faithful trustees of the life of the world. But it is one thing to know this and another to *do* it! The gospel of stewardship begins by overcoming that within us which prevents our being stewards—the pride of imagining ourselves owners; the sloth of irresponsibility, neglect, and apathy. And that gospel gives us the grace and courage that we need to exercise a love that is larger than our self-esteem or our anxiety about ourselves.

In short, the Christian view of stewardship starts with the stewardship of the One who did not grasp at equality with God, but was obedient (Phil. 2). It is *his* stewardship in which

by grace we participate—as those who are brought by the Spirit
through hearing the gospel and through the baptism of fire and
water into an ongoing process of identification with this One.

## c. The Ecclesiastical Dimension

Not only does the stewardship image provide a model for the
biblical picture of God and of Christ, it also quite naturally extends itself into the ecclesiological area of Christian theology.
The church is a stewarding community. As the body of Christ,
the disciple community is being incorporated into the work of
the great steward. As servants of the Suffering Servant, they are
being constituted "stewards of the mysteries of God" (1 Cor. 4:1)
through their witness to the Crucified One.—both their verbal
testimony and their own share in Christ's suffering. Their
whole life is to be an outpouring of God's varied grace.

Here as elsewhere there is an implicit polemic in the New
Testament against the church as end-in-itself. As we have already observed briefly in connection with the concept of divine
election, in contrast to the idea of an elite, the *koinonia* exists
for a purpose that is infinitely greater than itself. It is to serve
the God of a grace that is universally offered. It is to participate
in the extension of that grace throughout the world. It is to be
the harbinger of a reign in which it may or may not have a
place—nothing can be assumed! (Cf. 1 Cor. 10:1-12.)

But if the steward metaphor shines a critical light on any
narcissism in the church, there is an even more vigorous attack
upon the ecclesiastical pursuit of power. The steward exists not
only to serve his or her master, but in doing so to serve as well
those whose interests the master has at heart. When stewards
begin to allow their own ambition or desire to dictate what
should be done, they at once disqualify themselves: "the master
of *that* servant will come on a day when he does not expect
him . . . and will punish him, and put him with the unfaithful"
(Luke 12:46).

One could wish that the writers of the New Testament had

developed more fully the worldly meaning of the insight that the church of Christ is a community of stewards: how it applied to the Christian community's daily life in society; how it conditioned our dealings as Christians with institutions like government and economic structures; how it led to an ethic of social responsibility; or what it meant for our relation to the extrahuman world. As it is, the epistle and gospel writers concentrate almost exclusively on the spiritual and internal ecclesiastical implications of stewardship: "a bishop, as God's steward, must be blameless" (Titus 1:7); the gifts each has received should be shared with others in the *koinonia*. We must remember, however, that the earliest Christian communities were living under conditions significantly different from our own. In particular, their understanding of their mission was conditioned by their expectation of an imminent End (see *The Eschatological Dimension* that follows).

One of the great advantages of a metaphor like stewardship, on the other hand, is that it is not bound to these early Christian assumptions, as some other images used by the New Testament are bound (e.g., the bride of Christ imagery of Revelation). When the eschatological assumptions change, as they had begun to change already in the literature of the New Testament, the steward metaphor is just as applicable as in the earlier situation, and perhaps even more so. For there is something questionable about a complete spiritualization of such a concrete and worldly image as this; and in some ways the posteschatological situation brings the church back to the material and worldly meaning of its vocation as steward. At least it ought to have done so! In the next chapter we shall try to understand why it did not.

### d. The Anthropological Dimension

There is no doubt that the New Testament intends us to think of *Christians* as stewards. It does not develop in an explicit way the idea that *human beings as such* have a stewardly vocation, any more than it concerns itself directly with the worldly meaning of stewardship.

This does not detract, however, from the applicability of the metaphor to humanity as a whole. For one thing, as we have seen, the steward metaphor does not stand alone, but as one of many ways in which the Scriptures define humanity's posture vis-à-vis the Creator and the other creatures. In particular, the commandment to love God and neighbour by no means limits the neighbour to one's fellow Christians.

An even more important observation in this instance is that what is described and prescribed in the Scriptures of the New Testament as the appropriate life of the followers of the Christ is at the same time the authors' way of discussing humanity in God's intention. Christians are not aberrations or superhuman beings; they are essentially persons who are in process of becoming truly human. The "new humanity" that they are "putting on," to use the Pauline imagery (Col. 3:10), is the authentic humanity of Jesus. Jesus, whom the later christological discussions of the church declared to be *vere homo* (truly human), represents the humanity that the Creator desires for all human beings. God's object in establishing a witnessing people in the midst of the world is not to create a higher race (an elite), but through such a community to keep before humankind the identity and vocation that the Creator intends for all. As Irenaeus put it succinctly, *Gloria Dei vivens homo* ("the glory of God is humanity truly alive").

Though far too little has been made of it then, the New Testament certainly implies, both in its picture of the second and true Adam, Jesus, and in its discussion of the disciple community that is being conformed to Christ's genuine humanity, that stewardship is a human calling. It applies not only to those who are called into the life of explicit discipleship, but to the human species as such. God intends that the creature whom later scholarship designated (somewhat pretentiously!) Homo sapiens should live as God's steward within the creaturely sphere.

## e. The Eschatological Dimension

We have noted that within the metaphor of stewardship one is accountable. It is therefore not surprising that the eschatological dimension should appear so frequently in the New Testament's treatment of this metaphor, as well as implicitly in the Isaiah passage. The Lukan references are especially noteworthy in this connection:

> Who then is the faithful and wise steward, whom his master will set over his household, to give them their portion of food at the proper time? Blessed is that servant whom the master when he comes will find so doing. Truly I tell you, he will set him over all his possessions. (Luke 12:42-44)

The parable of the unjust steward also is full of eschatological significance. The whole context of that story is its consciousness of the End—which implies accountability. "Turn in the account of your stewardship!" the writer is saying. Stewards must be watchful (Luke 12), trustworthy (1 Cor. 4:2), blameless (Titus 1:7)—but not simply out of moralistic concern. Rather, they know that with which they are charged is the property of another. It is God's grace (Eph. 3:2), and therefore, like the servants who are given talents in Jesus' parable (certainly a cognate reference for any discussion of stewardship), they must finally report on their use or misuse of what they have been given.

This note of the impending judgment *(krisis)* of the steward is, as we have seen, especially the theme of the passage in the first epistle of Peter. The sense of apocalyptic urgency here is not necessarily diminished by alterations first-century Christians came to recognize in the timing of the anticipated eschaton. It remains true even after the End is no longer perceived as an immediate Parousia that "the judgment begins at the household of faith" (1 Pet. 4:17). Because those who are being incorporated into the life and work of the Great Steward have been given much, their failure to give much in return is especially serious.

## 6. Conclusion: The Gospel in Miniature

In summary, we may say that the steward metaphor as suggested in particular by the New Testament's appropriation of this Hebraic office and image is an inclusive concept, a kind of presentation of the gospel in a nutshell. Indeed, it seems to achieve a status beyond the metaphoric, though it would be wrong to say unqualifiedly that it is already a symbol. Even though it would be misleading and exaggerated to consider stewardship a full embodiment of gospel, still it possesses a potentially symbolic value that lifts it out of the category of a simple metaphor or image.

When therefore we speak of the need for an enlarged view of stewardship, and when in the subsequent pages of this study we shall attempt to open up such a view, it is not as though we were simply inventing a new set of ideas and weaving them around an old metaphor. On the contrary, we are exploring, in the light of contemporary circumstances, the depths of a biblical metaphor which already in its own historic context is potentially more than metaphoric.

Unlike signs, symbols, as Paul Tillich has taught us, cannot be invented at will. They belong or they do not belong. They happen. They are born and they die; but they can neither be produced nor extinguished by us. They are not arbitrary or manipulatable. We receive them as part of the heritage in which we stand as members of a culture or a religious tradition. Their meaning is never exhausted by this or that generation, this or that locale. Because they participate in the reality that they symbolize, their meaning is always unfolding. They are unlike theories in that their potential meaning always transcends every particular expression of their meaning.[13]

Stewardship belongs to the most ancient strands of our Judeo-Christian heritage. That much at least is clear from our

13. Paul Tillich, *Dynamics of Faith* (New York: Harper & Brothers, 1957), 41ff.

necessarily brief biblical investigations. Already with the New Testament appropriation of the concept, we have moved from the literal description of a social office or function to a quasi-symbolic or proto-symbolic manner of employing this category. From the first Christian century onwards, this category is present in the primary literature of the Christian movement, waiting for further development. The biblical authors themselves could and did realize much about the possibilities of this motif as a vehicle for communicating the meaning of the Christian message and the character of the Christian life. I have gone so far as to propose that they could employ it in such a way as to touch upon every aspect of biblical theology—not, of course, systematically, as we have done here, for they were not systematicians, but implicitly and in terms of their own modes of discourse.

We cannot ask these first Christians to have known in advance the significance of such a concept to an age like our own. They could not have guessed that it would become especially timely—that it would achieve a full symbolic status—in a world like ours, when the expectation of the End as they knew it has given place to an all-too-literal prospect of creation's termination, and when human beings who reject that sort of a future cast about for images and symbols of humanity that can offset the destructive impulses of the technocratic mindset. Nevertheless, what these biblical writers have bequeathed to us is far more than the bare skeleton of an idea or the mere hint of a foundation on which we might now boldly construct an impressive ediface of thought! The basics of the symbol are already there in the Bible, and they are closely enough bound to the core of the story told in the continuity of the two testaments that we are justified in thinking the steward metaphor an appropriate vehicle for the transmission of the gospel, and not just some aspect of Christian teaching. Under the socio-historical conditions in which we find ourselves, the potential for such a symbolic role that has been present in this metaphor from the earliest phases of the Christan movement is being actualized. While it is certainly not the only way in which gospel may and should be communicated in our time and place, it is a highly evocative and appropriate medium. It is for many, and can become for many more, the gospel in miniature.

How this is so must now become the subject of our subsequent meditations. But the above analysis leaves us with an implicit historical question, and our reflections about the present-day appropriateness of this symbol come of age will be deepened if we first try to deal with that question.

We have insisted that the Scriptures offered the developing Christian movement a particularly interesting metaphor, one which already contains potentiality for full symbolic connotation—that is, for being a linguistic and ideational device through which Christians could glimpse something of the whole thrust and meaning of their message and their life in the world. The question is this: Why was this metaphor not taken up by evolving Christianity? Why has it in fact played so minor a role in the unfolding of church history? Other biblical metaphors with less real potential for symbolic profundity achieved greater notice than "the steward." If this is truly such an inclusive metaphor as our biblical reflections suggest, how is it that more has not been made of it in the theology as well as the practice of Christianity in the world?

# CHAPTER II

# REFLECTIONS ON THE HISTORICAL TREATMENT OF STEWARDSHIP

## 1. Introduction: The Aim of the Chapter

Let me first interpret the heading of this chapter, which may be somewhat misleading. I do not intend to attempt here anything like a historical survey of the course of stewardship thinking in the church, though I believe that such an exercise would be a profitable one.[1] My aim is rather to venture certain historical reflections, which I suppose might be considered hypotheses or, taken together, a comprehensive thesis with various nuances. Naturally such generalizations would have to be tested by more minute and objective historical investigation. Even so, it would be difficult to prove the hypotheses I shall develop here: historical generalizations are never demonstrable in the strict sense.

1. There is a need for a serious, comprehensive study of the history of stewardship thought and practice in the Christian faith. Most of the available material concerns itself (quite understandably, in the light of the foregoing discussion) with the functional use of the metaphor. For further reading see: L. P. Powell, "Stewardship in the History of the Christian Church," in *Stewardship in Contemporary Theology*, ed. T. K. Thompson (New York: Association Press, 1960); by the same author, *Money and the Church* (New York: Association Press, 1962); George A. E. Salstrand, *The Story of Stewardship in the United States of America* (Grand Rapids: Baker Book House, 1956).

On the other hand, the mere review of data without the formulating of some such interpretive hypotheses would amount to an exercise in historical bookkeeping! It will be well for the reader to bear in mind that the purpose of the whole exercise is to respond in some comprehensive way to the question raised at the end of the previous chapter: since stewardship is a quite important biblical metaphor, and one with high potential for further development, why did this not happen significantly in the unfolding story of the Christian movement?

## 2. The Spiritualization of the Concept

During the first centuries of its history, Christianity underwent many changes. The great nineteenth-century historian of Christian dogma, Adolf von Harnack, believed that the transformation was so extensive that what emerged as the Christian religion was something quite different from what had been conceived by Jesus and his disciples. Franz Overbeck, the occupant of the chair of Critical Theology at Basel and friend of Friedrich Nietzsche, went even further: he believed that Christendom was a great mistake, a misunderstanding of the original message of Jesus.

One may not wish to go so far as either von Harnack or Overbeck; still, it is clear that very significant alterations did occur, and even scholars who are strongly committed to preserving the whole (Catholic) tradition of evolving Christendom realize that part of the work of Christian scholarship today is to recognize these changes and to recover original meanings that may be both more authentic biblically and more pertinent to our own historical moment.[2]

The general changes in Christian self-understanding occuring during the first four or five centuries of the church had an effect on many if not all aspects of Christian belief, including

2. See for example Leslie Dewart, *The Future of Belief: Theism in a World Come of Age* (London: Burns & Oates, 1966).

stewardship. Two eventualities within these centuries materially affected the direction that would be taken by this incipient symbol of the Christian message and life: first, the movement of Christianity away from its Hebraic matrix into the cultural milieu of the so-called Hellenistic world; second, the adoption of the Christian religion by Constantine and his successors as the official religion of the Roman Empire. We begin with the former.

The Hellenistic culture, to be distinguished from the Hellenic or Greek civilization as such, refers to that mishmash of Egyptian, Persian, Greek, and other cultures created largely by the military exploits of Alexander the Great. This was the arena that early Christianity had to enter as soon as it moved outside the Judaic homeland. Even in that homeland it could not escape the influence of Hellenistic civilization. Judaism itself, as one can see from the work of its most renowned contemporary scholar, Philo of Alexandria (B.C.E. 20?–C.E. 42?), had been greatly hellenized. Hellenization was, so to speak, the "Americanization factor" of the period. While Rome exercised military and political power over the civilized world of the Mediterranean area, its cultural values, mores, and goals were set by the earlier Hellenistic civilization which Rome absorbed. As soon as Christianity became a consciously missionary faith, its representatives, beginning with Paul, had to relate their gospel to the language and the ways of the hellenized world. Naturally this meant its partial adaptation to the existing culture, for nobody ever shares an idea, experience, or worldview without losing some of its original meaning, and in the process gaining other connotations that stem from the rudimentary assumptions of the receiving party. The most obvious aspect of this adaptation process—something still readily traceable—was the manner in which many of the feast days and holy seasons of the pagan, Gentile world were "baptized" with Christian names and meanings, though they frequently continued to carry the deep undertones of the original pre-Christian festivals and events.

At a more subtle level, the adaptation of Christianity to the social conditions of the Hellenistic world meant certain alterations in basic tenets of belief. For example, there was no word in Greek, the common language of that culture, to express precisely what Jesus, Paul, and other Jewish people meant by the key term "sin." In the Hebraic tradition, sin at its most fundamental level means the radical breaking of a relationship—disobedience, rebellion against God, confrontation, and alienation. The Greek word that the Christians did pick up to translate that essentially relational concept (the word *hamartia*, from *hamartano*) is not a term of relationship, but refers rather to personal lack or failure. It means "missing the mark," "falling short"—that is, failure to achieve one's potential, or underachieving. Popularly employed, this soon gave way to thinking of sin in moralistic and even legalistic ways: sins are wrong thoughts, words, and deeds that detract from one's potential for moral perfection. Perhaps that in itself is not an unworthy notion, wisely understood and handled; but it is certainly different from the Hebraic sense of sin as the abrogation of relationship and the estrangement that comes of it. In the Jewish sense, the trouble with human unrighteousness and sin is not that it takes away from my personal fulfilment but that it introduces "dividing walls of hostility" between myself and my neighbour; myself and God who is the source and ground of my life; and myself and creation. I become alienated from others. This conception of sin particularly should be remembered when we discuss (Chapter VII) the theology of nature. For "the other" in relation to whom one sins could as well be otherkind (i.e., nonhuman beings), as one's own kind.

To trace what changes in the cultural context of Christianity affect the theology of stewardship is more difficult because they are indirect. Of course stewardship is also a much less prominent article of belief than such a central idea as sin. With the latter, a failure to find the linguistic materials suitable to the idea at once introduces significant and conspicuous change to the idea. The change affecting the fate of the stewardship motif was not so conspicuous. As we have already noted, the Greek language could serve the steward metaphor rather well, and it does so in the New Testament, as well as in the thought of some of the early church fathers.[3] But there were other, very subtle but ultimately powerful influences in the atmosphere of Hellenistic society which gave the stewardship idea the direction that it assumed subsequently—or, to put it more accurately, which prevented it from blossoming in the manner promised by its biblical beginnings.

To grasp this, it is necessary to understand that one of the strongest tendencies in Hellenistic culture and religion was an abiding suspicion of matter. The material world, including the human body, was regarded as inferior; it was the locus of temptation, of evil, of danger, and therefore it was fundamentally *unreal*. Reality was thought to transcend matter and to be essentially spiritual. Matter is not only inert, but it positively resists spirit; and so long as we, through our bodily preoccupations, are fixated on the material world, we are deprived both of truth and of being itself. To get into touch with the "really real," one has to slough off, so far as possible, one's physicalness, together with its associated passions. Through such detachment, one might rise to the realm of spirit. Hence, the function of religion in Hellenistic civilization, as well as of most philosophy, was to lift persons out of their bondage to the flesh and put them into proximity to the transcendent, supramundane realm of pure spirit. To state it perhaps too bluntly but nonetheless with considerable accuracy—salvation in the typical religions and philosophies of this civilization meant salvation *from* the world.

By contrast, as even a cursory reading of the Old Testament will show, Hebraic faith was very earthy. For the Jews, God was the very Creator of the material universe and all of its creatures. In the creation narrative (Genesis 2), God is depicted personally fashioning the human body, and blowing breath into its mouth to "get it going"! Such a conception of deity is positively repulsive to Hellenistic religion. Moreover, the Jews believed

3. See in this connection Reumann, "The Use of 'Oikonomia' and Related Terms."

(and still do!) that the material world, and therefore also the body and its functions—eating, drinking, sexuality, work, and recreation—are good. "And God saw everything that had been made, and behold, it was very good" (Gen. 1:31). That evil is also real and terrible was never doubted by the tradition of Jerusalem; but it did not and does not locate the source of evil in matter per se. In fact, it regards evil as a product of spirit— perhaps transcendent spirit (Satan, the demonic), but also the human spirit, which as we have already noted craves on the one hand a status more than human (pride) and on the other settles for something less than truly human (sloth). In this tradition, matter is the pawn and victim of a distorted human spirit, not the other way around.

What happened in the move of the Christian faith into the Hellenistic world was that Christianity, which at first was an essentially Jewish offspring, underwent a process of spiritualization that robbed it of its potential for "world orientation" that it had inherited from its parental faith. Archbishop William Temple once remarked that of all the world's religions Christianity is the most materialistic. That claim still shocks many Christians, whenever it is heard (which is seldom enough!). But our shock only demonstrates how far we have come from Jerusalem, and how much closer to Athens and Alexandria and their later counterparts. In terms of the biblical sources of our faith, when they themselves are not distorted through our acquired ambiguity about creaturehood, Christianity shares with its parental faith, Judaism, a profound world orientation: for the tradition of Jerusalem, the world is both real and good. This is the presupposition without which the whole notion of the Incarnation would be meaningless.

But while one must acknowledge this in faithfulness to the Scriptures of both testaments, one is obliged at the same time to recognize that from the start the Christian religion has manifested a strong tendency towards an antimaterial, antiworld spiritualism. Conrad Bonifazi, writing about a subject to which we shall have to turn our attention later ("Biblical Roots of an Ecological Conscience"), puts the matter succinctly when he writes:

> The religion of the *incarnate* Word was all too quickly attacked by an ascetic virus which undermined its natural elements in favor of the supernatural. This atrophy of interest in the natural makes nonsense of the whole concept of Incarnation whereby the New Testament wished to affirm that the God who is personal Love is indissolubly united not only with the human race but also with the entire universe of matter.[4]

What Jürgen Moltmann calls "the nihilism practiced in our dealings with nature"[5] must certainly be traced in part to this spiritualistic denigration of matter. It is there in second-century Gnosticism, which orthodox Christianity officially rejected but did not defeat; it is strongly present in Manichaeanism, by which Augustine of Hippo was influenced and which he never entirely shook off; it cropped up in militant form in some of the more stringent experiments in monasticism, and in movements such as those of the Catharists and Albigensians and countless other groups throughout the ages.[6] But it was never only a minority form of the faith, because these groups and persons had the effect of exemplifying for the larger and looser body of the faithful what it would mean to be really Christian!

It is thus not accidental that the story of the church is full of heroes and saints whose chief claim to prominence, at least in the popular imagination, is their promethean struggle against every worldly attachment. This image of the faith is still the one that is held up—albeit with perennial ambiguity and periodically disastrous contradictions!—by the electronic church's presentation of Christianity. What is usually being denounced by televi-

4. In Michael Hamilton, ed., *This Little Planet* (New York: Charles Scribner's Sons, 1970), 207.
5. Moltmann, *God in Creation*, xi.
6. See Christopher Derrick, *The Delicate Creation: Towards a Theology of the Environment* (Old Greenwich, Conn.: Devin-Adair, n.d.), 35ff. The whole of chap. 3 is relevant to this topic.

sion evangelists and their sweet musical backup artists is not just the sin of the world (and certainly never the economic and political sins of the First World!) but the worldly condition as such. Like their Manichaean, Gnostic, and Docetic progenitors, these people feel imprisoned in "a hostile environment"; they are "nostalgic" for "home,"[7] and home can never be a reality for them under the conditions of time and space. The apocalyptic intuition of our present historical situation of course aggravates this otherworldliness, but the results are just exaggerated and often bizarre forms of a spiritualism that has plagued historic Christianity almost from its inception.

But how does all this shape the destiny of the stewardship motif within the evolution of Christian thought? The answer, briefly stated, is that it leaves the Christian movement with a highly spiritualized version of the biblical metaphor; therefore it discourages the development of the stewardship theme as a way of thinking about human existence in its totality—in the psychosomatic unity of its creaturely condition. To put the matter more concretely, the spiritualization of the Christian message occuring under this general Hellenistic influence meant that a concept with as much worldly potential as that of the steward metaphor could not be nourished by its environment. It atrophied before it had had a chance to prove itself. Its unfolding was limited to the spiritual side, and therefore the worldly meaning of stewardship remained at best dormant. A phrase like Paul's—that as Christ's servants we are "stewards of the mysteries of God" (1 Cor. 4:1)—could very readily fit the mindset of Gnostic and other Christian spiritualizers, and not only fail to suggest that our stewarding has something to do with the creation but actually confirm such persons in their belief that the gospel is a secret code through which to overcome and escape this lost and inferior sphere.

One can easily appreciate how such a spiritualistic reduction of the stewardship motif could achieve a foothold in early

7. *Ibid.*

Christianity. Remember that one of the most prominent features of the earliest form of the Christian religion was its expectation of an imminent parousia or triumphant return of the conquering Christ. "The end of all things is at hand!" (1 Pet. 4:7). As we have seen, this kind of expectancy tended to discourage the early Christians from carrying the stewardship idea into the arena of everyday worldly responsibility. Although the metaphor of the steward in its biblical expression does contain great potential as a symbol of human responsibility within creation, New Testament faith already tended towards a more exclusively religious or sacred interpretation of Christian stewardship: as Christians we are stewards of "God's varied grace," and of "the mysteries of God," of the gospel. The prominence of the End in the consciousness of the early church naturally favoured this religious side of the metaphor.

But surely one does not have to indulge in wild conjecture to think that had the culture into which the early church moved in the second and third centuries itself been more this-worldly, Christians, as they gradually abandoned the most literal interpretations of the parousia, would have discerned in the steward symbol something having a profound and concrete worldly meaning. There are indeed some hints of this possibility in the writings of the second-century apologists. But the longings of the ancient world, like many of the human longings in our own uncertain age, were not in fact directed towards reconciliation with and transformation of this good earth. People longed rather for the permanence, tranquility, and security of life beyond the fluctuations and sufferings of "this vale of tears." This is what they expected of religion; and this, for the most part, is what they caused the Christian religion to offer them. Hence the worldly meaning of stewardship was nipped in the bud. Insofar as it was retained in that spirit-ladened atmosphere, it was retained in a highly religious form, and not infrequently with Gnostic overtones: Christians are the keepers of the secret mysteries of God's revelation in Christ!

## 3. Consequences for Stewardship of Christian Establishment

In the Introduction, I have devoted a little attention to the disestablishment of Christianity that has been occurring, with varying levels of intensity, in our own era; and I have noted there that this process carries with it certain consequences for the Christian life that are provocative for the question of stewardship. What we have to observe in the present discussion is in a sense the opposite end of that long process, namely, the establishment of Christianity in the fourth century, and the consequences that this had with respect to our subject.

If the "dehellenization" (Leslie Dewart) of Christian belief is one of the most urgent requirements of Christian theology in our time, the disestablishment of Christianity is the other. It is a mistake to think that establishment meant only external, political changes in the life of the Christian church. The changes occurred also at the level of belief and theology, so that the disestablishment of Christianity entails a great deal of discernment, not only regarding church polity and practical issues, but also in our fundamental comprehension of the faith. Since I have written a good deal about this in other places,[8] I shall not do so here extensively. Suffice it to say that until the adoption of Christianity by Rome, the Christian faith existed only as a voluntary, countercultural movement, embraced by persons at their own risk. Persecution of the church was neither uniform nor always severe during those earliest centuries (exaggerated accounts of martyrdom and the like should be distrusted by anyone who wishes to get to the bottom of the matter). Yet to be Christian prior to 313 C.E. was to opt for a life outside the pale of respectability and against the stream of the dominant culture. All that was changed by the seemingly sudden but nonetheless politically sagacious

8. See my *Future of the Church*; see also *Has the Church a Future?* (Philadelphia: Westminster Press, 1980) and *The Reality of the Gospel and the Unreality of the Churches* (Philadelphia: Westminster Press, 1975).

decision of Constantine to bring the faith of Jesus into the imperial court. Having become a kind of Christian himself, Constantine began politically and economically to favour the Christian religion; and before the end of the same century Christianity had become, under Theodosius the Great, the only legal religion of the empire.

Now a sociological transformation of this magnitude does not occur without drastic changes at every level, including basic beliefs. I suspect that we are only at the beginning of the process of historical and theological reflection that is needed to unearth the full meaning of Christian establishment. Part of what retards this process within the churches is the desire on the part of many Christians, perhaps most, to retain the supposed benefits of establishment. Certainly the effects of this marriage of church and empire are to be observed in every major doctrinal area of faith. What does it mean, for example, that the most decisive theological formulations of the two most central and complex doctrines of Christianity—the Trinity and Christology—were both constructed *after* 313 C.E.? The Council of Nicaea (325) was in fact convened by Constantine himself.

In what way did these changes alter or influence the direction of the stewardship motif? Really, in a whole spectrum of ways. For one thing, in the preestablished situation still assumed by the biblical writers, the apostolic fathers, second-century apologists, and others, the Christians had to take direct responsibility for their own life and work. Thus we learn from Acts 2:44ff. that the earliest Christians "had all things in common." Part of their individual stewardship was this cooperative pooling of resources—what has been called "primitive communism." They had to "bear one another's burdens" (just as the earliest settlers in North America had to do), because they could expect no help from outside, whether from public or private sources. After the establishment of the Christian religion, however, Christianity became an officially supported cult, and the support extended to material as well as less tangible matters.

It does not take a great deal of imagination to realize how

such a socioeconomic transformation could easily and in a very short time effect changes in attitudes, expectations, and practices. For its fulness, stewardship depends upon a sense of immediate responsibility on the part of all who claim membership in the body of Christ. When it can be assumed, however, that much of what is needful for the well-being of the church will be provided by the state, or simply by the society at large (whether this means economic support or a constant influx of members, generation after generation), there is no longer any pressing need for inculcating such an attitude of personal responsibility in every Christian person or congregation.

In any case, it would have been extremely difficult to achieve such an indoctrination; for from the fourth century onwards, the great bulk of those who became Christian did so as a matter of routine, without any fundamental change of heart *(metanoia)* or experience of special grace. Indeed, after the reign of Theodosius the Great (346-395) it was sheer political necessity to be a "Christian." It was illegal to be anything else! This is a far cry from the diaspora (dispersed) situation of the earliest congregations—from the situation of Paul of Tarsus, for instance, an important part of whose ministry was convincing his converts in the Gentile world that their new faith obligated them to share their money not only with one another but with congregations poorer and more persecuted than themselves.

Besides this rather obvious change, the new sociological condition of the church in the established situation brought about very subtle but very real alterations in the Christian understanding of the mission of the church. In the preestablished diaspora situation, the Christian community as a countercultural movement was able to feel a certain solidarity with other oppressed groups and peoples—with the poor, the political outcasts, the lower classes including slaves (many of whom were the first converts), and others. Such solidarity is reflected in the parables they remembered (Matt. 25, for example) as well as in the stories told in Acts of the imprisonment of the apostles, their feeling for other prisoners and for others oppressed. The same sense permeates the literature of early martyrdom.

Stewardship in this setting could mean (not that it always did) identification with the victims of power, and thus vigilance for justice and liberty—a constant theme of the Hebrew prophets. Under the conditions of establishment, however, Christianity permitted itself more and more to be identified with the dominant political and economic classes of society. As I have put it elsewhere, the *modus operandi* of the church became the quest for power through proximity to power. And power seeking, as we have seen in connection with our biblical exposition, is no fit attitude for the steward to cultivate! As Joseph Conrad wrote in *Heart of Darkness*, "The conquest of the earth, which mostly means taking it away from those who have a different complexion or slightly flatter noses than ourselves, is not a pretty thing when you look into it too much."[9]

It was quite unlikely that any church bent upon achieving a foothold with the powerful would ever seriously explore the meaning of stewardship—especially its worldly meaning. Imperial Christianity learned how to use the language of service; but for the most part this language was more rhetorical and liturgical than it was descriptive of the actual life of the church. The church that was inaugurated at the Edict of Milan, unlike the church born at Pentecost, was, I fear, largely bent upon *self*-service. The losers had become winners by a strange twist of fate, and they quickly demonstrated to the world that they were determined to win everything and everyone—for Christ, of course![10]

Fortunately for our present edification and encouragement there were always a few who resisted this ecclesiastical power trip; a few who remembered that "the servant is not above his master"; a few who found conquest and stewardship incom-

9. Joseph Conrad, *Heart of Darkness* (Harmondsworth, Eng.: Penguin, 1983), 33.
10. See my fuller discussion of this theme in my *Has the Church a Future?*

patible bedfellows. It is chiefly in these that the subsequent history of the stewardship motif must be traced.

## 4. Remnants of the Stewardship Motif among the Disinherited

It would be an understatement to say that the two factors named above—the spiritualization of the faith and its political establishment—have continued to influence the development of stewardship down to our own time. The fact is, the symbol has played almost no role at all in the history of European Christianity. One looks in vain in the great systems of dogmatic theology for any mention of the theme. Recently some of the encyclopedias dealing with Christian faith have introduced articles on stewardship, but still its definition fails to appear in many standard works of this sort—including, for example, the well-researched *Oxford Dictionary of the Christian Church*. It is true that ideas approaching, or cognate to, the stewardship theme are developed in major works of theology; but the very presence of these makes one wonder why their authors were not at once drawn to the symbol itself. The reason, I suspect, is that there was very little in the actual life of the church that would have made the symbol meaningful. There is a much closer relation between the practical realities of ecclesiastical life and the themes pursued by theologians than is sometimes appreciated. With little necessity of pursuing stewardship at the level of their material life, the great churches of Europe had no need to ask about that theme as a theological issue.

It is in fact part of the historical generalization that I am in process of developing here that at least in the history of its conscious usage, the symbol of stewardship must be traced in those groups and movements that broke away from the Christian establishment, and who therefore needed to reorganize their corporate life and mission in a different way. Something of this can already be observed in the earliest breakaway movements, such as the monastic communities, which began to develop shortly after the time of Constantine as part of the response of those who were not satisfied with the perfunctory Christianity of the majority.

The relation between disestablishment and stewardship is made transparent in the experience of the first great pre-Reformer, John Wyclif. Wyclif was one of the few historical figures of note in the Christian movement explicitly to use the metaphor of the steward. In the thought of Wyclif, stewardship is associated with his critique of *dominium* (lordship or sovereignty). He took very seriously the biblical declaration that "the earth is the Lord's and the fulness thereof" (Ps. 24:1). The human condition, if it is rightly discerned, is that of a steward. It is the calling of the church to exemplify concretely in its life the universal Lordship of God, that is, to have done with the sinful desire to seek security through possessions, and, on the contrary, to behave towards all creatures, human as well as non-human, as stewards. Humanity assumes the posture of possession and dominion only in its sinful state, when it has persuaded itself that God is absent. In the presence of God, human beings know that *dominium* is not an appropriate stance for creatures of God to assume. They may bear a certain authority as stewards, but it is a borrowed authority and radically qualified by the sole dominion of God.

> God loans us lordship, but it is not ours: a human being is improperly called a lord, but is rather a steward of the supreme Lord. It is clear from this that every creature is a servant of the Lord, possessing whatsoever he has of pure grace that he may husband it.[11]

Obviously Wyclif intended this doctrine of stewardship, with its inherent critique of both authority and property, to apply explicitly to the church—a church which he believed to be in a state of radical disobedience because of its pretention to power

11. Matthew Spinka, *Advocates of Reform: From Wyclif to Erasmus*, Library of Christian Classics, vol. 14 (London: SCM Press, 1953), 22.

and its wealth. But though he addressed the church he could not avoid the implication that such an understanding applied in general to the human condition, for he believed that the church was the doorway to a renewed and authentic humanity. His rich and powerful supporters, like John of Gaunt, also saw these implications, and did not like them!

Ernst Troeltsch in fact finds these aspects of Wyclif's teaching his most original contributions to reform.

> In this theory, Wyclif had no intention of attacking the property rights of the secular classes. . . . The primary aim of this conception . . . was simply that of restoring the ideal of the "poor church," and its radical social implications were not developed to their logical conclusion in the temporal sphere. It is, however, very significant that in this strict conception of the *Lex Dei et Naturae* radical social consequences *do* emerge over against the whole existing order, even although at first they were only practically applied to Church property; more far-reaching consequences were inevitable.[12]

For our present purposes, the point to be stressed is that Wyclif's tentative though highly provocative ventures into this area contributed very significantly, along with his later attack upon the eucharistic doctrine of transubstantiation, to his expulsion from Oxford and his fall from grace. He had only come to his radical critique of dominion after he had already distanced himself from the ruling authorities of the realm and the church; and his critique of property and sovereignty, with its almost socialistic undertones, cost him the support of many of his powerful friends.

There are aspects of the later Reformation of the sixteenth century which contribute to stewardship theology—for instance Luther's concept of vocations and Calvin's covenant theology. One can also hear in the Geneva Reformer's strong emphasis upon the sovereignty of God a very important presupposition of the stewardship concept—as it was quite explicitly

12. *Ibid.*, 24.

for Wyclif. Luther too, as we shall see, provides significant material for the development of a stewardship theology in relation to the natural world. All the same, the steward motif seems not to achieve any special prominence in either of the chief Reformers. It begins, rather, to make a hesitant appearance on the periphery of the Reformation, amongst those not-quite-legal, sometimes rejected and persecuted Protestant bodies—such as the Anabaptists and (later) the Methodists—who unlike the mainline Protestant movements were not able to rely upon the state for either material or moral support.

This being so, it was natural enough that the most self-conscious and explicit development of the stewardship idea should have occurred on the North American continent. For it was in this New World that the rejected religious bodies of European society found a place to belong. They brought two attitudes with them that were fodder for the growth of at least a remnant of the theology of stewardship suggested by the Scriptures: a well-earned suspicion of Christian establishment, and a readiness to assume personal responsibility for the maintenance of free religion to the point of personal sacrifice.

### 5. Stewardship in the North American Experience

Even in the New World, stewardship as a specific theme and emphasis did not immediately emerge. As Professor Salstrand reports in his book, *The Story of Stewardship in the United States of America:* "In the literature of the colonial period, the term 'stewardship' seems to have no place."[13] The churches in some cases tried to emulate Old World patterns of giving, though this was never very satisfactory. Some of the conditions necessary to the evolution of stewardship practice in the life of the churches had been met in the wilderness of the new continent; other conditions were still awaited.

13. Salstrand, *Story of Stewardship,* 13.

These latter cannot be dealt with adequately here, for they are part and parcel of very complex historical currents. We may relate them however to two, perhaps antithetical, movements in the unfolding of the religious history of the continent.

One is the movement called "secularism." A consequence of the religious freedom marking the history of North America was the growing awareness of the freedom not to be religious at all, if one so chose. Or, if one preferred a less drastic alternative, one might be privately religious without denominational affiliation. Secularism, whether of the more philosophic sort or simply of the practical variety that allowed one to be a decent citizen without going to church, was a necessary condition to the development of stewardship practices. It provided a background in which it became necessary for the churches to appeal to individual faith and responsibility for the support of the work of the church. Secularism meant that such support could no longer be counted upon as a matter of course. People had an alternative, and a respectable one. In other words, we are speaking of the beginning of a process of disestablishment that reaches far beyond the organizational structures of church and society, into the cultural assumptions and beliefs that are the spiritual foundation stones of those structures. One began to develop a conscious stewardship indoctrination at the point where large numbers of the populace, including church members, openly entertained the secular option.

The second movement that provided a necessary boost to the stewardship concept is in some ways the other side of this same coin. We may call it the evangelistic movement, although this term has been rendered unsatisfactory by subsequent usage. What I am referring to is of course the awareness that in a world that offers people the choice not to believe and not to support the community of believers, the church must work to propagate the faith. It cannot be assumed that belief will occur, generation after generation, without effort on the part of the witnessing community. Christian witness may be the responsibility of every Christian and therefore the church ought naturally to evangelize; but practically this does not occur with great success or regularity, and therefore the mission must be organized, must be equipped with the best resources and persons, and must be financed. Stewardship begins to be a special theme at the point where all these necessities come together.

Moreover, if the necessity of engaging in an active mission to the world is combined with a growing sense of the this-worldly orientation of the Christian gospel, this too will add incentive to the quest for adequate stewardship practices. Were it only for the eternal destiny of the souls of human beings, personal witness might suffice. But if it is felt that the Christian message is meant to bring a better life to people here and now, such a mission cannot be met without funds and without personnel who are highly equipped—medical missionaries as well as preachers; clothers of the body as well as of the soul; and teachers of the mind, not only of the spirit.

Those who are more or less acquainted with the history of stewardship in the United States and Canada will realize that I have not arbitrarily arrived at these two conditions for stewardship development. It is not accidental that the "Great Stewardship Awakening," as Professor Salstrand has designated it, occurred in the nineteenth century and in particular in the forties and fifties of that century. For that is also the period in which the movements I have briefly characterized above began to be felt. The secular alternative, which was already well under way in Europe, was of course not the popular route that it has since become in North America. At the same time, it was a definite presence, and its very novelty made it seem to the religious instinct all the more threatening. It gave zest and direction to the evangelistic spirit, which at the same time was spurred on by the beginnings of that liberal sense of expectancy that hopes for the kingdom of God in our time. The shaping of stewardship as we know it occurred in the press and excitement of these days. "Only one more revival is needed," declared Horace Bushnell of Hartford, "namely of Christian Stewardship or the 'consecration of the money power of the church.' 'When that revival comes, the kingdom of God will come in a day.'"[14]

## 6. Conclusion and Transition

In the Introduction, I said that my intention in this study was to engage in an exercise in theological praxis, meaning in part the kind of critical reflection on historical practice that enables people to enter into their historical destiny. In both the biblical exposition of the first chapter and the present discussions we have been considering critically the history of the church's relation to stewardship. What may we conclude at this point that might enable us to move on, in the subsequent phases of the study, to investigate more explicitly the destiny that could be present for us in this dimension of our history?

We may, I think, conclude something like this: The metaphor of the steward is sufficiently rich and inclusive in its original conception to be regarded an important symbol of the faith, with special reference to the vocation of Christians and implications for the whole anthropology of the biblical tradition. For a variety of reasons, however, this symbol was not selected by the empirical church as it developed; for most of the history of Christianity it has remained peripheral at best, and on the whole quite inactive.

As the church began to emerge into the modern world, however, the stewardship motif gradually acquired currency. It was perhaps inevitable that the power of the symbol was evoked at first by the very practical needs of Christian denominations—largely in North America—as they found themselves increasingly confronted by the need to develop a biblical rationale for their appeals for financial and other material support. Until the

14. Salstrand, *Story of Stewardship*, 31.

present time, the stewardship concept in the churches has been confined chiefly to this functional office.

But we know from the biblical origins of this concept that it is much more expansive than the use to which, until now, it has been put. This we have begun to realize, and this incipient knowledge could be the point of entry into a new phase in Christian stewardship. Like all lively, authentic symbols, the symbol of the steward will permit itself to be used for purposes—including purely utilitarian purposes—that are less profound than the reality to which it points. But when we take on the use of symbols, even if we do so innocently and merely for pragmatic ends, we open ourselves to the truly deep and sometimes frightening power and potential that they possess. As the greatest symbol of our faith, the cross ought to have imprinted that lesson indelibly on our spirits. For the symbol "participates in the reality that it symbolizes" (Tillich); and therefore to associate oneself with it is to open oneself to the awareness of that reality. Thus the cross is the mediatory symbol through which we are exposed to the whole suffering of the world, and of the God who loves it. To have begun to know the expansiveness of the symbol of the steward is to have begun to make the transition from the functional meaning of stewardship to a meaning whose proportions and depth most of us, in all probability, have not yet fully anticipated.

Such transitions cannot be engineered. They can only happen. We have already observed that real symbols are not invented as signs are. They come to be. Similarly it may be said that the transition from the dormant or incomplete state to something more radical cannot be engineered by us: symbols grow when the situation is ripe for them.

Our increasing interest in the language of the steward, our very dissatisfaction with its conventional articulation, accompanied as this is by a growing curiosity about stewardship on the part of sensitive persons outside the faith—all this indicates that the situation may well be ripe. And if that is so, then no power on earth will prevent this symbol from leaping out of the small, utilitarian harnesses to which we have bound it, and unleashing its power where it is really needed. As for us Christians, who are the inheritors of the tradition that has produced this symbol, we must either let it go along without us or prepare ourselves to be carried by it, perhaps in directions "where [we] do not wish to go" (John 21:18).

CHAPTER III

# WHAT TIME IS IT?

## 1. Discerning the Signs

Christian theology is never pure theory. It is a type of reflection upon our concrete involvement in existence, undertaken from the perspective of a message about God's involvement in our existence. This message transcends any of its specific articulations, including the biblical one, because it is always addressed to the specific realities of our "here and now"—our context. That is to say, it is a living Word of the living God intended for living human beings.

According to the Protestant insistence upon the primacy of Scripture (*sola Scriptura*), however, the Bible is indispensable to this reflection. The witness of the biblical words to this living Word is unique and normative for Christians, because the message of God's involvement in the life of the world is for us inseparable from the story of Jesus, of the people in whose lineage he stood, and of the people who first recognized that he is the Christ, God's redemptive response to the human predicament. This biblical witness functions for the church of Jesus Christ as the "lens"[1] through which it views and interprets the world.

1. George Lindbeck, *The Nature of Doctrine: Religion and Theology in*

But this means that the world, that is, the situation in which the church actually finds itself, has constantly to be interpreted—deciphered, as it were. What is really going on in it, appearances notwithstanding? What is the character of the age? What time is it? Unless the disciple community can at least risk answering this question, its rendition of God's Word will be something less than gospel. For the gospel is good news only in relation to what is transpiring in the life of the world to which it is addressed. This is why Jesus berated his hearers for their failure to interpret the present time:

> When you see a cloud rising in the west, you say at once, "A shower is coming"; and so it happens. And when you see the south wind blowing, you say, "There will be scorching heat"; and it happens. You hypocrites! You know how to interpret the appearance of earth and sky; but why do you not know how to interpret the present time? (Luke 12:54-56)

Two interfacing points of concentration or orientation are necessary, then, to the witnessing community: an ongoing struggle to comprehend the Scriptures and the long tradition of those who in the past have done the same thing; and a continuous attempt to decipher the worldly context in which the community is to make its witness. Theology is what happens when these two orientations intersect—that is, when the biblical testimony to the Word encounters the spirit of the age, and when the Word encounters that spirit (Zeitgeist).

Our fundamental proposition, communicated by the title of this book, is that the concept of human stewardship is pertinent for articulating the gospel today. Looking through the lens of Scripture at the world in which we are living, we are being impelled to conclude this: Ours is a world in which human beings are required to find a new way of conceiving of their identity and vocation; otherwise there can be no averting the cat-

---

a *Post-Liberal Age* (Philadelphia: Westminster Press, 1984), 119. Lindbeck writes that the Bible "supplies the interpretive framework within which believers seek to live their lives and understand reality" (*Ibid.*, 117).

astrophic future we are courting. Simultaneously we bring to our reflection on the biblical text this existential concern for the future and the specific demand for a new image of the human implicit in it, and we find ourselves searching the Scriptures for appropriate clues to such an image. And amongst these clues the biblical metaphor of the steward becomes highly suggestive. It is an ancient metaphor that, in view of the present intricate constellation of problems which conditions our context, has become newly accessible to the community of faith as a medium for its message. That is to say, the steward metaphor of the biblical lens ought now to be considered a full-fledged symbol. It has come of age.

In a nutshell, that is our underlying proposition. So far we have only investigated part of it—the scriptural and historical background. While our research of this background has certainly not been exhaustive, it is sufficient to assure us at least of this much: that the metaphor of the steward is conspicuously present in the biblical tradition, even though it has never been consistently or profoundly appropriated by evolving church doctrine. It is there for our pedagogical and kerygmatic deployment, and it is there as a metaphor which already contains symbolic potential—a potential which has only been sporadically and imperfectly glimpsed in the Christian past.

What we have yet to show, if our thesis is to be adequately defended, is that the spirit of the times in which we live is such that this potential for symbolic usage may and must now be actualized in the teaching and preaching of the Christian community. What is the character of our context? And why does such a time evoke from us the strong suspicion that the steward metaphor of this ancient literature is one on which we may draw now for the timely articulation of our message and the accomplishment of our mission?

This is now our task, and we should not mistake it: there is enormous risk involved in it! One must say this in sympathy with those whom Jesus rebuked for their dullness and lack of perception: it is one thing to predict the weather a day or so in advance; it is something else to decode the mysterious signs of the times. Even weather predictions can be misleading and wrong, as we know well enough despite today's sophisticated forecasting technology. Our world also is full of expertise for social analysis. Sociologists, economists, geographers, ecologists, demographers, historians, political scientists, futurologists, and representatives of many other disciplines daily provide us with more information than anyone could possibly assimilate in a lifetime; and much of it is contradictory. What is really going on? Even at the intellectual level it is hard to say. Who can assess with accuracy what is the truth about the here and the now?

Hindsight is of course easier. But the sort of obedience that is required of faith is never a matter of knowing what one might have done *then*. It is a matter of believing and deciding what one ought *now* to do: here and now. The wise ones of every age will always judge such obedience presumptuous, because the wise always want to wait until all the facts are in. But of course all the facts are never in. Is that why the wise so seldom act?—why for instance European intellectuals in two world wars were so silent? Obedient stewards of God's varied grace must act—unlike that clearly judicious servant who feared his actions might end in the loss of his paltry talent (Matt. 25:14ff.). They must be ready to risk, to rush in where the angels of the intellect fear to tread. They must be prepared, too, to hear that they are fools. All they can do is to hope that their necessary folly might at last, through God's transforming grace, serve the cause of that ultimate wisdom that the wise ones and "debaters of this age" regularly miss (1 Cor. 1:18-19). Perhaps they will turn out to have been "fools for Christ," after all (1 Cor. 4:10).

But the risk of discerning the signs of the times is not only a risk of the intellect. It is a risk of the self, of the spirit-body. For especially in times of great unrest and manifold crisis, the whole inclination of the human heart is to "flee from the wrath to come." By all accounts but those of the most doctrinaire optimists, ours is such a time. The problem of our world is so complex and overwhelming in its scope and ubiquity that it is somehow natural to flee all contemplation of it. Perhaps the desire to escape from reality has never been so strong as it is in our present context. It can be observed that the most popular activities in the Western world today are activities that offer the illusion of escape: sex, sports, food, travel, and entertainment. Our kind of frenzied preoccupation with such things is incomprehensible apart from the escapism that fires it. And perhaps the most escapist activity of all is religion. Bizarre religions and quasi-religions spring up everywhere, as in the last days of Rome. Christianity itself becomes a happy hunting ground for all manner of religious pursuits and presuppositions which have virtually no connection with any of the major streams of the faith. Indeed, the forms of the Christian religion most popular today (to the point of displacing traditional mainline Christianity) are those that offer the most effective techniques for escape from history. Whether they do this through spiritualistic flights of fantasy or by the continuous reassurance that there are no real crises in the affairs of the world makes little difference. One evades the real world just as effectively by eliminating its dark side as by creating a secondary world (heaven) in which there is no shadow or turning.

Genuine escape from the world—and I mean this very explicit world of the late twentieth century—is nevertheless impossible. To illustrate: I wrote these words originally in southern France, inside a house that is perhaps centuries old, situated in the valley of a quiet river and sheltered by ancient foothills, far from the tumultuous and violent cities of restless, frightened Homo sapiens. There were moments in that setting when, forgetting some of the objects by which I was surrounded (including the television set and my PaperMate pen!) I could think myself far away from the twentieth century—perhaps a contemporary of the monks of Cluny or the peasants of the nineteenth century working in their fields of lavender. But just as I was basking in the quietness of such imaginings, the serene Provence skies would be shattered by the vulgar, sickening shrieks of supersonic military jets from a nearby base, and I would be brought back to the realization that I am after all a child of the "Age of Anxiety" (W. H. Auden). It is in this age that I must think and do and live. It is in this age that I must try to comprehend what it means to be a steward of God's varied grace. To attempt to transcend this age is to court the judgment meted out to that unjust steward, who for his comfort decided that the time of his obedience was not yet; that in the meantime he might take advantage of the delay of his master.

But how shall we characterize this age? Of all the ages of humankind is it not the most perplexing? Who can subject himself or herself even to a fraction of the data available in one discipline alone? The world is full of books and documentaries and reports that try to tell us who and where we are. Whole institutions, research teams, think tanks, and commissions are devoted to the analysis of our society. It is a never-ending task, and never wholly successful either. How can we hope to comprehend it?

Certainly we cannot do so in the chapter of a small book. Yet even here we are bound again to make the attempt. For without coming to terms with ourselves and the spirit of the age in at least a preliminary way and in relation to the subject we are pursuing here, we cannot discover the appropriate expression of this dimension of the gospel. We cannot even demonstrate convincingly that it is an appropriate expression of the Christian message. We have claimed that the particularities of our context have created an atmosphere in which this ancient metaphor can come to life—can achieve symbolic status. But the life, the shape, and the direction our stewardship thinking and acting should take depends upon a more decisive and explicit articulation of the character of our time and place. Let us therefore risk it![2]

---

[2]. For a fuller discussion of the method on which I am drawing here, see my discussion of contextuality in Christian theology in *Thinking the Faith*.

## 2. The Polarities of the Age

Two pervasive attitudes can be detected in First World societies. At first glance the two appear to be opposites—as though a tug of war were going on in the soul of the body politic. But on closer inspection it appears that there are inherent connections between the two, that they are by no means unrelated, that one in fact begets and sustains the other. Like so many apparent contradictions, they are in reality of a piece. The logic of their relationship may be obscure, but it is not at all illogical.

### a. The Technocratic Mind-Set

The first attitude is what we may designate, with others, the technocratic mind-set. Let me be quite precise: I am not referring to machinery, not even to the complex and (for average minds) almost magical machinery of which the computer upon which I am writing these lines is part. The machinery itself— those "dark satanic mills" of Blake that in these latter days are often more hygenic and full of light than cathedrals!—is nothing but the consequence of a frame of mind. As such it may be frightening enough, especially since much of the most advanced of it is designated for horribly destructive ends ("Nothing equals the perfection of our war machines!").[3] But what is more appalling is the collective mentality that produces the machinery, sets priorities for its production, and selects the ends to which it is put. It is the technocratic mind-set, not merely the technology, that must be understood and challenged by all persons of good will. The dilemma of our civilization will not be met by Luddite-like striking out at computers or military hardware, even though the symbolic value of such acts may sometimes be great. Chances are, as Kurt Vonnegut so cleverly demonstrates in his fiction, and the Japanese and German economic miracles dem-

3. Jacques Ellul, *The Technological Society* (New York: Alfred A. Knopf, 1964), 16.

onstrate in their nonfiction, that even if all the machinery in the world were destroyed it would be remade and improved upon within a generation. What is "wrong" about us is not our gadgetry so much as the spirit that it incarnates.

Jacques Ellul has defined that attitude in terms of the "systematization, unification, and clarification" of experience:

> Technique is the translation into action of man's concern to master things by means of reason, to account for what is subconscious, make quantitative what is qualitative, make clear and precise the outlines of nature, take hold of chaos and put order into it.[4]

Technique is in short the reigning mythology of our epoch. "We *are* technique," is the simple formula of the late George P. Grant, the Canadian philosopher.[5] Novelist Hugh MacLennan has expressed the same judgment in a way that is theologically provocative:

> Technology, which developed as a system of tools and labour-saving devices, greatest of boons to muscle-wearth, earth-bound men, now has developed into a kind of universal church with a faith all its own, with a hierarchy of bishoprics and an army of lay brethren known as specialists. Its faith, like the Christian faith in the Middle Ages, is simply this: that its way is the only way to heaven, because it assumes that earth is the only heaven or hell we can know . . . *Vox scientia, vox Dei.*

However, continues MacLennan, "despite these miracles, nobody could call the human psyche today heavenly, happy, or overly confident."[6]

The lack of happiness, that elusive element the pursuit of which was given modernity's seal of approval in the American Declaration of Independence, can be related to two concom-

---

4. Ibid., 43.

5. George P. Grant, *Technology and Empire: Perspectives on North America* (Toronto: House of Anansi, 1969), 137.

6. Report of author's speech on "Literature and Technology," in *Toronto Star*, 1 March 1972, 10.

itants of the quest for technocratic mastery of the world. One is the loss of any operative sense of meaning or purpose—any teleological sense—and the consequent lack of direction that is conspicuous in the pathetic posturing of the great technocracies. The other is the direct implication of the quest for mastery itself—the tragic flaw in the whole exercise, namely that when Homo sapiens sets out to master nature it must eventually subject itself, being part of nature, to the same process of mastery that it applies to the natural world at large. And herein lies the connecting link between the two attitudes to which I am alluding. But before we elaborate on that point, we need to consider briefly what I have named the concomitants of the quest for mastery.

The loss of meaning that has been depicted in thousands of novels, plays, and films, and celebrated by atheistic existentialism, is the great spiritual fact of our era. Persons who still think and live within the framework of some system of meaning, such as Christianity or Marxism, frequently fail to grasp what it means that for multitudes of human beings throughout this present century there has been no transcendent purpose in existence. Only a few of those who have lived with this sense of purposelessness, to be sure, have had either the courage or the imagination overtly to indulge it, to contemplate it, to write about it, to express it in word, symbol, or song. The majority, as always, has simply lived it—many of them content out of habit to repeat the rituals and proverbs of the past, but in their deeds betraying a vast spiritual vacuum, a moral wilderness so inclusive that it is itself the most potent ingredient in our cultural dilemma.

To have lost sight of a horizon of meaning within which personal dreams and ambitions can seem significant is perhaps the most devastating thing that could happen to a people—potentially far worse than even grave physical crises like the crisis of nature. And this lostness certainly is the cause of most physical crises. The loss is crucial, for as Abraham Heschel has so cogently stated it, "Man's vocation is not acceptance of being, but relating it to meaning; and his unique problem is not how to come into being, but how to come into meaning."[7] It is indicative of the primal importance of meaning for a human community that its loss can be expressed in a symbol like "the death of God"—which could as accurately be named "the death of man," as Elie Wiesel and others do in fact name it. If the term "civilization" has any nonspecific connotation, it is that of a society that is born and that grows on the foundations of some system of meaning; and it is seriously to be questioned whether, in the absence of any such system, human community is even possible.

Today we are busying ourselves with attempts to find substitutes for the sense of transcendent meaning. Educators devise curricula for prioritizing our values; legislators construct, and then try to implement, codes of human rights and the like. Obviously these activities are necessary if any sense of public morality and decency is to apply in a civilization that has lost touch with its own traditions of meaning and behaviour. But it remains to be seen whether any of these highly self-conscious attempts can stave off the crudity and violence against which they are pitted. Without some foundation in reality beyond our own conscious devising, such efforts appear arbitrary at best, a matter of wishful thinking at worst. If they are created by the will of a public, there is no reason why they cannot be dismantled and rejected by the will of another public. Anyone who has been half alive during the last five decades will have noticed, surely, that public opinion is a very fickle thing!

By comparison, the ancients (whether of Jerusalem or Athens) did not engage in morality by consensus, but assumed that the Good preceded and conditioned our valuing:

> The pre-modern universe was shot through and through with value: there was a hierarchy of purposes into which man with his purposes could fit and feel at home. By contrast, the universe

7. Abraham Heschel, *Who Is Man?* (Stanford: Stanford University Press, 1965), 67.

of modern science is a universe of fact without purpose; and because man cannot live without purpose there arises a dichotomy between "fact" and "value." Values are now human only: man finds that he and his values have no counterpart in the world of sheer fact around him—he is radically alone. When Aristotle gazed at the stars, he could regard them as manifesting purposes somehow akin to human purposes. When the stranger of Albert Camus' novel gazes at the stars, he must regard them as neutral. Thus it seems that man is not only a marginal being within the universe of modern science but also that his purposes and values, inextricably bound up with any conceivable religion, lack the kind of "objective" warrant which could be given them by some Archimedian point outside himself.[8]

The consequence for technique of the loss of a teleological sense is, to put it in a word (Martin Buber's), that technology is "leaderless." The inventive genius of humanity goes on, of course, even after the demise of meaning. Perhaps then it even continues at a pace greatly accelerated, because it knows no boundaries, no "limits to growth" (Club of Rome). But it also knows no goals, no points beyond which it would not be good to go. Its progress is directed only by its own inherent voraciousness. Because the thing can be done, it will and must be done. Sheer brilliance, curiosity, competition, and the lust for power sweep technology onwards, endlessly—or perhaps towards a catastrophic end that is all too logically bound up with its leaderless drive. Walter M. Miller in his unforgettable novel, *A Canticle for Leibowitz*, a story set after the nuclear holocaust, recalls that the first great destruction occurred simply because of the unbridled curiosity of a collective technocratic spirit that has lost the capacity for asking about the good.[9] Those who still today have been given the grace of belief (even if it is only belief in humanity, or history, or reason) need to contemplate long

8. Emil Fackenheim, *Quest for Past and Future: Essays in Jewis Theology* (Bloomington, Ind.: Indiana University Press, 1968), 232.

9. Walter M. Miller, *A Canticle for Leibowitz* (Montreal: Bantam Books of Canada, 1959).

and seriously that the world may already be in the grip of forces that are accountable to no belief system whatsoever; that only the logic of unrelenting progress remains. "What demons obsess our technology," asks the German physicist and theologian C. F. von Weizsäcker, "to make that contemplation impossible to which we ought to turn from time to time if we want to find the right use of technology itself?"[10] That humanity has lost its raison d'être just at the point where it had developed the means to realize some of its greatest dreams is either the ultimate historical irony or the work of some strange power that senses again the proximity of the Babel syndrome.

The destruction of Babel occurred not—as is sometimes naively thought—because Yahweh was jealous, but because Yahweh was gracious. God knew that the pride of mastery leads inevitably to the Fall, for mastery is the illusion of all illusions. The confusion and alienation of a failed Babel is terrible to contemplate; yet the degradation of the earth that could be achieved through a successful Babel is infinitely worse.

The *hubris* (inordinate pride) of the technocratic mindset contains a sort of aboriginal Catch 22: Whoever sets out to control the world must sooner or later control the controller— that is, the internal world that is the human spirit must be rendered predictable and harmless if the control is to be complete. Both the personal and the collective will must be placed under the command of the system, i.e., the rational means by which the chaos and infinite diversity of nature can be ordered and its impulsive powers constrained. You cannot afford to have human beings running about at random, each one pursuing her or his private goals, if your aim is the aim of technocracy, that is, to "eliminate chance" (George Grant).

The full consequences of this necessity were not noticed until the present century, and there are of course many still who are blithely oblivious to them. So long as it was possible for the majority to believe in a transcendent purpose in the very move-

10. Weizsäcker, *Relevance of Science*, 9.

ment of time (progress), it could be supposed that individual freedom, however self-serving, could only ultimately serve the common good. It was of course this belief that gave the necessary spiritual rationale to capitalism. Adam Smith's famous "Invisible Hand" could take the selfish, random deeds of the profit seekers and make them produce the best of all possible worlds for the majority.[11]

But the disappearance of objective purpose,[12] or, to state it another way, the emergence of the finally secularized society, means that the random or egotistic thoughts, words, and deeds of billions of human beings are not seen to blend nicely into a symphony of order and beauty. Of course, the harmony assumed by the progressive view of history in general and the liberal capitalist system in particular was always more credible to the rich than it was to the poor; and in fact part of the reason for the disappearance of meaning is precisely the failure of this modern vehicle of Western humanity's system of meaning to produce the utopia that it promised.

The assumption of the secular, postliberal, postmodern world is consequently that the ordering of society, which is no longer accomplished by invisible authority, must now be achieved by visible authorities, especially states. It makes a considerable difference of course whether the state is influenced by humane ends, and how far it will go towards compelling conformity. But what is shared by most of the states of our present world is the assumption that chaos can only be avoided if order is imposed from above. It becomes increasingly difficult for persons who want to uphold the freedom of individuals to obtain or hold office in any of our societies. Even elementary public

11. See the discussion of stewardship and capitalism in Chapter V.

12. "The natural science of Darwin and Newton has shown us that nature can be understood without the idea of final purpose. In that understanding nature appears to us as indifferent to what have been considered the highest moral purposes. We can control nature, but it does not sustain good." George Grant, *Time as History*, Massey Lectures (Toronto: Canadian Broadcasting Corporation, 1969), chap. IV.

opinion seems now to be ready to hand over its birthright to whatever Augustus can guarantee survival, and it is not over-scrupulous about the spiritual quality of that survival.

The logic of this mind-set has found its most brilliant amanuensis in B. F. Skinner. Skinner is, like most of us, concerned for the survival of the species. But he believes that Homo sapiens can survive only if a technology of behaviour is developed. Freedom and dignity must go.[13] What we call freedom is in any case only an illusion. We are willy-nilly conditioned creatures. Why not condition people deliberately—for ends that are good, such as social survival, benevolence, and pleasure? So long as we permit the sort of arbitrary decision-making that Western peoples have designated rationality to dominate, we are inviting destruction and oblivion in a society that is beset by a magnitude of survival problems. Why not permit the true rationality of mastery to be applied to human beings as it has been applied to everything else? This is no time to stop progress! "The simple fact is that man is able, and now as never before, to lift himself by his own bootstraps. In achieving control of the world of which he is a part, he may at last learn to control himself."[14]

Such logic fits almost exactly the formula for the kind of death of Homo sapiens depicted in the stories of the great anti-utopians from Zamiatin's *We* to Huxley's *Brave New World*, or from Michael Frayne's *A Very Private Life* to Margaret Atwood's *The Handmaid's Tale*. In order to ensure the survival of the species, those very qualities that led our predecessors to name our species (somewhat pretentiously, it is true!) *Homo sapiens* are willingly sacrificed! In this recognition lies the transition to the second attitude that informs our culture and that I suspect becomes daily the more characteristic of the two.

13. B. F. Skinner, *Beyond Freedom and Dignity* (New York: Alfred A. Knopf, 1971).

14. B. F. Skinner, "Freedom and the Control of Man," in George Kateb, ed., *Utopia* (New York: Atherton Press, 1971), 59.

## b. Programmed Indifference: The Soul as a Black Hole

When Howard Hughes died at the biblical age of seventy, he was reputed to be "worth" more than 2.5 billion dollars, and had become a complete recluse. *Time* magazine wrote of him: "In his latter years, Hughes had become the epitome of the 20th century tragedy, a man so preoccupied with gadgets and power that he severed the bond with his fellow men."[15]

Of another and later multimillionaire, Donald Trump, a recent edition of the same magazine, in which Mr. Trump was the feature presentation, ended with these words:

> One man who knows Trump well does see a rhyme and reason. Trump is a brilliant dealmaker with almost no sense of his own emotions or his own identity, this man says. He is a kind of black hole in space, which cannot be filled no matter what Trump does. Looking toward the future, this associate foresees Trump building bigger and bigger projects in his attempts to fill the hole but finally ending, like Howard Hughes, a multibillionaire living all alone in one room.[16]

The cases of Hughes and Trump may be exaggerated in certain respects. Few human beings ever amass so many dollars! But the Willy Loman character of so many of the public figures of our era (so different in this respect from the Carnegies and Vanderbilts of the past) highlights a general malaise, a drama of pathos that is played out silently and unnoticed in the living rooms and offices of our nations. The lives of ordinary people have always been routine and often boring; but in the past, which those of us over fifty can still remember, even the most banal of those lives were provided with a sense of worth and periodic dignity by the conventions, ceremonials, festivals, and expressed goals of the community. In the village in which I grew up, there

15. "The Hughes Legacy: Scramble for the Billions," *Time*, 19 April 1976, 30.
16. Otto Friedrich, "Flashy Symbol of an Acquisitive Age," *Time*, 16 January 1989, 54.

were individuals whose lives were so ordinary and inconspicu-
ous as to seem to provide little more than props on the stage of
our youthful dramas; still, these prosaic souls could at least count
upon the marriage of a son or the visit of a relative from the city—
or at very least their own funeral—to bring them into some
special prominence and even general esteem. All that seems to
have gone with the wind, but for exceptions here and there. Not
only in our cities, where the humble old await their inevitable
end in the anonymity of hospital wards or rooming houses, but
even in the villages that remain (and few remain *as villages*),
death itself goes almost unnoticed. Death is unremarkable because life is also unremarkable.

It is as if twentieth-century humanity had acquiesced quite
naturally and without a breath of protest to the absurdly reduced
status assigned it by time. The framers of the modern credo could
sing the praises of the ingenious being at the helm of the historical procession: "Man is the measure of all things." But between
their wild boast and our grey reality is fixed a great gulf. The gulf
perhaps bears the names of Auschwitz, Hiroshima, Vietnam, El
Salvador, South Africa, and many other places that have conclu-
sively revealed the utter cheapness of human life. Societies before
ours have known degradation, and their degradation has produced
a sense of guilt and shame. But we do not rise so high as these.
Guilt and shame presuppose the remembrance of righteousness
and innocence, and in a day when values have replaced goods
righteousness seems little more than an old-fashioned name for
outmoded morality and innocence is now called naivety.

We have become small. And there is no undergirding
greatness to give our smallness any glory. When the psalmist
"considered the heavens" he too felt small, but his smallness
did not crush him; for one who was very great was "mindful" of
him (Ps. 8). When late twentieth-century Adam or Eve contem-
plates the boundless spaces into which we hurl our costly space-
ships and satellites, the sensation produced is very different.
Not only the vastly expanded universe, but the very machinery
we thrust into it confirms our own insignificance. Our own in-

ventions have robbed us of some of the qualities on which we
had most prided ourselves. We thought ourselves "rational animals" (Aristotle). But beside the rapid and accurate calculations
of the complex computer, our brains seem heavy-laden; now we
seem to ourselves more animal than rational. Great seers tell
us that our human genius is in any case not to be found in cal-
culation but in meditation.[17] But we scarcely know what
thought could mean if it does not mean that calculating capacity of the brain that serves the drive to mastery. Honoring above
all effective technique, we fall short of the canon by which we
have come to measure perfection: the perfect machine!

> Every generation has a definition of man it deserves. But it seems
> to me that we of this generation have fared worse than we de-
> serve. Accepting a definition is man's way of identifying himself,
> holding up a mirror in which to see his own face. It is charac-
> teristic of the inner situation of contemporary man that the
> plausible way to identify himself is to see himself in the image
> of a machine. "The human machine" is today a more acceptable
> description of man than the human animal.[18]

Our glorification of the machine at the level of spirit and
intellect manifests itself powerfully in our daily existence. Unemployment, one of the most devastating problems of most
Western societies, is to be traced to this strangely unwarranted
apotheosis of efficient technique at the expense and denigration
of human beings. "Poor people are victimized by the very inventions and machines which improve standards of living for the
rest of society," writes Michael Kammen—onesidedly, in my
view, for he assumes all too willingly that automation necessarily entails the improvement of our standards of living.[19] Cer-

17. E.g., Martin Heidegger's distinction between *rechnendes Denken*
and *besinnliches Denken*.

18. Heschel, *Who is Man?* 23.

19. Michael Kammen, *People of Paradox: An Inquiry Concerning the
Origins of American Civilization* (New York: Oxford University Press, 1972),
281-82.

tainly the poor are the primary victims of the technocratic society, but there is also an impoverishment of spirit that in the long haul may be more damaging even than material poverty. Unemployment, as well as meaningless employment, are symptomatic of a much deeper malaise.

The failure of meaning at the level of public life has resulted in a new privatism that threatens to rob society of those most suitably equipped to serve the public good. This "immigration into the interior" *(innere Immigration)* has been described by Christopher Lasch as a culture of narcissism:

> Americans have retreated to purely personal preoccupations. Having no hope of improving their lives in any of the ways that matter, people have convinced themselves that what matters is psychic self-improvement: getting in touch with their feelings, eating health foods, taking lessons in ballet or belly-dancing, immersing themselves in the wisdom of the East, jogging, learning how to "relate," overcoming the "fear of pleasure." Harmless in themselves, these pursuits, elevated to a program and wrapped in the rhetoric of authenticity and awareness, signify a retreat from politics and a repudiation of . . . the past.[20]

To summarize: We find ourselves at the end of a process that began with the Renaissance and expressed itself mightily in the Industrial Revolution: the great thrust forward, the bid for sovereignty over nature and history. But just as such sovereignty seems within reach the whole vision has ceased to charm us. It has in fact turned sour.

Partly this is because we have sensed a little the flaw that was in it all along (the Catch 22); partly it is because we have lost, in the meantime, the whole ontic foundation of the vision. We have inherited a dream of glory and we do not apprehend ourselves as glorious. The role was written for someone else, perhaps for Prometheus, as some have suggested—and we are

---

20. Christopher Lasch, *The Culture of Narcissism: American Life in an Age of Diminishing Expectations* (New York: W. W. Norton, 1978), 4.

Sisyphus. Where our soul ought to be, there is a black hole which absorbs everything but is not increased.

## 3. Old Names for New Phenomena

One does not expect universal agreement with such a portrait of society, and yet I think it is not merely arbitrary or one-sided. Many students of our age (it is true for instance of most of the contemporary imaginative literature of our own continent) have analyzed Western civilization in similar terms. I have purposely attempted in this brief statement to incorporate the opinions of many others, especially of persons who do not speak out of Christian or even religious conviction, because Christians do not have a vested interest in making the world seem bleak. It is, to be sure, an assumption of our faith-tradition that existence is flawed at its core; this is the meaning of the so-called doctrine of sin. But this aboriginal flaw does not always take the same form; in fact, sin has an infinite variety of expressions. The public mood of the nineteenth century was very different from our "Age of Anxiety." But sin was as much present then as now—and if anything it was more deadly then because it was so seldom acknowledged, even by Christians, who were swept along by the general tide of euphoric progressivism. It is in many ways easier for Christians to acknowledge this darker side of our tradition today, because they can find all kinds of support from countless other sources. Indeed, by comparison with much societal analysis today, the Christian assessment of the human condition seems generous and hopeful in the extreme!

Sin is not a category of morality but a category of being. It describes the distortion of being that is the consequence of distrust. And, precisely as in the foregoing analysis of our society, this distortion involves two apparently contradictory but really complementary movements. Traditionally the two are named pride and sloth.

In pride the human creature reaches beyond the limits of its creaturehood. It grasps at equality with God:

> So when the woman saw that . . . the tree was to be desired to make one wise, she took of its fruit and ate; and she also gave some to her husband, and he ate. (Gen. 3:6)

Pride is born of the deep dissatisfaction of the creature with the limits of its creaturehood, its lack of permanency, wisdom, and power. Pride is behind the Babel search for mastery—"Come, let us build a city and a tower . . . and let us make a name for ourselves lest we be scattered abroad" (Gen. 11:4). Sloth, on the other hand, describes the state of indifference to our fallen condition. It means adapting oneself to less than righteous, less than just, less than peaceful, to less than human circumstances. If pride implies reaching too high, sloth means sinking too low, settling for something less than real humanity. If pride means forgetting that one is human and therefore "capable of failing"[21] (Paul Ricoeur), sloth means adjusting to failure and being fatalized by one's conditions.

Given such a definition of sin, it is hard to imagine a society more illustrative of the state of sin than our own! On the one hand we grasp pridefully after a technical sovereignty over nature and history; on the other hand we wallow in a fatalistic acceptance of our destiny, and slothfully withdraw from the arena of public life, pursuing our stingy, private happiness (the yuppie phenomenon). Pride drives us to pit our inventions and our inventiveness destructively against one another in a buildup of arms and economic defences that is patently absurd. Sloth keeps us away from the election polls (even so minor a public act as that!) and convinces us that mere individuals can do nothing to change things. Pride causes us to engage in a collective egotism, a ridiculous and boastful and promotional optimism that assigns exaggerated meaning to our space explorations and other scientific

21. Paul Ricoeur, *Fallible Man*, trans. C. Kelbley (Chicago: Regnery, 1965), 223.

achievements. Sloth counsels us in our privacy to cease hoping for any kind of long-term future and to prepare our offspring for small and highly personalized futures.

Beyond this, the logic of the relation between these two prongs of sin is also wondrously demonstrated in our societal polarities. Sloth is the other side and consequence of pride. It is pride driven to its final state—to the point where the secret spirit of the race, disillusioned and sulking, seeks its little revenge against life. Since we were apparently not cut out for the Promethean mastery to which our industrial pride beckoned us, we shall play the role of "unhappy gods" (Camus). Because we cannot achieve our superhuman ambitions, we seek compensation in the frenetic pursuit of subhuman pleasures (and pains!). We have sensed at some deep level of knowing that the vaunted modern dream of human lordship, including that special version dubbed "the American Dream," has been wrecked on the rocks of twentieth-century realities. Our response is not unpredictable, if one recollects this ancient dialectic of pride and sloth: we are sinking into a corporate depression. At the rhetorical level we continue halfheartedly to mouth the language of official optimism; but in fact we are losing the very capacity to hope.

An old proverb affirms, "Where there is life, there is hope." But human societies before our own have shown that there may be some sort of biological existence without an inherent thrust towards the future. Besides, as Freud has reminded us, life also contains a thrust towards oblivion (the death wish). The real question is whether, without any lively and operative hope, there can for long continue to be life—real life, not just existence. "Hope," says the prophetic, drunken priest who is the antihero of Graham Greene's *The Power and the Glory*, "is an instinct only the reasoning human mind can kill."[22] Have we been reduced to the necessity of killing our hope in order that we may survive?

22. Graham Greene, *The Power and the Glory* (Harmondsworth, Eng.: Penguin Books, 1962), 141.

## 4. Stewardship: A Matter of Direct Confrontation

Where does such an analysis leave us in relation to our topic, the theology of stewardship? It leaves us, I would suggest, at the very centre of the conflict! For if the analysis has any truth, it means that the image and symbol of the steward can only be explored and put forward today in the form of an explicit challenge and alternative to both sides of the anthropological distortion informing our society. Stewardship, rightly conceived, constitutes a direct confrontation with the image of the human *(imago hominis)* by which we are enthralled.

Against the concept of human sovereignty that modern industrial *hubris* taught us to covet for our species, the symbol of the steward challenges human beings to assume the posture of those who serve. And contrary to the retreat from the world into which we have been seduced by our failure at mastering it, stewardship challenges us to serve responsibly and as those committed to creation.

So, to "think stewardship" in our time is to think in very bold terms. It is to be plummeted into the center of the spiritual struggle of late-twentieth-century civilization—the struggle to find a future that is neither a pretentious and unfounded lordship of the universe leading with a dread logic to oblivion, nor on the other hand a cowardly slinking away from all thought, planning, and action that believes in the possibility of change.

In short, stewardship is no longer concerned with matters—including religious matters—on the periphery of existence; it belongs to the essence of things. It is for us today very close to what the prophets and apostles meant by the Word of God. For the call to responsible stewardship encounters us precisely at the heart of our present-day dilemma and impasse. When this biblical metaphor is brought to life by the Spirit of God blowing through the psychic desolations, the spiritual emptiness and future shock of our corporate life, it has the effect of direct address: "Will you at last assume your rightful role in this creation, child of Adam and Eve? Can you find it in yourself to take responsibility without being carried away by your own cleverness and power? Can you act the servant without grovelling and demeaning yourself? You have it in your power to love and to change the world! Can you at last take hold of that vocation, without thinking it either too high or too low a calling?"

We have seen enough of the biblical and historical background of this symbol to know that it will bear more truth (direct address) than the church has allowed it to bear. And now we have also seen enough of our world to know that the truth this symbol could bear is sorely needed. What we have still to ask is how, as a Christian community, we might liberate and enlarge this symbol, so that it could begin to achieve its potential for radical truth in such a world.

# CHAPTER IV

# GETTING OUR
# PRIORITIES STRAIGHT

## 1. Stewardship and "the Revolution of Humankind"

Latin American Christian spirituality has taught us about the biblical God's "preferential option for the poor." Many sensitive Europeans and North Americans have been moved in our times by the plight of the oppressed peoples of the world—statistically the majority! Christians can only be grateful for this contemporary sense of solidarity with the impoverished, hungry, and oppressed, wherever we find such concern and by whatever ideas it is inspired; for it renews our tie with the prophetic side of the tradition of Jerusalem, and therefore with that One who fulfils the office of prophet.

At the same time, Christian realism requires that we recognize that the condition of the world's dispossessed will not be greatly altered until the character of the oppressing forces of our own First World has been comprehended, confronted, judged, and changed. For citizens of the North Atlantic affluent nations it means this: until we have significantly examined and altered our own expectations; until we have ceased to demand of earth more than our just share of its bounty.[1] Liberation theology chal-

1. "North Americans comprise about 6% of the world's population and

lenges Christians everywhere to behave in accordance with their own declared ideals of justice, and it attracts many of our young who are (rightly!) bored and frustrated by the business-as-usual mentality of so much bourgeois Christianity. Liberation theology is a theology of action, of revolution. Whether in its Catholic or its Protestant expressions, it is a protesting theology, for it emboldens the wretched of the earth to rebel against what they have been conditioned to believe is their fate, and to explore new avenues of worldly hope. Liberation theology is a theology for those who have fallen among thieves.

But we are the thieves. Our question must be: "How do you develop a Christian theology for thieves?" Not the obvious thieves, like those crucified for their crimes on either side of Jesus; but unwilling thieves, unknowing thieves, thieves whose crimes would be recognized in no court of law, thieves who are for the most part "very nice people."

It was just this sense of the need for a truly critical theology within the First World that prompted one of the greatest exemplars of Christian theological praxis in our time to discourage young idealistic Christians of Europe and North America from seeking their Christian obedience too exclusively within Third World contexts. In 1969, Dom Hélder Camara wrote:

> Instead of planning to go to the Third World to try and arouse violence there, stay at home in order to help your rich countries to discover that they too are in need of a cultural revolution which will produce a new hierarchy of values, a new world vision, a global strategy of development, the revolution of mankind.[2]

A cultural revolution! A revolution of mankind! The gentle priest of Recife is no wild-eyed ideologue calling for the violent overthrow of the capitalist system. He is asking, rather,

---

consume approximately 40% of the world's raw materials." *Consumer Society Notes* 1 (December 1975): 2.

2. Dom Hélder Camara, *Church and Colonialism,* trans. William McSweeney (Danville, N.J.: Dimension Books, 1969), 111.

that we white Euro-Americans explore the potential of our own best past and present for alternatives to the ethics of greed that have guided our dealings at home and abroad. (I shall never forget his simple but spirit-penetrating words as he stood before an amphitheatre filled with students and professors of our large, secular university and pleaded: "Give us a *human* economics! Give us a *human* sociology! Give us a *human* chemistry, physics, historiography, etc." He dared to *exhort* in that temple of the gods Reason and Research!) Dom Hélder knows that the only significant revolutions are revolutions that take shape from within the spirit and experience of a people. They cannot be imported. And he knows that apart from such an internalized transformation of our First World behaviour and self-understanding, the burdens of his Third World will not be lifted.

There are in fact many facets of our heritage in North America that counteract, and could further counteract, the exploitation of humanity and nature that has characterized so much of our behaviour in the universe. These are aspects of our life which, if they were revived and refurbished in the light of contemporary realities, could create some of the stuff of the indigenous North American revolution for which Third World voices are calling.[3] One thinks for example of that fierce determination of our pioneer ancestors, themselves in so many cases victims of oppression, refusing to import to the New World the noxious distinctions of birth, wealth, and class from which they suffered in the old European homelands. One could think too of that tradition of political idealism which led some of our great statesmen and dreamers to envisage a unified society with equal opportunity for all; or of the spirit of indignation and native justice that, even if it did not always follow through wisely or nobly, at least freed the slaves; or of that sense of human interdependence which led to the cooperative movement in Sas-

3. See in this connection Robert N. Bellah, Richard Madsen, William M. Sullivan, Ann Swidler, and Steven M. Tipton, *Habits of the Heart: Individualism and Commitment in American Life* (Berkeley: University of California Press, 1985), especially chap. 11.

katchewan and other Canadian provinces. These and similar aspects of our heritage, in which there is an inherent vision of the common good that curbs the selfishness of fallen egos, can, if they are not allowed to be consumed by the rust of collective forgetfulness or the decay of sentimentality, constitute a treasury from which much good can still be drawn.

Amongst these treasures, the practice of stewardship is one that is of particular importance to Christians, as we have already seen. If it were liberated from certain cloying impediments, if it were enlarged to incorporate in fact the radical implications that it already contains in principle, it could become one of the most effective agents for change within the churches and, through their work and witness, in our First World society at large. There is *dunamis* (power, potentiality) in this symbol. We have shamefully domesticated it, blunting its revolutionary potential. Yet it persists, and today it almost openly begs to be set free to perform its radical, humanizing work in our midst— humanizing both for those who make that image their own and for those who benefit from their stewardship.

Moreover, it has one quality that is essential to radical symbols: it is indigenous to this continent. We do not have to import it, as we do so much of our theology. It belongs to our own experience; indeed, it could become one of the genuine exports of our particular province of the ecumenical church, if we free it and let it grow.[4]

---

4. It is one small indicator of the truth of this claim that one of the two study guides independently produced for the first edition of this book—the larger and more detailed of the two—was created in Britain: *The Steward: A Biblical Symbol.* The changed circumstances of the church in Britain, financially as well as in other ways, means that stewardship has become a very existential concern amongst Christians there. In a recent and very enlightening article Ralph C. Wood notes that "British Christianity, once the bastion of European culture-Protestantism, now approaches something akin to the New Testament situation." "British Churches Encounter the Challenge of Pluralism," *The Christian Century,* 19 Oct. 1988, 923ff.

## 2. The Basic Impediment

What would freeing the symbol of the steward mean concretely? What impedes its potential to effect spiritual and intellectual transformation, the internal condition without which external change cannot occur at depth?

Many things, of course. Some of them, including the ecclesiastical captivity of the symbol, we have already noticed; others shall become the subject of the subsequent chapter. But first we have to deal in basics, for that is what theology must always try to do—get to the bottom of things! And it seems to me that at the most fundamental level what holds back the full revolutionary force of the steward symbol is a certain abiding ambiguity in our Christian attitude towards This World.

Perhaps this ambiguity has been there from the beginning. Perhaps it belongs to the foundational assumptions of the faith. One can sense it in the Fourth Gospel, for example, which on the one hand presents God's love for the world (*kosmos*) as the fundamental rationale of the Incarnation, and on the other exhibits a permanent distrust of the world and great skepticism about its prospects for salvation. The same ambiguity sometimes informs the Pauline writings. At times, the apostle can seem very earthy and universalistic in his soteriological pronouncements:

> God was in Christ reconciling the world [*kosmos*] to himself, not counting their trespasses against them, and entrusting to us the message of reconciliation. So we are ambassadors for Christ. (2 Cor. 5:19-20a)

At other times he appears to harbour a typically "religious" distaste for the flesh, the body, and matter, and vows that personally he would be glad enough to get away from this world in order to "be with the Lord," as if the Lord were himself not with us in the world! The author of James even declares that "friendship with the world [*kosmos*] is enmity with God" (James 4:4). It is of course possible to soften the impact of such statements through careful exegesis and by balancing texts of this sort with

101

those that are more world-affirming. Nevertheless it would be hard to explain away this ambiguity of the New Testament writings altogether, and even if that could be done through inventive exegesis it would not alter the historical effect of such texts on the evolving faith of Christendom.

This ambiguity, frequently manifesting itself in practice as a straightforward world rejection, presents itself significantly in the history and theology of stewardship. As we have already observed, the great tendency in early Christianity as it moved out into the non-Judaic, hellenized setting of the first and second centuries was a spiritualization of the *kerygma*, which meant that stewardship was not allowed to develop its worldly potential. (When the church did become worldly in the fourth century, it was not the worldliness of gratitude for creation but of a thirst to possess the world.) Under the conditions of imperial Christianity, it was not stewardship but lordliness that appealed to the mentality of the church's policy makers. Thus, historic Christianity has seemed either to ignore and escape from the world, or else to wish to possess it.

Such ambiguity is at the core of incisive thought about stewardship today because if we cannot be sure that this world is the immediate object of the divine *agape* and the locus of God's "mending" (Emil Fackenheim), then neither can we embrace a theology of stewardship that can meet the explicitly worldly demands described in the foregoing chapter.

Nor is this problem one that can be safely relegated to the Christian past. Today the perennial Christian ambiguity about this world amounts to a profound confusion. This confusion has become visible for us in the split of Christianity into two quite distinct groupings or types. That grouping, or rather regrouping, has apparently little to do with older denominational identities and loyalties. It cuts across denominational lines and even across creedal and doctrinal heritages. It seems to me in fact that the real differences between Christians must now be seen in terms of this issue rather than the other distinctions and emphases that gave rise to the various historic splits in Christendom. The point of great division comes over two different ways of ordering our Christian priorities. For purposes of convenience, we may call these the theocentric way and the way of Christian humanism.

## 3. The Theocentric Way

One type of Christianity is clear in its priority to God and "the things of God." It believes that the primary mission of the church in the world is to turn human beings towards the eternal. Its object is the conversion of the unbelieving, or at least that all should be confronted by the claims of Christ and have opportunity to accept or reject them.[5]

In its theology, its liturgy, its evangelism, and all phases of its life, this type of Christianity prides itself on being theocentric or Christocentric. That is, it conceives of the Christian life as the cultivation and perfecting of an orientation towards the divine. This glorification of God does not always or necessarily entail a neglect or denigration of the creation, though in practice it very often does so.[6] But even where it leads to a more positive attitude towards creation, this type of Christianity makes a clear distinc-

5. This objective is given even greater impetus as the year 2000 approaches. For example, in 1977 the Southern Baptist Church adopted what it called a "Bold Mission Thrust," which (in an undated mimeographed circular on the subject) is described as follows: The "B.M.T. [Bold Mission Thrust] asks the convention to set as 'its primary missions challenge that every person in the world shall have the opportunity to hear the gospel of Christ in the next 25 years (2000), and that in the presentation of the message, the biblical faith be magnified so that all people can understand the claim that Jesus Christ has on their lives.'" This "Recommendation 1" is accompanied by a *stewardship* clause: "The Stewardship Commission's B.M.T. Task Force set as its goal: 'That the Southern Baptists double the 1977 Cooperative Program at least three times by the year 2000.'"

6. Dorothee Sölle writes: "Mythology and withdrawal from the world are only two sides of the same coin of hopelessness. Such hopelessness expects nothing more from man, and it triumphs today in the form of . . . [an] orthodoxy, which is not yet rid of that disdain for humanity characteristic of late antiquity and the late Middle Ages, a disdain that sees itself as devotion to God." *Political Theology*, trans. John Shelley (Philadelphia: Fortress Press, 1971), 52.

tion between obedience to God and the service of the neighbour, particularly the neighbour collectively and corporately conceived. What Christians do in and for the world is a second step after their primary duty to God. Those who belong to this camp are very often heard to expatiate on the theme that in Jesus's summary of the Law, the love of God has priority over the love of neighbour, and indeed that the first love (love of God) leads to a kind of love for neighbour that may not be experienced by the neighbour as anything like love. Translated into practical terms, this often means that real love for the neighbour means doing everything in one's power to convert the neighbour to Christ (an emphasis I have failed to detect in that classical parable in which Jesus defines for us who our neighbour is and what it would mean to love her or him! [Luke 10:29ff.]).

There are many variations on this theme of theocentric religion, and not all of those who would embrace the prioritization to which I am referring here would be compatible with one another in every respect. There is a vast difference in this respect between the grave doctrinal faith of the old Protestant orthodoxy of the seventeenth century and the Bible-thumping vulgarity of the television "prophet." There is also an immense distinction between those conventional believers who are committed to an a priori doctrinal theocentrism and some contemporary Christians who adopt what I would call a "strategic theocentrism" to offset the unwarranted anthropocentrism of liberal Christianity. The latter, of whom James M. Gustafson is a notable instance,[7] are rightly concerned about the fact that a theology too exclusively devoted to the human condition runs the danger not only of reducing the deity to an answering service for the felt needs of Homo sapiens but also of neglecting the extrahuman species and the larger universe. Insofar as this is a contextually important emphasis—a strategic theology—it is commendable. Yet it does not, I think, entirely avoid the danger of all theocentric religion.

7. James Gustafson, *Ethics from a Theocentric Perspective*, 2 vols. (Chicago: University of Chicago Press, 1981-84).

The danger is that of setting up a God-consciousness which is not only distinct but at least potentially antithetical to creation consciousness. Orientation towards God too easily becomes an alternative to world orientation, rather than a way of qualifying and deepening one's awareness of and involvement in the life of the world. Theocentric faith manifests an abiding suspicion of all forms of Christianity that demonstrate a too direct interest in this world. In every one of our churches today there are theocentric watchdogs who periodically warn the fellowship that it is going too far towards humanism, apparently (despite the fact that Calvin, Zwingli, Melanchthon, and other Protestant Reformers were educated in the humanist tradition) a very dangerous heresy. Theocentric religion guards against mixing up its priority for God with anything like an equal, simultaneous, and immediate passion for creation.

Today this type of Christianity is very strong, particularly in North America. As we have already suggested, it is in fact increasingly the dominant type, and the norm on whose basis true belief is measured. Moreover, it would appear that the more blatantly theocentric and more militantly anti-world elements within this general type of Christianity are increasingly prominent. These elements have taken the perennial ambiguity of the Christian attitude towards the world and turned it into a rather clear-cut abhorrence of the world. For such Christians, the life of obedience to Christ is a life of calculated avoidance of this world, with its temptations and evils. It expresses itself in the attempt to create "an alternative Christian environment."[8] So thoroughly incompatible is the sinful, lost world with the life of obedience to Christ that belief must segregate itself as completely as possible from ordinary life and fashion a world of its own in which everything is expressly "Christian."

The popularity of God-affirming/world-denying forms of Christianity is not difficult to explain. Is it not almost a rule of

8. Jeremy Rifkin and Ted Howard, *The Emerging Order: God in the Age of Scarcity* (New York: G. P. Putnam's Sons, 1979), especially 125-26.

history that religion becomes ever more otherworldly during times of world crises? When history is incendiary, people look about for fire escapes. That is human, natural, and understandable. Every honest news broadcast in these days tempts sane minds to find a way out of "burning Rome." But as the beautiful legend of *Quo Vadis?* expresses it so poignantly, Christ's way is not out of Rome but into it. And is that legend not just a mythic illustration of what stands at the very centre of our faith—the Incarnation and humiliation of the Word? The cross? Theocentric religion is, or is always in danger of becoming, a religion that is conspicuously anti-Christocentric—and this is no less a danger when it uses the rhetoric of christocentrism; for its "Christ" is too often a Docetic Christ, clearly enough identified with *Theos* but hardly made flesh, hardly *anthropos*.

A final irony of so much of the current religion that is seeking alternatives to this world is that it very often represents no genuine alternative but a mirror image of what it claims to be fleeing. It turns out to be a variation on the very consumerism and narcissism that it fancies itself to be rejecting. Often it is little more than a coy, stained glass version of old-fashioned North American self-centeredness and isolationism. Thus it is hardly surprising that these types of Christians can join hands with gunslingers and pronuclear fanatics to vote into power the most reactionary forces available, sensing that such forces will keep from our doors the beaten, angry, frightened world of the hungry majority and permit us to enjoy our dream a little longer.

## 4. Christian Humanism

While one grouping of Christians embraces a God-centered faith that in times of global distress expresses itself in ever more eccentric and duplicitous attempts at world denial, the second grouping centers its attention upon the intention of the gospel as a world-building message and posture. It is convinced that the ethical, world-directed thrust of the Christian message is the goal of true faith and therefore our priority as churches. Working for the transformation of the world is not an option for Christian faith, it insists. Moral responsibility, concern for the neighbour, the betterment of the social order—these things are built into the faith as such. It is not merely a consequence, not a second step. It is already part of the first step. You discover God's love as you attempt to love your neighbour. You discover God's peace, the peace that "passes understanding," as you immerse yourself in the activities of those who strive for world peace. You find out the meaning of divine grace as you act graciously towards the ungracious and undeserving. In short, this type of Christianity insists that the human impetus of the gospel is its primary orientation. "The sabbath was made for man, not man for the sabbath" (Mark 2:27). The gospel exists for the world, not the world for the gospel! The object of the whole enterprise is not that we should get everyone repeating the Apostles' Creed and intoning "Lord, Lord," but that the will of the Christ should be performed in the habitat of those whom he himself befriended; that the hungry should be fed and the sick healed and the imprisoned liberated and the proud humbled and the self-righteous made to know their need for forgiveness and the broken community of humankind reconciled.

It is no secret that the chief intellectual and spiritual impulse behind this type of Christianity emanates from nineteenth- and early twentieth-century Christian Liberalism, and in a special sense from the Social Gospel movement, which many Christians nowadays feel was prematurely dismissed by Neoorthodox theology. Nor is it any secret that stewardship, as it is practiced in most denominations on this continent, was given a special impetus and directedness by the Liberal movement. This is not the least surprising, for only Liberalism had the courage or the audacity to answer unambiguously the question that I am posing in these pages, or at least part of it. Yes, said the Liberals, Christians are committed to the world, and that by definition! Other individuals and movements have sometimes approximated such an affirmation. All Christianity has in one way or another insisted that faith must manifest itself in good works, that it must bear fruit. That side could hardly be neglected altogether, even by the most God-enchanted! But at least when it comes to major movements of theology and faith, only Christian Liberalism dared to say that the world—notably humanity—is our Christian priority; and that not even God must be put before the neighbour.

For that reason, all of us who wish to pursue the theme of stewardship in something more than truncated forms will retain a healthy respect for Liberalism, with its passion for Christian humanism. For stewardship can be regarded as a way of being in and for the world only if the human dimension and direction of the gospel is the heart of the matter. I suspect that the return to the study of great Liberal thinkers that can be observed in many theological circles today (including centers behind the Iron Curtain) is to be explained on just such grounds. Those who want to put humanity first, as Christians, know that they cannot dismiss Liberalism as easily as in fact happened earlier under the impact of Barth, Brunner, the Niebuhrs, and others. For only the Liberals were able to embrace an unabashedly anthropocentric version of Christian belief.

### 5. The Inadequacy of Liberalism

It will be obvious from the foregoing comparison that, at least in ordering basic priorities, my own sympathies lie with Liberalism. I do not think, however, that the appelation "liberal" is generally a very helpful one; it is usually employed by its enemies, both the old enemies of the Right and the new enemies of the Left, and it is usually intended to dismiss anyone so named without a discussion.[9] Historically, Liberalism meant and means a whole spectrum of opinion, so far as the content

9. See Ernst Käsemann, *Jesus Means Freedom*, trans. Frank Clarke (Philadelphia: Fortress Press, 1969), especially chap. 1.

of this opinion is concerned—all the way from the modernists who discarded almost every traditional dogma of the faith to moderate and cautious Christians who tried very hard to retain all the traditional doctrines. At base, liberalism must be understood as a spirit and a method, rather than a specific theological content; and at the heart of this spirit and method there is precisely what I have insisted upon in the foregoing subsection, namely, an abiding commitment to humanity.

It is this commitment that binds me to "liberalism," and in this respect I have no regret whatsoever that I am sometimes identified as "a liberal"! For any faith that puts at its centre a God whose heart yearns for broken and suffering humanity cannot allow itself the luxuries of an untrammelled conventional theism! Let us recognize it once and for all: the God of Abraham, Isaac and Jacob, the One whom Jesus called "Abba"—this God is anthropocentric! There is something dreadfully ironic when, as has happened with such abysmal regularity in Christian history, people are exhorted in the name of Jesus Christ to embrace a faith in God that effectively insulates them from the pain of God's beloved world!

This rudimentary acceptance of the liberal spirit and method, however, does not mean that Liberalism is adequate as a permanent expression of Christian theology and faithfulness. While Liberalism takes seriously the human orientation of the gospel, it is nevertheless inadequate as the theological basis for a Christian ethic of radical worldly concern today.

This inadequacy manifests itself at two particular points: first, in its general assumptions about humanity and history; second, in its failure to provide the groundwork for an acceptable theology of nature. The first inadequacy has been remarked upon in theology and church ever since Karl Barth launched his attack upon Liberalism just prior to World War I. The second inadequacy, however, is only just beginning to be recognized, and it is perhaps the more decisive where stewardship concerns today are the issue. We shall examine briefly each of these.

## a. Liberalism's Naivety about Humanity and History

Although the criticism of Liberal doctrines of humanity and history offered by the commanding theological presences of our immediate past is a lesson that some of us have learned almost too well, there is, it seems to me, a certain need again today to rehearse it. Partly through contact with Roman Catholic theology, which has always been more optimistic about humanity than was classical Protestantism; partly through dialogue with Marxism, which as a child of modernity rejected the biblical concept of radical sin and embraced a version of historical progress that made history as such redemptive; partly simply as a natural reaction against the overemphasis upon the "dark side" on the part of the Neoorthodox and later disciples of this school (e.g., Jacques Ellul)—for these and other reasons, a substantial trend in contemporary Protestantism appears to have forgotten why Liberalism failed. There is again a danger that those who (in my opinion, quite rightly!) follow in the Liberal tradition of allowing the gospel to make good its human and historical orientation will do so on the basis of a worldview that is less than realistic about evil. This danger is only accentuated by the typical North American capacity for public philosophy full of optimism. Even though this optimism is today more rhetorical than real, it winces still at any suggestion of negativity.

Liberalism in theology failed because there came a day when its assumptions about the essential goodness and rationality of the human creature, as well as the progressive march of time towards the divine kingdom, were no longer confirmed by experience. In fact, for sensitive Christians and non-Christians alike, the assumptions were totally and devastatingly rejected. The formative events of our century, beginning even before "the guns of August" (1914), have rendered the utopian dreams of pre-twentieth-century humanity inaccessible to us forever. The old categories of sin (even Original Sin!) and the demonic and death (as a spiritual and not only physical reality) had to be reintroduced into the theological vocabulary to account for what happened already decades ago. And nothing that has happened since then has warranted their being regarded as merely temporary measures. Whoever after Buchenwald, Nagasaki, Stalin's Gulags, My Lai, Soweto, Afghanistan, El Salvador, and countless other events; whoever in the face of "the future Hiroshima" (Wiesel) talks easily about establishing the reign of God on earth only demonstrates his or her shallowness. That route is closed to us, perhaps forever. Was it ever open?

There is of course no doubt that some Christians were all too willing to hear the criticism of Liberalism provided by the Neoorthodox theologians and others. Unlike the great figures at the centre of the so-called Neoorthodox movement, many of their disciples settled down into a kind of fatalism about existence, a permanent distrust of any kind of change! What can one expect in such a world? they asked. This too must be fought against mightily by all who seek to develop a responsible theology of stewardship.

In other words what we must aim for is a theology that is as passionately orientated towards humanity as Liberalism was but that, unlike Liberalism, is perfectly alert to the negative dimension of historical experience and capable of discerning and naming evil. Our priority must be this world, its present and its future. But we can only assume such a priority wisely and with some prospect of its making a difference if we keep our eyes wide open to the extreme difficulties of sustaining precisely such an affirmation.

What I mean here is stated with her usual eloquence by Hannah Arendt in her essay on Waldemar Gurian:

His uncompromising realism, which formed perhaps the outstanding trait of his contributions to history and political science, was to him the natural result of Christian teachings. . . . (He had a deep contempt for all sorts of perfectionists and never tired of denouncing their lack of courage to face reality.) He knew very well what he owned to [these teachings] for having been able to remain what he was, a stranger in the world, never quite at home in it, and at the same time a realist. It would have been easy for

111

him to conform, for he knew the world very well; it would have
been easier for him, a greater temptation in all probability, to
escape into some utopianism. His whole spiritual existence was
built on the decision never to conform and never to escape, which
is only another way of saying that it was built on courage.[10]

The Christian is "a stranger in the world, never quite at
home in it," because he or she remembers—and hopes for—a
righteousness, justice, and peace that the world does not know,
though it is of its essence and the very thing towards which it
is daily beckoned. Yet this homelessness must not tempt the
Christian into otherworldliness, whether of the religious or the
secular utopian variety; *this* is the world God loves, and it must
not be substituted for by some other, no matter how desirable.
The courage to walk between these two pitfalls—conformity
and escapism—is a courage that Liberalism cannot give us now,
though it may have served that end for some of our forebears.[11]

### b. No Basis for a Theology of Nature

The second inadequacy of Liberal theology and ethics is one that
it shares with most Christian theology, including the Neoor-
thodoxy that succeeded and criticized it: it did not provide a

10. Hannah Arendt, *Men in Dark Times* (New York: Harcourt Brace
Jovanovich, 1955), 261-62.
11. The best contemporary statement that I know about the present
status of Christian Liberalism is Joseph C. Hough Jr.'s essay, "The Loss of Optimism as a Problem for Liberal Christian Faith," in *Liberal Protestantism*, ed.
Robert S. Michaelsen and Wade Clark Roof (New York: Pilgrim Press, 1986),
145ff. Professor Hough notes that "The deepest problem for contemporary liberal faith is the concrete possibility of the end of all history." He traces "three
theological proposals" (the Barthian, represented particularly by Ellul, which
"has not made a significant impact on American Christianity"; the theocentric
perspective represented by James Gustafson; and Process theology), in all three
of which it is possible to trace some "continuity" with Liberal Christianity. But
"all these theological proposals call into serious question any sustained optimism about the human prospect," and "the confidence about history is so
thoroughly qualified in all of them that they represent the end of the liberal
theological program as we have known it."

basis for a theology of nature. In theology as in every other expression of the liberal spirit of the nineteenth and early twentieth centuries, Liberalism put the kind of emphasis upon humanity that had in the long run a deleterious effect upon the extrahuman environment, which is after all necessary to human well-being. Following the lead of the whole modern Western mentality from the Renaissance and Enlightenment onwards, theological Liberalism put "man" at the centre. It even dignified the secular image of humanity as technocratic master of the natural world by depicting this wondrous creature as the very crown and jewel of God's creation.

In doing so, the Liberals of course were only taking their cue from history. The whole tradition, including the Reformers, knew how to use the language of "crown and jewel." But Liberalism went far beyond every previous Christian anthropology, both by its outright praise of Homo sapiens and (more to the point) by neglecting to mention with any consistency the other side of the traditional Christian story: that this no doubt marvellous creature who is clearly at the centre of the biblical narrative, is also profoundly distorted. Fallen! While Liberals often waxed eloquent about the divine immanence in creation and with the Romantics indulged sometimes in excesses of sentimentality about nature (to the point of turning Jesus into a caricature of St. Francis), their highly positive anthropology guaranteed that they would not challenge the plunder of nature by industrial society. Not only did Liberalism refrain from raising objections to the modern project, but it added to the secular world's quest for human sovereignty its own peculiar litanies and exhortations to humanity's lordship of the earth. The human being had a mandate from God to assume mastery. Without any strong countervailing sense that human dominion under the conditions of the Fall is a prideful attempt to wrest power from God, Christianity under the Liberal impact lacked any really prophetic bite in the face of industrial Prometheanism. It is no wonder that those who seek to understand the roots of the ecological crisis today, most of whom have grown up in a culture deeply influenced by theological and other forms of Liberalism, have conceived the notion that the Christian religion is at the bottom of the crisis. For without a radical doctrine of sin, Christianity's high anthropology lends to the human creature a preeminence that biblical and traditional forms of the faith do not warrant.

The question that is put to Christians today is not simply, "Do you care about humanity?" but "Do you care about the world?" Religious Liberalism, like its secular cousins, tended to concentrate so exclusively on human worth and dignity that it failed to provide an adequate critique of humanity's (sinful) encroachment upon the rest of the created order—a note that orthodox forms of the faith sounded through their insistence that the fall of man entailed grave distortions within the natural order as well. Liberalism's anthropocentrism can be understood, if not excused, over against the backdrop of the pessimism about human possibilities generated by old orthodox concentration on original sin, total depravity, and the like. But the optimistic reaction against this pessimism produced its own problems, and from the present perspective they must be considered worse than the former. It is our lot today to work out a theology of radical worldly concern that is aware of human possibilities, yet not naive about human pretention, greed, and apathy. A theology of stewardship needs to know that the human creature is capable of responsibility; it also needs to know that this creature is prone to turn responsibility into an unconditional management.

## 6. Beyond Christian Humanism

What basis could be found for such a theology of stewardship?

Liberal theology took shape before the modern world began to darken. Older forms of the Christian faith, such as those of Augustine or Calvin, would have said that the world is always dark, that darkness is our condition. But modernity convinced itself to everyone's satisfaction except the "losers" and some of the great poets and intellectuals, that all that was past and over. From now on it would "grow ever lighter" (Buber).

Given the general character of eighteenth- and nineteenth-century expectations in Europe and North America, it was not asking for a very momentous leap of faith when the great Liberal preachers and theologians of that age beseeched their contemporaries to believe in "the Fatherhood of God and the Brotherhood of Man," in "the infinite value of the human personality," in the inevitable progress of history towards God's kingdom, and similar very positive articles of faith. To go a step beyond this and to ask their contemporaries to align themselves with the general kingdom-direction of history, to involve themselves actively in the humanly-edifying work of the divine Spirit—in short, to become good stewards of God's bounty in their conduct of their affairs—this really was not an extravagant demand. In a world that seemed to almost everybody (at least to most of those in the leadership of the church) eminently prosperous and on the upward way, exhorting one's congregation to lend to the historical process the weight of their wills, the energies of their spirits, and the substance of their material gains was almost expected of the forward-looking clergyman. In fact, such a proposal could seem as reasonable as asking one's business associates to buy into an obviously flourishing concern.

But what does today's preacher do? How can we promote a theology of stewardship in a world that from so many accounts seems less than worthy of our best efforts—perhaps already a losing proposition?

One thing is certain: a simple humanism no longer suffices. Without any backing in a more realistic system of meaning, simple humanism, lovely as it often is, falls victim to its own innocence in such a world. Sometimes it ends in despair and narcissistic withdrawal, as happened to many in the aftermath of the romantic activism of the 1960s; sometimes it is co-opted by the dominant culture; sometimes it becomes fodder for the many ideologies, some of them admirable enough, some violent and frightening, that can seem to give it the backbone that it needs in a world no longer fitting its gentle assumptions about the human spirit.

For Christians, the experience of the world's darkening must mean a return to those depths of our tradition that still understood the dark, acknowledged it, knew that it could not be reckoned with easily, but nevertheless found the courage to confront it. I am not ready to say that only religious belief can deal adequately with the present shock of historical existence; I have too much respect for profound secular systems of meaning, such as the less doctrinaire forms of socialism, to make such a claim. But I do know that as a Christian I am caused by the character of my epoch to search for a reason to be—to be involved, to care, to assume the posture of steward in God's world—that is more clear-eyed about evil and the experience of failure and meaninglessness than simple humanism can be.

What has been for me the most encouraging and even exciting aspect of these past two or three decades—years during which, with many of my contemporaries, I have had to abandon my New World innocency about the world—is to discover that Christianity does in fact possess unique resources for just this wisdom and this courage. It is possible, under the aegis of this faith, to be honest without becoming hopeless. There are depths in this tradition of Jerusalem, hidden beneath its sentimental versions, that have gripped the remnants of classical Protestantism, and which are sorely needed now. Recovering these depths, we are enabled to be truthful about the world's wickedness without concluding in our hearts that wickedness is the last word to be uttered about this world. We may keep our eyes open to the real degradation of creation without letting go of the faith in a God who so loved it.

For the God who is identified with this world, in our tradition, is not a God of power and glory, an omnipotent deity who is forever immune to the experience of suffering and humiliation; and the world as it is understood in this tradition is not a world that must always be getting better and better. It is a vulnerable world, forever slipping into nothingness, forever verging on self-destruction; a world on a collision course, not with other planets but with its own spiritual satellite, called by the ancients hell. And the God who looks with anxious eyes into the dark places of creation—with the eyes of a parent powerless to alter the course of the child's life from outside it— is a God who suffers, who weeps, and who is able to break the ultimate power of our hell only through personal subjection to it. "God is dead," wrote Friedrich Nietzsche, and believers still smart from that smart remark. But few believers contemplate the second part of Nietzsche's statement, which perhaps in spite of the author's intention carries a burden of the truth that this son of a Lutheran pastor imbibed with his mother's milk: "God is dead. He has died of his pity for humanity."[12] Only a God who can be understood to participate in a world that is court- ing "catastrophe" (von Weizsäcker)—only a "crucified God" (Luther)—could give us the courage to believe that such a world is nevertheless worth caring about, perhaps even dying for.

This will, I trust, make it quite clear that in claiming that all biblical theocentrism is immediately anthropocentric and geocentric I am not opting for a simple, nontheistic humanism. Stronger medicine than that is needed for our present malaise. I remain convinced that the direction of the Christian gospel is human-ward and earthward. For that reason I am able gladly to join hands with every sort of humanism. But as a Christian my own reason for taking up the cause of humankind and earth will not be found in any humanism, altruism, socialism, or ethical culturism. It will be found in a faith whose God is the God of Golgotha—that is, a faith that is more honest about the dark- ness of the world than the most determined realist; a faith whose God inhabits the darkness and is "not overcome" (John 1:5). But (and this is to me the crux of the matter), woe unto me if I ever turn this theological priority into an ethical one! Woe unto me if I regard this faith in this God, granted to me as

12. Walter Kaufmann, ed., *The Portable Nietzsche* (New York: Viking Press, 1954), 202.

a means to worldly involvement, as an end in itself. Those who are God-oriented have understood well enough, perhaps, that God is indeed the presupposition of our life and love. But they have become fixated at the level of means. They have not yet found the end. To follow through, they must learn to look where God is looking and to go where God is dying of compassion for creation.

### 7. The World Must Not Be Prematurely Abandoned!

Translating the foregoing into the more technical language of systematic theology, what I have been insisting is that the only workable basis for a theology of stewardship is a newly appropriated and contextualized theology of the cross *(theologia crucis)*. Since I have written fairly extensively elsewhere about that theological tradition, and since it is itself a vast and complex subject, I shall not attempt to elaborate on it here, except to say that the fundamental thrust of what Luther named "theology of the cross" is precisely its radical this-worldliness—not, of course, in the sense of an easy conformity with or acceptance of this world, but in the sense of its being firmly rooted in the realities of our life, and its refusal to seek refuge in easy theoretical answers to difficult existential questions. Liberalism was committed to the world—or at least to the human project within it. But Liberalism had not faced the impossibilities that biblical and Reformation thought about the world took for granted. Paul and Luther developed their theologies of grace in the presence of the impossible: grace was "the impossible possibility" (Reinhold Niebuhr). The theology of the cross expresses this succinctly: the cross symbolizes the impossibility of the human condition; but as the point of God's deepest solidarity with us it also stands for the grace that overcomes our impossibility, the negation of that which negates.

We have hardly even touched the surface of the worldly orientation of the gospel of the cross. Partly, this is because

Christianity has been so thoroughly mixed up with philosophical, religious, and political views that fought shy of any rudimentary commitment to this world. We have already seen this in connection with the hellenization of the faith in its earliest expressions, and also in connection with its establishment. Perhaps we are only now emerging from a long period of the misuse of biblical faith. Perhaps we stand at the crossroads where this faith could become what it is: a religion of worldly stewardship. But this can occur only if we steadfastly and consistently resist the age-old temptation of all religion to conduct its adherents out of history, to provide for them ladders to the gods. The courage and the wisdom to resist this temptation has been granted so far only to a few amongst the Christians of nearly two thousand years. Dietrich Bonhoeffer, in the last years of his short life, was one of the most articulate of these.

A few days before he was hanged at Flossenbürg near the German-Czech border, Bonhoeffer wrote some paragraphs which, better than any words I know, express the indelible connection between the formula of Paul, "Jesus Christ and him crucified" (1 Cor. 2:2) and the kind of world-commitment that is the sine qua non of any responsible theology of stewardship.

Now for some further thoughts about the Old Testament. Unlike the other oriental religions, the faith of the Old Testament isn't a religion of redemption. It's true that Christianity has always been regarded as a religion of redemption. But isn't this a cardinal error, which separates Christ from the Old Testament and interprets him on the lines of the myths about redemption: To the objection that a crucial importance is given in the Old Testament to redemption (from Egypt, and later from Babylon . . .) it may be answered that the redemptions referred to here are *historical*, i.e. on *this* side of death, whereas everywhere else the myths about redemption are concerned to overcome the barrier of death. Israel is delivered out of Egypt so that it may live before God as God's people on *earth*. The redemption myths try unhistorically to find an eternity after death. Sheol and Hades are no metaphysical constructions, but images which imply that the "past," while it still exists, has only a shadowy existence in the present.

The decisive factor is said to be that in Christianity the hope for resurrection is proclaimed, and that that means the emergence of a genuine religion of redemption, the main emphasis now being on the far side of the boundary drawn by death. But it seems to me that this is just where the mistake and the danger lie. Redemption now means redemption from cares, distress, fears, and longings, from sin and death, in a better world beyond the grave. But is this really the essential character of the proclamation of Christ in the gospels and by Paul? I should say it is not. The difference between the Christian hope of resurrection and the mythological hope is that the former sends a man back to his life on earth in a wholly new way which is even more sharply defined than it is in the Old Testament. The Christian, unlike the devotees of the redemption myths, has no last line of escape available from earthly tasks and difficulties into the eternal. . . .This world must not be prematurely written off.[13]

When he wrote these paragraphs, Dietrich Bonhoeffer was only a few hours away from his own worldly omega—at age thirty-nine! In the face of such an end to his own mundane possibilities, he could have been forgiven for taking up, at that juncture, an otherworldly "religion of redemption." Yet here he was, urging his fellow Christians not to take refuge in a form of Christianity that in effect abandons this world. This world, for all its pain and anguish of spirit, in spite of its injustice and cruelty, the deadly competition of the species and their never wholly successful struggle to survive—this world is the world for which God offered up his "only begotten Son." It was precisely the belief in a God crucified for the world that gave Bonhoeffer the courage to go to his own death affirming the life of the world.

This, I am convinced, is where the theology of stewardship must seek its real foundation. If this foundation is missing, then no amount of beating the drum for God and money will

13. Dietrich Bonhoeffer, *Letters and Papers from Prison* (New York: Macmillan, 1971), 336-37.

make the least difference. If this world and its "fate" (Jonathan Schell) are not the "ultimate concern" of the Christian, then stewardship in and of this world is no logical consequence of Christian faith but just an addendum; and we can expect it to be treated as such, as something tacked on. But if this world matters—*really* matters!—and if the secret for its mattering is felt in the very depths and centre of the community of the crucified one, then the stewarding of this beloved world is of the very essence of our belief, and every attempt to shove it off to the sidelines will have to be regarded as a matter of apostasy and blasphemy!

There are many things that shall have to be accomplished if a genuine theology and praxis of stewardship is to take its appropriate place in the church today. But this is the basic necessity, the "bottom line": the resurrection faith of the people of the cross must mean, quite concretely, that this world must not be abandoned; that this world is worth all the care and love and sacrifice that we can devote to it. Just that, after all the centuries of Christian ambiguity, is the priority that we have to get straight.

# CHAPTER V

# ENLARGING OUR VISION

## 1. Principles of Contemporary Stewardship Praxis

The biblical metaphor of the steward has assumed the status of a symbol in our time. That, in its briefest form, is the thesis of this book. And if we ask why this is so—why stewardship has come of age just at this point in time—then we must answer that Christians are realizing, under the impact of the many-sided threat to its future, that it is the world that they and all of God's human creatures have been called to serve and to keep. Stewardship is no longer to be conceived in purely spiritual or ecclesiastical terms. It is a worldly category; it describes the vocation that God intended and intends for the human creature in the midst of God's good creation.

All the remaining chapters of this book are informed by the intention of spelling out concretely the consequences of that realization. My aim is to put together the radically worldly calling of Christian stewards with the explicit character and problem of our historical context, and to ask what sorts of directives emerge from this meeting.

We begin this process in the present chapter by identifying some of the basic principles that are involved in the enlargement of our thinking about this symbol. What is meant by principles in this connection? It is easier to say what they are not: they are not mere abstractions, deduced from a theoretical speculation about the meaning of the symbol. The methodology of praxis for which we have opted in this study precludes such a procedure. The principles I shall name in the following pages (certainly they are not the only ones that could be named) have been arrived at, therefore, through a reflective process that combines two basic points of reference: the Christian tradition and experience of stewardship on the one hand, and the explicit problems and needs of our own historical moment on the other. I would not say that these principles are merely relevant, because they seem to me to be implicit in the symbol itself and as such, as it was evolved in the faith of Israel and the church. At the same time, neither would I claim that they are eternal or timeless—as theoretical abstractions from the symbol could seem to be. Not every time and place would need to stress these particular principles. It is even conceivable that there could be times and places where some of these principles would be inappropriate. Our time and place—our context—on the other hand, appears to me to evoke from the ancient metaphor conceptualizations like these. It means that the ideas are there, in the symbol, to be evoked; hence they are not simply arbitrary, or superimposed upon the symbol by our contextual need for them. At the same time, they must be evoked—quite literally called forth—by an informed awareness of the exegencies of our context. They manifest and clarify themselves as we allow ourselves to become the meeting place between text and context, tradition and world situation, "Bible and newspaper" (Barth).

Perhaps it would be useful to compare this employment of the term "principle" with what John C. Bennett and others have named "middle axiom." A middle axiom in Christian ethics is a principle of ethical reflection that stands between a broad theological/ethical motif on the one hand (e.g., redemption) and on the other hand the deed or act of redeeming a specific situation, person, or group (e.g., the freeing of slaves).

In the case of the examples given here parenthetically, the middle axiom could be named the principle of liberation. In other words, it is implied in the Christian concept of redemption, as this is reflected upon by faith in the context of oppression (slavery), that the liberation of the oppressed is demanded of those who take seriously the gospel of redemption through Jesus Christ. The middle axiom of liberation is a stage on the way from thought to deed, but it is also a movement from deed (or the arena of the deed) to thought; because without involvement in the situation of oppression on the part of the Christian thinkers it would not occur to them that redemption implies the liberation of the oppressed. In other words, thought which is not informed or is insufficiently informed by participation in the actual life of the world too easily remains at the level of theory. At the same time, active involvement in the life of the world does not by itself guarantee profundity of analysis or appropriateness of act. The middle axiom describes a conclusion that is gleaned from a process of subjection to both the actual situation and the faith perspective by which the situation is deciphered. Hence the combination of human oppression and the biblical and traditional doctrine of redemption evokes the middle axiom—liberation of the oppressed.

There is another connotation of the middle axiom concept that is applicable to what I intend here by the use of the term "principle"; namely, it refers to an idea or program of action that is accessible to those who do not stand within our particular faith tradition. Redemption, at least in its explicitly Christian articulation, cannot be for those outside the Christian faith a basis for their moral sensibility. We cannot expect the humanists of whom we have spoken in the foregoing discussion to be motivated towards freeing those in bondage by contemplating the meaning of the redemptive work of Christ. If such persons are active in movements of liberation (and they certainly are!) it is not because the Christian gospel of redemption drives them to this kind of ethical behaviour; it is rather for many different reasons—e.g., for Marxists it may be participation in the "class struggle"; for liberal humanists the ideals of justice and human rights; for persons of other faiths the moral codes that flow from these faiths, and so on.

Does this mean, then, that Christians cannot work together with these others? Or that, supposing they do work with the others (and of course they do), they can find no common ground for their acts in the realm of motives and ideas? Such a thing would be sad indeed. For while human beings may of course engage together in a piece of work for purely pragmatic reasons, there is no joy in it (and probably no endurance either!) unless they can find some way of communicating with one another concerning the reasons for their work. Horses teamed together do not seem to need any mutually comprehensive rationale for their labor. Human beings do. For thinking is already part of our doing, and vice versa. The middle axiom is a way of speaking about principles that are at the same time fundamentally related to Christian faith (e.g., liberation is implicit in the biblical concept of redemption) and accessible to many others who take part in the vigils, protest marches, international presence, fund-raising, and other activities geared to human liberation. Both the Christians and the non-Christians understand the language of "liberation of the oppressed," and therefore their actual deeds of liberation can be achieved in the spirit of joy and solidarity even when the most rudimentary motivation differs from group to group.

It seems to me important to establish the same sort of broad accessibility for the principles that I shall name below. It can be demonstrated that they are thoroughly Christian principles: that is, they derive from the gospel of Jesus Christ; they are implicit in the stewardship motif as it is contemplated in the light of contemporary problems. But at the same time they are not narrowly or exclusively Christian. All of them can be (and are) taken up into the programs and platforms of many others "who are not of this fold." And why should Christians be troubled by such a thing? (Some actually are.) Jesus once had to rebuke his own disciples for that kind of exclusiveness (Mark

9:38-40). Is it not possible, given the sovereignty of God, that the world is full of women and men who are doing the bidding of Jesus Christ, perhaps under the aegis of many other names and systems, including perhaps the names and systems of those whom we avowed disciples of the Christ are prone to fear or distrust?

Our primary concern here, however, is not to show how these conceptions are or ought to be honoured by non-Christians. I am writing quite intentionally for those who are "of the household of faith"; and, to be honest, what concerns me most is that many of our own Christian household seem not to have grasped these principles as firmly as have significant numbers of outsiders. It is our Christian vision that I desire to enlarge. All the same, one of the many benefits that can come to us through such an expansion of the stewardship symbol is that if we allow ourselves to be drawn into this enlargement of our own Christian vision we shall indeed find ourselves in the company of many others today who can also embrace such principles. And there will be great joy in this. It will not be the joy of Babel, which was false joy, and very short-lived, because it was based on anxiety and pride; but it may be something approaching the joy of Pentecost, where people of many different backgrounds and worlds began to understand one another a little, and could therefore not only work together but also communicate with one another despite the barriers created by their previous assumptions and commitments.

After we have identified the principles that require our attention today, as stewards of the Great Steward, we shall press on to the deed—specifically, to the working out of these principles in three specific areas of our worldly problem: the quest for justice; the quest for a more acceptable relation between humankind and the extrahuman creation; and the quest for world peace. The process of concretizing the symbol of the steward will then, finally, move to a consideration of the implications of all this for Christian persons and for the mission of the church.

What we discover in this process is that once we have made the great leap—the leap into the worldly orientation of the gospel as this is upheld in the symbol of the steward—we are willy-nilly engaged in an increasingly explicit attempt to bring the symbol more and more concretely "down to earth." This is the internal logic of the theological praxis of stewardship, and it is grounded in the "logic of the cross" (Reinhold Niebuhr): that is, it will not have done with us until it has become wholly incarnated in the life of the world. This study will succeed, therefore, only if and insofar as it encourages its readers to carry the spirit and method it has suggested ever more exactingly into the unique circumstances of their own lives.

## 2. Globalization

The first principle that emerges in the confrontation of the stewardship tradition and our present-day reality is globalization. What this means, to state the matter in the most direct and rudimentary way, is that the whole earth is a steward's responsibility.

Let us begin our deliberations on this subject by acknowledging that few of us have grasped this. It is of course very hard to grasp. Thinking *wholly* about anything, including our own persons, involves for most of us a stupendous effort of mind and will. We regularly compartmentalize even our own lives—as the ancient body/soul dichotomy indicates. If even the microcosm of our own body/soul is difficult for us to get together, this certainly applies to the macrocosm. No one has ever seen the whole earth. Not even the astronauts who look at this precious ball of green and blue from on high can see the whole. To be sure, their image of our planet (that is, the images of their cameras) has helped considerably to enlarge our vision of the beautiful globe that has been entrusted to our keeping; some believe that is the most important "spin-off" of the whole space program. But as even space exploration demonstrates, becoming aware of the marvellous unity and interrelatedness of the whole earth is not just a matter of seeing, in the usual sense. It is finally a matter of decision, of belief, and of wonder. Evidence one can have, of course. Much evidence! Yet between the evidence and the sense of wholeness a leap must be made.

And most of us in the global village have still not made that leap. With our intellects we perhaps understand something of it; but the heart, the spirit, the gut—or whatever it is that makes our most characteristic decisions at the supermarket and the election booth!—is still living on a flat earth with nicely segregated sections. This is very convenient for those who inhabit the more affluent sections, of course. But it is also precisely the regionalism—the "parochialism"—of such societies that militates most effectively against the evolution of global consciousness.

We do not think "whole," we think "parts." Rather small parts indeed, for most of us. What strikes me again and again in my travels in North America and Europe is our utter provincialism. We don't even know very much about one another in the so-called First World. We hardly care to! We prefer our prejudices to good, solid information. Through the marvels of satellite communications, I can telephone my scattered family almost anywhere in the world. But in spite of this closeness of all who inhabit "spaceship earth," we remain as ignorant of people five hundred miles away as were our untravelled forebears.

That does not mean that the concern for part of the earth—in particular "my own, my native land"—is always wrong, or always at loggerheads with global concern and involvement. On the contrary, as I have argued elsewhere,[1] I seriously doubt that it is possible for anyone to love the whole without loving this or that particular part. For we do not love universals directly. If we love dogs, for instance, it is because we

1. Douglas John Hall, *The Canada Crisis: A Christian Perspective* (Toronto: Anglican Book Centre, 1980).

have known and loved and been loved by certain quite specific dogs. To be truthful, I always distrust people who say that they love the world, or humanity, or nature, or young people, or women. Especially women! Men who boast that they love women are almost always despisers of particular women—probably chauvinists, quite possibly Don Juans. Who has ever met humanity? One meets particular men, women, and children. These individual persons alone are our access to humanity. Christians and others who speak much about loving humanity are not infrequently the spiritual equivalents of the male chauvinists who love women. I am not, therefore, proposing that we should all immerse ourselves in a kind of love for the world that would in fact function as a way of avoiding love for particular parts of the world. There is a kind of universalism that is finally just as escapist as any otherworldly religion.

At the same time, there is also a narrow particularism that, instead of functioning to put me in touch with something even bigger than itself, keeps my attention riveted to it alone. This is the culprit that I am trying to isolate just now—this petty parochialism, which like a jealous lover insists that I should have eyes only for it, for "my own." It is especially obnoxious when it occurs amongst the affluent—which is in fact where it usually occurs (for reasons that are obvious enough). Love for the particular, if it is really love, does not narrow down one's vision; it enlarges it. If what is going on between me and my wife is really love and not just mutual self-aggrandizement, then that love will enable both of us to be more (not less!) hospitable to other persons. Through this particular woman, I am given an astonishing gift: the possibility of being open to other human beings who, because I am a male being, would otherwise remain to an appreciable degree beyond my range of comprehension. Through particular children, the world of the child—and therefore the future—becomes accessible. The discovery of one love makes more love possible. Isn't that precisely what the First Epistle of John means—"We love, because [God] first loved us" (4:19)?

Love of the whole is a consequence of genuine love for some part or parts. If one loves "one's own" profoundly, then one cannot love one's own (child, husband, parent, native land) exclusively. Love which is true is expansive. All other love—the love that tries to get us off into a corner and keep us for itself!— is finally simply untrue. It has no foundation in reality. There are no such corners, away from all those others. Love, at least as we know it, takes place in this world; everyone is affected by it (or the lack of it), and everyone and everything is involved in it. The world will only honour our need to find corners, to isolate ourselves, on a temporary basis!

This is today wonderfully (and to the localized mentality devastatingly) demonstrated by our global unity and ecological interrelatedness. Although we indulge in such divisions as First, Second, and Third Worlds; north and south; rich and poor; or developed and developing, and although these divisions are historically, sociologically, and economically real enough, at another level they are patently lacking in any ontic basis. They are even absurd. The globe simply does not have four corners. Spheres don't have corners! There are no corners around which people can hide and consume their goodies all by themselves forever. There are no walls that can establish a permanent border between this and that part. There are no moats that can keep out the hungry—not even the large moats called oceans. There are no defense systems that can shoot down explosive ideas.

In short, there are no parts any more, if by parts we mean separable entities whose destiny can be lived out in isolation from all the rest. The globe is one single and continuous whole. It will either survive as one or it will not survive. The boundaries between earth's historical parts are geographically and biospherically untenable. No border between nations, no matter how well-armed, can prevent the fall of acid rain or the fallout from nuclear accidents. From outer space, it is said, the only visible historical boundary is the Great Wall of China.

Our thinking, which is conditioned by knowledge that is

limited and love that is tainted by inordinate self-love, has simply not yet taken in the reality of our condition as inhabitants of a global village. Not only individually, but as whole societies, we behave in ways that are outmoded, dangerous, and finally ridiculous. To imagine that the national debts, the overcrowding, the hunger, the political oppression and violence present in many Third World nations can be contained is a delusion that may be brought home to us sooner than we think. As a wise and outspoken moderator of the United Church of Canada, Dr. Bob McClure, once stated: It is as absurd for First and Second World people to look upon the Third World with unconcern as it is for passengers in a ship's first class section to look down on those in steerage and remark, "It seems your part of the ship is sinking." Barbara Ward and countless other sensitive students of earth's condition have told us repeatedly: You *are* one world. You must learn how to *be* one, or else you will not be at all.

Today the physical interrelatedness of our habitat has become the primary spiritual truth by which all our faiths and ideologies and values are tested and judged. Any system of meaning, religious or secular, which lacks the capacity to see things whole is quite simply irrelevant—and possibly pernicious. The tradition of Jerusalem in its biblical and best traditional expressions not only has this capacity, but places its concern for wholeness of vision, reconciliation of the parts, and the breaking down of "dividing walls of hostility" at the very centre of its message. In this as in other matters, however, Christianity in its empirical reality by no means upholds its own best tradition. Jesus' prayer "that all may be one" (John 17) is hardly even taken seriously by the denominations of Christendom itself, which often continue in mutual suspicion, ignorance of one another, and sometimes open hostility. In many parts of the globe, moreover, the Christian religion undergirds jingoistic sentiments and neurotic forms of nationalism, racism, ethnocentrism, and other types of estrangement. (How many times a day does one hear on the media terms like "Christian militia"?) It is no longer mere doctrinal and biblical faithfulness that drives responsible

Christians to try to make good their own message of reconciliation; the biblical injunction to global unity has become a political necessity—indeed, a matter of life and death.

For stewardship, the principle of globalization means, on the negative side, liberating churches and all within the sphere of their witness from the practice of localism. The gospel, we must finally learn, frees us from equating the love of God with what one loves naturally and as a matter of course (see Matt. 5:26, par.) Grace not only perfects, it also critiques and transcends nature. The steward is called to a service that extends way beyond the boundaries of her or his own family, race, gender, generation, nation, and world. Positively speaking, globalization means learning how to love "our own" in such a way that that particular love leads us—as it certainly will, if we allow ourselves to be led!—to the larger reality of which that particular is part. In this sense, the motto "think globally, act locally" is instructive: that is, insist upon acting within your immediate context from the perspective of a knowledge and love for the whole of which is it part; and in your reflection upon the world situation allow your involvement in your own little world to become deep and broad enough to carry you well beyond its own imagined limits. There are no such limits, anyway. Our stewardship will be stunted if it occurs within the limits that we have conditioned to think our own. Confined to such supposed limits, we shall not even serve our own wisely and well. Nothing less than global consciousness will facilitate a stewardship which is prepared to serve responsibly in the local situation.

### 3. Communalization

A second principle that suggests itself in the juxtaposition of tradition and situation is communalization. The steward in the biblical tradition is not first of all an individual but a community. This does not imply that individuals are excluded. But it means that our personal stewardship is a participation in the stewardship of a community—a community whose corporate stewardship is in turn its participation in the still greater and more expansive work of the chief steward, Jesus. This from the side of our tradition.

But our situation also calls for a more wholehearted effort to think corporately—to communalize our theology of stewardship. The sense of frustration that is felt by many of us today as we confront the enormous and apparently unalterable patterns of societies that are driven by a leaderless technology is partly the consequence of that individualism that has been the matrix of our New World experience.[2] At a level deeper than most of us realize, we are conditioned to think that nearly everything worth doing can, may, and must be done by us as individuals. It is as individuals that we must succeed—all the way from kindergarten to a happy and well-adjusted retirement. If we fail, we fail as individuals—even though it is patently obvious that the causes of so much individual failure in our society (unemployment, environmental tensions and illnesses, psychic stress due to overcrowding in cities, that overweening sense of purposelessness of which we have already written) is attributable directly to *societal* disorders. But we have been so successfully conditioned by individualistic thinking that we almost always attribute personal failure directly to the persons concerned.

To illustrate: A conference on the farm crisis had been organized by a presbytery in the state of Michigan. The need for such a consultation was obvious in that area, as in many others on this continent and elsewhere: many farmers had "gone under"—some pathetically and even tragically. "Christmas!" quipped a lawyer who addressed the conference—"Christmas!— the season to be jolly! I haven't had a happy Christmas for seven years. Invariably at Christmas or New Year's I am taken away from my family circle by the suicide of some farmer, a client of mine." All the same, the conference was very poorly attended—

2. See in this connection Robert Bellah et al., *Habits of the Heart*.

despite months of planning, publicity, and a splendid panel of speakers and leaders. I asked why. "Because," said one of the organizers, "we are still well enough off in these parts that farmers can attribute the failure of their neighbours to poor management. They themselves may be bankrupt in two or three years' time, but they continue to mouth the rhetoric of individual initiative and responsibility. The situation has not yet become bad enough for them to look about for other explanations."

The habit of corporate thought and action is very difficult for North Americans to learn. Even the pioneer experience, which necessitated the kind of communal cooperation that here and there is still valued, seems on the whole to have given way to the need or desire to make it on our own (which was of course another dimension of the same pioneer spirit). Part of our abhorence of communism is explicable on these same grounds. We manifest an almost adolescent attachment to self-sufficiency, and pathetically imagine that our individuality and freedom would be forfeited if we merged our efforts in a common struggle.

This very individualism, however, is one of the chief ingredients in the fatalization that is overtaking us today. Because the forces over against which we must assert ourselves—violence in the cities, scarcity of meaningful work, the threat of war, economic recession or inflation, the failure of public institutions, and others—*are* too great for us to handle as private persons. In the face of the complexity and enormity of the threat to our way of life, maybe to life itself, it is perhaps natural to turn one's back on public life and retreat narcissistically into one's privacy. When one assumes that individuals make or break their own lives and fortunes, it is somehow even logical that one retreats from an unmanageable larger world into one's own little world, where the illusion of freedom and mastery can still for a time be indulged.

But the discernment of the signs of the times today must entail underscoring the phrase "for a time" in that last sentence. The forces of both nature and history are driving us towards the need to think and act communally. This is felt as a terrifying threat to all who are committed to an ideological individualism—as many in our society are; as many in our churches are! But such individualism, under whatever influence and nomenclature, needs to consider the situation carefully. Is there any major problem in the world today that can be confronted without human solidarity?

The truth of the matter, surely, is that this rugged individualism is itself a luxury that has been permitted to endure as long as it has—in very circumscribed sectors of the planet—because meanwhile other forces, including the energies of millions of other persons, have been devoted to the survival of the world community. Where would the few rich families of Central American capitalist nations be were it not for the many poor upon whose patient and backbreaking labours their wealth has been accumulated? Where would the middle-class business and professional people of the North Atlantic nations be were it not for the thousands who devote their lives to protecting the environment against the ecological collapse that is continually threatened by the very pursuits of those business and professional people? Where would any of us be today had not millions of persons of peace and good will engaged in mass demonstrations against the buildup of nuclear armaments and cold war, bringing sufficient pressure to bear upon the leaders of empires that they at least began to desist from their folly? The highly acclaimed and propagandized "individual initiative" of our official rhetoric never acknowledges that it would be strictly impossible apart from the individual sacrifice of untold millions who, through sheer economic or biological necessity or through deliberate acts of will, sacrificed their personal desires on the altar of the public good.

But in our attempt to defend the principle of communalization, we who are Christians have other resources to draw upon besides common-sense observations of this sort. For the gospel not only positively upholds the communal ideal but it insists that the only authentic individuality is one that is kept in dialectical relationship with communality. It does this in a great many different ways—in its theology of creation, of redemption, of the covenant, of church and kingdom; in its ethic of marriage, of the family, of friendship—in fact, in every conceivable aspect of the tradition one encounters the dialectic of individual and corporate life. We cannot elaborate extensively on the theme in this place; but one important biblical metaphor—which is more than a mere metaphor—captures the whole character of this dialectic: the image of the church as *soma Christou* (body of Christ).

In the Pauline imagery of the body (e.g., 1 Cor. 12:12ff.), it is obvious enough that the controlling thought is communality: that is, what is most important is that the whole body, the church, should be built up, to the end that it can function with something like singleness of purpose in the world. *But*—and here we glimpse the intricacy of the dialectic under discussion—the body will only be able to act in unity and harmony if its various members perform the tasks that, individually, they are intended to perform and are capable of performing. Thus it is of vital concern to the whole body that the hand should be what it can be and do what it can do—and the same is true of all the other members. By the same token, however, it is of vital concern to the whole body that the hand should not assume an importance greater than its real worth and begin to think other parts of the body unnecessary.

Here is an affirmation of individuality that assumes communality, and vice versa. It would be a contradiction of this affirmation of communality to deny the importance of the individual member. Bodies without hands, or eyes, or "less honourable parts" are handicapped. But it would be still more questionable to take from this metaphor its affirmation of individual worth and leave out the communal context which functions here as the end (purpose) to which individual worth makes its contribution. A body without a hand is handicapped. A hand without a body is simply useless, dead.

It must seriously be asked within the remnants of classical Protestantism on this continent how, with this kind of dialectic of individuality and communality informing our sacred Scriptures from one end to the other, we managed to become the spiritual bulwark of an undialectical accentuation of the individual. Not only have we contributed substantially to the spiritual wherewithal necessary to construct a society which makes a totem of individual enterprise and freedom, including (as has frequently been demonstrated) economic capitalism; we have also incorporated this same fetish of individualism into our interpretation of the faith. We have made religion a very private affair—"what a man does with his solitude." Our stewardship practice itself has fostered this same individualism. What we have said, in effect, is this: Let individuals make as much money and develop as much power and influence and leisure as they can; and then let them philanthropically contribute of these treasures to the church (yes, chiefly to the church of course!).

It is not necessary to denigrate philanthropy. Thank heaven there have been a few very generous persons of wealth who, through religious and other forms of motivation, have been moved to share their wealth, as well as their time and talents, with others. But we must stop equating philanthropy with stewardship. When we do so, we neglect or deliberately ignore the whole basis of our faith, which does not glorify the prudent or aggressive individual (contrary to some interpretations of the parable of the talents) but which aims at the creation of a community, a *koinonia*, which can exist in the world both as a model of human reconciliation and God's great project of the reunification of all that is divided: the divine reign (kingdom).

Again therefore, in summary we may say that the enlargement of stewardship means, on the negative side, freeing the practice from the individualism and privatism with which it has been too consistently bound up, and, on the positive side, learning how to live our oneness in Christ in such a way that we may at least approximate the *koinonia* we say we are and support the drive towards community, wherever we find it in the world.

## 4. Ecologization

Summarizing the first two principles in a word, we may say they insist that as stewards we are responsible for the globe (globalization) and that we are *together* responsible for the globe (communalization). But now we must move out beyond the human community, which has been our particular preoccupation up to this point, and insist that stewardship today means that our corporate responsibility both as Christians and as human beings generally includes the stewardship of many creatures and created things, the greater share of which by far are not human. And it means, furthermore, the recognition that the existence of all these extrahuman creatures and of their and our environment constitutes a complex state of mutual dependency, so that the fate of one is also in some measure the fate of all the others, including us.

The most problematic aspect of this subject will be treated in Chapter VII, where we shall consider the rudiments of a theology of nature. But here we should already introduce the principle which enlarges our stewardship vision, which for want of a better word we may call the principle of ecologization. At base, what it would mean to expand our horizons through the application of this principle is that when as Christians today we reflect on the tradition of stewardship in the light of our contemporary problem, we are bound to confess that our stewardship applies not only to concern for our own kind but for all created life. To confine stewardship to the human sphere is finally not even to assume responsibility for the human sphere; because the human sphere is in reality no sphere, no separate realm, but part of a totality without which it would not have been and cannot continue to be.

Now it may be argued with some plausibility, I suppose, that this particular principle need not have manifested itself in earlier times; that it is only in view of the present crisis of the biosphere that Christians could be expected to perceive the need for such a principle as this. Perhaps. Certainly the multifold crisis of the environment has had to become extraordinarily conspicuous before most Christians (or anyone else!) took any particular notice of nonhuman beings. And yet, as I shall want to argue more fully later on, there are dimensions of the Hebraic-Christian anthropology that point unmistakably to an important if ignored and underdeveloped awareness in our tradition of human responsibility within the biosphere. Some recent commentators on this dimension have singled out individual Christians in whom the awareness of the nonhuman species and nature was highly developed. St. Francis of Assisi is of course a favorite instance. But there were others. Listen to Dostoevsky's Father Zosima in this passage from *The Brothers Karamazov*:

> Brothers . . . love all God's creation, the whole and every grain of sand in it. Love every leaf, every ray of God's light. Love the animals, love the plants, love everything. If you love everything, you will perceive the divine mystery in things. Once you perceive it, you will begin to comprehend it better every day. And you will come at last to love the whole world with an all-embracing love. Love the animals: God has given them the rudiments of thought and joy untroubled. Do not trouble it, don't harass them, don't deprive them of their happiness, don't work against God's intent. Man, do not pride yourself on superiority to the animals; they are without sin, and you, with your greatness, defile the earth by your appearance on it, and leave traces of your foulness after you—alas, it is true of every one of us![3]

Like St. Francis, Teilhard de Chardin, his fellow countryman Tolstoy, and many others, Dostoevsky belonged to that tradition of Christian mysticism which believed that all created things have a capacity to manifest the divine (*finitum capax infiniti* —"the finite has a capacity for the infinite"). Martin Luther, in this respect unlike the Reformers whose primary historical influence beyond the Scriptures was the newly emergent

---

3. Fyodor Dostoevsky, *The Brothers Karamazov*, trans. Constance Garnett (London: William Heinemann, 1912), 332.

humanist movement, stood in this same tradition. This is not the mysticism that wants to transcend the earth, to live at least two feet above time, to engage in flights of supramundane rapture (what Tillich named "abstract mysticism"); it is rather what Tillich called "concrete mysticism" and others "creation-mysticism," and still others (especially in the case of Luther) Christ mysticism. By whatever name, this refers to a type of spirituality which plants its feet firmly on the earth, and gives its adherents a greater sense of participation in creation than, apart from such faith, they had known. This type of mysticism does not entice one away from earth; on the contrary, it causes one to embrace creation all the more unreservedly. It shares with all forms of mysticism the sense of another, unseen dimension, i.e., of transcendence; but it locates the transcendent, not beyond but rather in creation. To say the same thing somewhat differently, concrete mysticism does not think of transcendence in terms of height, but in terms of depth. The basic (ontological) assumption here is that matter, far from being alien to spirit, is the enfleshment of the spiritual, and that therefore true spirituality does not entail a flight from the material world but a more profound affirmation of and participation in it.[4] With the authority of this whole side of the long mystical tradition, as well as on the basis of much unacknowledged and untapped Scripture,[5] we may say that the principle of ecologization truly belongs to our faith. That it is also an overwhelm-

4. I have tried to exemplify this creation- or Christ- or "concrete" type of mysticism in relation to *prayer* in my book, *When You Pray: Thinking Your Way into God's World* (Valley Forge, Pa.: Judson Press, 1987). As the title suggests, I consider the essence of prayer to be a type of thought (meditation, contemplation) which, far from "weening us from earth," gives us the grace and courage that is needed to affirm all the more unreservedly our *creaturehood*, and to find in it depths of wonder and mystery that are unknown to those for whom prayer is essentially escape from the world.

5. See for example the careful study of the biblical and historical background of the theology of nature in H. Paul Santmire, *The Travail of Nature: The Ambiguous Ecological Promise of Christian Theology* (Philadelphia: Fortress Press, 1985).

ing need within our contemporary situation hardly needs to be demonstrated.

In her work on the world as God's body, Sallie McFague seems to me to stand within this same tradition of concrete mysticism, and certainly the ethical object of her theological reflections seems continuous with my ecologization principle. "The world as God's body," she writes, "may be seen as a way to remythologize the suffering love of the cross of Jesus of Nazareth. In both instances, God is at risk in human hands." The concretization of the agape of God manifested in the crucified one is also manifested in the vulnerability of the world as God's creation. We shall discover in a new way the reality and depth of this divine love if we reflect upon the beauty and fragility of the natural order:

> We should dwell upon the specialness, the distinctiveness, the value of these things until the pain of contemplating their permanent loss, not just to one individual but to all for all time, becomes unbearable. This is a form of prayer for the world as the body of God, which we, as lovers and friends of the world, are summoned to practice. This prayer, while not the only one in an ecological, nuclear age, is a necessary and permanent one. It is a form of meditation to help us think differently about the world and to work together with God to save our beleaguered planet, our beautiful, vulnerable Earth.[6]

But once again the principle in question can be evoked within the Christian church only with difficulty. For while we may cite Francis and Dostoevsky and Eckhardt and Luther and de Chardin and Matthew Fox and Sallie McFague and others on the side of the flora and fauna, so to speak, we must in all honesty point to a much more powerful Christian convention that has been perfectly willing to add the weight of divine authority to the managerial approach to nature. We have already observed that this was a feature of religious Liberalism in most of its expressions. But before Liberalism, indeed from the beginnings of the

---

6. Sallie McFague, "The World as God's Body," *The Christian Century*, 20-27 July 1988, 671ff.

modern epoch and the demise of the Middle Ages, there were many avowed Christians who contributed in their way to the evolution of that attitude towards nature which has typified our New World particularly. The ecologist Barry Commoner in a radio broadcast characterized this attitude in the motto: "If it grows cut it down, if it moves shoot it!" This is no doubt a little crass; but it makes the point with considerable accuracy.

That this approach to nature is a phenomenon predating the Industrial Revolution is illustrated by Michael Kammen in his Pulitzer Prize-winning study of "the origins of American civilization." Kammen reports that in 1705 Robert Beverley complained about the Virginians in these words:

> They depend altogether upon the Liberality of Nature, without endeavouring to improve its Gifts, by Art or Industry. They spunge upon the Blessings of a warm Sun, and a fruitful Soil, and almost grutch the Pains of gathering in the Bounties of the Earth.

Carrying the same observation a little farther into the eighteenth century, Kammen writes of William Byrd's *Journey to the Land of Eden in 1733*, where Byrd discovers a group of land surveyors who, having located several large chestnut trees full of ripe fruit, simply destroyed the trees in order to have the chestnuts more conveniently at hand. "Our men were too lazy to climb the trees for the sake of the fruit but . . . chose rather to cut them down, regardless of those that were to come after."[7]

The medieval sense of an eternal, internal depth inhabiting all the creatures of time gave way in the modern epoch to a "thingification" of the natural world. It saw nothing in trees but lumber and paper—or at best sap, shade, or decoration for the aggrandizement of humans. And from the heights of a sort of Protestantism that celebrated the utter transcendence of the divine (the "monarchical model of God"),[8] this utilitarian attitude towards the created order could quite readily find a

---

7. Kammen, *People of Paradox*, 150.
8. McFague, *God's Body*, 672.

churchly blessing. If God is altogether beyond the world and spirit is a category applicable only to humankind, then all else is reduced to pure matter (stuff) and we need have no compunctions whatever about putting it to our own uses. Besides, if nature is overabundant, as it has always seemed in this new Eden, what might in other situations be considered waste is here scarcely noticeable. Who, even with the increasingly effective machinery of the twentieth century, could make a dent on the vast forests of British Columbia, or the endless fresh-water supplies of the Great Lakes?

Or so we thought—so, apparently, significant numbers of us still think! In the meantime, however, certain consequences of this same utilitarian and wastrel attitude have begun to dawn on our civilization; and the question that this raises for Christians is not only an ethical one but a theological one: What theological adjustments are called for by the environmental crisis?

The answer, as Sallie McFague's bold imagery of the world as God's body suggests, is that these adjustments are more extensive than most of us have yet realized. The problem cannot be solved by a more responsible theology of stewardship alone; it reaches into the very core of the gospel, affecting not only our doctrine of creation but, perhaps even more intensely, our doctrine of redemption. We have allowed ourselves to entertain the thought of the redemption of the human species as though this species were entirely separable from all the others. The Christian faith will not escape the critique of the environment today by making a few alterations here and there!

Insofar as our present subject is concerned, however, this much must now be said: the development of the principle of ecologization as a dimension of stewardship must entail, on the negative side, a rejection of all religion that in the name of the supernatural denigrates the natural, and on the positive side a new openness to the mystery of all created life, including the willingness to undertake sometimes the sacrifice of our human well-being for the sake of the extrahuman.

## 5. Politicization

A fourth principle that is evoked by the meeting of the steward-ship tradition with the great issues of our context today is politicization.

There are two implications here. The first is that politicization could mean that stewardship has to be rescued from sentimentality and private morality and articulated in ways that are realistically addressed to the hard political data of our endangered world. The familiar manner of appealing to the spirit of charity and philanthropy in individuals has simply not worked. It is too hit-and-miss. Besides, it has been too consistently concerned to make the philanthropically-minded feel good to achieve any real good in the world. As Philip Potter wrote, "In the past, too much was left to good will and fine statements and it has been shown that that is not enough."[9] The critique of this side of the matter has already been touched upon in our earlier discussion of the principle of communalization. Our stewardship practice has been far too individualistic.

But the politicization of stewardship also points to a second and no doubt more controversial issue, namely, the extrication of stewardship from its almost indelible association with economic capitalism.

The truth is of course that stewardship has never been apolitical in our North American ecclesiastical experience. It has been subtly married to the politics of free enterprise and the market economy.[10] In the last century no one even tried to camouflage the fact! "It is," wrote the Reverend Josiah Strong, a great advocate of stewardship, "the *duty* of some men to make a great deal of money."[11] Strong was of course picking up an old theme in North American religion, namely, the Calvinist-Puritan belief

9. Philip Potter, "Looking Back Into the History of Ecumenical Sharing," in *Empty Hands*, 53.
10. See the new study by M. Douglas Meeks, *God the Economist: The Doctrine of God and Political Economy* (Minneapolis: Fortress Press, 1989).
11. Salstrand, *Story of Stewardship*, 31.

that earthly reward was a sign of divine blessing, and that the tithing of one's wealth was a means of tapping supernatural resources for further success—or, as the concept is sometimes called in promotional literature of this sort: "seed money."[12] It was this sense of an almost impersonal law of reward that fired the minds of great philanthropists like Andrew Carnegie. As a child who gained much (I hope) lasting benefit from hours spent in a Carnegie-endowed public library, I should be the last to question that such philanthropists often contributed substantially to the life of the community. But we are not judging persons here; we are considering principles. The ill effects of associating Christian stewardship with the philanthropy of religious capitalists have been far-reaching.

Already in 1930, Reinhold Niebuhr, noticing these ill effects, wrote an article for *The Christian Century* provocatively entitled "Is Stewardship Enough?" Niebuhr's argument is if anything more valid today, given the fact of multinationals and income-tax reductions for contributions to charity, than it was in 1930. He said that "philanthropy is not stewardship," and that when it was passed off as stewardship it in fact frequently covered up a great deal of injustice perpetrated by the same Christian philanthropists, who were held up as models of charity.

> How inadequate [our alleged stewardship is] . . . may be recognized from the fact that in the year 1929 the total philanthropies of America amounted to two and a half billion dollars, a sum that does not equal the accretion of values in stocks on the New York exchange in a single day. . . . It is, of course, not impossible to interpret the doctrine of stewardship realistically. But to do so would require an honest discussion of every moral and social problem involved in modern industry, the displacement of work-

---

12. "Nothing in Calvinism *per se* led automatically to capitalism. But in a society already becoming capitalistic, Reformed Protestantism reinforced the triumph of new values. Puritanism undermined obstacles which the more rigid customs of Catholicism had imposed." Kammer, *People of Paradox*, 155. T. A. Kantonen writes: "Our stewardship literature abounds in promises of prosperity to those who fulfill their obligations to God." *Christian Stewardship*, 6.

ers by the machine, the inequality of income, the ethics of vary-ing standards of living, the democratic rights of workers, and all the rest. If this is not done, it is ideal to think of the church as a moral guide in our civilization.[13]

As Niebuhr implies, the politicization—more accurately, the re-politicization—of stewardship may involve the churches in a new look at the socialist alternative to capitalism. Surely it is no longer radical to suggest such a thing. Even a study as mild in its critical cultural appraisal as that of Holmes Rolston pre-sents a similar proposal. Commenting upon the "Differing Forms of the Economic Order" present in our contemporary world, Rolston notes that

the very fact that millions of men do live under an economic order which is radically different from our own must raise even in the mind of the most unthinking Christian some question as to the permanence of the form of economic order within which he lives.[14]

While it is true that "many of the great fortunes of North America have been dedicated, in part at least, to the great causes of human welfare," still, "the Christian faith is not identified with the preser-vation of the existing form of the economic order." Of course, there will always be subtle attempts on the part of those who benefit from the economic order to lend it supernatural sanction.

From this point of view, the history of Christianity often makes painful reading. Men have sought to throw the whole power of the church behind the preservation of slavery in America, or the tyranny of the feudalism of Russia, or the interests of the landed aristocracy of Spain."[15]

13. D. B. Robertson, ed., *Love and Justice: Selections from the Shorter Writings of Reinhold Niebuhr* (Cleveland and New York: World Pub. Co., 1967), 89ff.

14. Holmes Rolston, *Stewardship in the New Testament Church: A Study in the Teachings of Saint Paul Concerning Christian Stewardship* (Rich-mond: John Knox Press, 1946), 143.

15. *Ibid.*

It is just possible, Rolston concludes, that Christians could eventually find socialized forms for the economic and political order more compatible with basic Christian beliefs than the older forms with which the church of the centuries has been yoked:

> Christianity has lived with slavery, and feudalism, and capitalism. She may learn to live in the more socialized forms of society towards which modern society seems to be moving. In fact, she may find some of the newer forms of society more congenial to her life than the more ancient forms of the economic order. In this respect, Christianity must judge all orders of society. She must point to the evils in the existing economic order. She must be prepared also to examine from the point of view of the insights of the Christian any form of the economic order which may be established in the future.[16]

This statement summarizes rather well the principle I am discussing here. It is not a matter of all Christians becoming doctrinaire socialists—though it is high time that North American (and especially U.S.) Christians recognize that a very large percentage of their fellow Christians in the world today, including Canada, are socialists at the political level. Under whatever form the social order may assume, Christians will always have to be prophetically vigilant.[17] But the assumption, so firmly entrenched on this continent, that Christianity assumes or can make an easy alliance with economic capitalism, must

16. *Ibid.*, 147.

17. In a recent television documentary on the role of the (Protestant) church in the German Democratic Republic (East Germany) today, the well-known East German theologian, Heino Falcke, Dean of Erfurt, made this point quite explicitly. Christians, he affirmed, must maintain a critical vigilance in respect to *all* political authority, capitalist or socialist. "After 40 years of socialism," he said, "we Christians in East Germany know that there are definitive links between Christianity and socialism, particuarly in the concern of socialism for the underprivileged classes of society. Yet we also know that we cannot assume anything about socialism *in power*. Power must be watched carefully, no matter what political party wields it." (" 'Ihr seid das Salz der Erde': Evangelische Christen in der DDR," von Roman Barner, Helmut Nemetschek; West German television station ZDF, 17 January 1990, 22.10 [my translation].)

be recognized as an assumption—and a highly questionable one at that. It is quite possible that our economic system makes it more difficult to pursue a life of responsible Christian steward-ship than do systems which accentuate less the individual and facilitate corporate action and concern. This is the negative di-mension of the politicization principle. On the positive side, politicization means that Christians are called upon to search for and support new forms, of community, including their economic dimensions, which reflect more adequately than do existing orders our faith's inherent concern for justice, equality of opportunity, and compassion.

## 6. Futurization

The final principle that I shall name here (I leave it to the reader to continue this investigation) is what I should call the principle of futurization. Stewardship implies that we are responsible for the whole earth (first principle); that we are together responsible for the whole earth (second principle); that this responsibility includes the nonhuman as well as the human world (third prin-ciple); that this responsibility must seek to express itself in just and merciful political forms (fourth principle)—and (fifth prin-ciple) that this responsibility must be exercised in the light not only of the immediate situation but of the near and distant fu-ture as well.

It is (or should be) impossible to avoid the high conscious-ness of the future that permeates the Hebraic Scriptures. They are always speaking about "the children's children," and "unto the third and fourth generation," and way beyond. This future orientation seems to disappear in the New Testament—or rather, it tends to be redirected there. The anticipated future of the gospels is a new order inaugurated by the returning Christ: the reign of God. This, at least as it has influenced the church his-torically, too easily implies a nonhistorical or trans-historical fu-ture. We have already seen that the eschatological dimension of

148

the New Testament's stewardship theology contains important positive connotations: it reminds the disciple community of its stewardly accountability. But an unfortunate effect of the New Testament's more apocalyptic rendering of the future—and one which did permanent damage when it combined with the Hellenistic spiritualization of the Christian message—was the conspicuous diminishment of an Hebraic idea: our responsibility towards those who will inherit the earth (the "children's children"). Under the impact of the more openly apocalyptic side of the New Testament's eschatology, Christians have been tempted to embrace such a preoccupation with the afterlife that they have left the fate of the earth not to the meek to whom Jesus promised it, but to the ravenous, the power-hungry, the plunderers, grabbers, and developers. If it is the Christian West that has spawned a technological society that persons of principle must today describe as rapacious and leaderless, this ought to make us ponder some of the deficiencies of our Christianity! And it would be less than serious pondering if it did not bring us back once more to the basic issue treated in the previous chapter: whether this world ought to matter to Christians in an ultimate way.

If it does matter, then quite obviously its future matters. That follows not only logically, as it would under any kinds of societal circumstances; but today it follows as a matter of grave critical concern. For precisely the future of the planet is at stake.

Our immediate predecessors, at least in First World settings, took the future more or less for granted. They assumed that history would go on and on—indeed, that it would get better and better. In Victorian England it was possible to lease a box in the Albert Hall for 999 years, "and many citizens did so."[18] How different it is now, less than a hundred years later! As Arthur T. Clarke has said, "The future ain't what it used to be."[19] The future is no longer "assured" (a favorite word of the architects of

18. Michael Crichton, *The Great Train Robbery* (New York: Bantam Books, 1976), xiii.
19. Quoted by Michael MacClear in the CBC broadcast entitled "The American Century," Cineworld Inc., CBC 10.9.86.

---

modernity). On the contrary, it is all but assumed now that what future we have before us will be fraught with ever-increasing hazards (famine; a poisoned environment; a burdensome population; AIDS, and other dread communicable diseases; wars leading to possible nuclear holocaust; and unpredictable and diminishing economies). "Humanity has become mortal."[20] The phrase "It can't go on like this" and similar turns of speech are more indigenous to our epoch than is anything approaching Dr. Coué's nineteenth-century motto, "Every day in every way we're getting better and better." With alarming frequency, one hears older persons commenting to the effect that they are "just as glad" that they will "not be around" to face the future by which our age seems held hostage. Compare with this ancient Israel's patriarchs, who were always looking off into the far distant future when their progeny would be "more in number than the stars of the heavens or the sands of the earth." Today we appear to be capable of entertaining the idea of the future only by cultivating an almost cynical indifference to it, or else feverishly trying to immerse ourselves so mindlessly in the present moment that the thought "Tomorrow we die" cannot affect us too often.

This is to abandon the world more and more unconditionally to the demonic forces, including the force of inertia and leaderlessness, that will certainly destroy it if left uncountered. It is also to destroy ourselves, psychically and spiritually, in the very act of making ourselves indifferent to the future. For, as Dorothee Sölle has stated succinctly, to be human is to have "an elemental relation to the future."[21] It is no more feasible to live only in the present than it is to live only in the past. Physically and spiritually we are creatures who know ourselves to be moving from a past to a future; and the momentary, unmeasurable thing that we call "the present" is comprised of nothing else except remembrance and hope. How pathetic we are, then,

20. From an unpublished lecture by Jürgen Moltmann, in a series entitled "Christian Hope in a Dangerous World," given in Montreal, 2 October 1988.
21. Sölle, Political Theology, 47.

when we try to live wholly in the present, without thinking of the future, without living for the future—not in it, but for it nonetheless: for the life that it holds, the fulfilment that it promises, the unrealized possibilities that it enables us to entertain as real. Perhaps the "hollowness" (T. S. Eliot) of so much of contemporary life is to be traced just to this attempt to have "nothing but the present" (Jean-Paul Sartre). It is of course a luxury entertainable only by those whose present is relatively pleasurable; and that means, on the whole, the dominant classes of the First and to some extent the Second Worlds. Cut off from the past, with its unwanted memories of quite different expectations, and fearful of the future, the comfortable classes of the "developed" world lose themselves in the exaggerated pursuit of momentary happiness. Thus they complicate even further the misery of the other two-thirds of the world's people, and hasten the day when they themselves—or their "children's children"—will reap the whirlwind.

To speak of stewardship in such a context is to insist that Christians have the responsibility of encouraging human beings individually and corporately to reclaim the future. It is no simple mandate, given both our Christian and (in the West particularly) our generally human record! For the whole notion of "reclaiming the future" is bound up with the very modernity that has brought us to the present impasse. Thinking ourselves lords and masters of time, makers of history, we determined to create a technological civilization that would of necessity conform to our bright designs for the future. We know now, if we are alert, that as designers we are not to be trusted.

Yet the alternative to mastery is not sheer passivity. To resign from public life, to "let it be," is as sure a way to future devastation as is the continuation of the illusion of human sovereignty. There is, after all, an alternative to both mastery and the fatalized and cynical posture that is so often displayed by those who have failed at mastery. It is precisely the alternative that is the subject of these reflections: stewardship.

Stewardship occurs under the conditions of an awareness

that sovereignty belongs to Another. "The earth is the Lord's"; the future is in God's hands. The patriarchs and matriarchs of Israel knew this perfectly well when they looked with such hope to the future that would belong to the "children's children." They knew, accordingly, that they could by no means control the future, making it always safe, lovely, and better. They were not so foolish or so egotistical as to consider themselves "masters of their fate." Trust, not assurance, was their stance vis-à-vis the future; confidence [con + fide = with faith], not certitude, was their posture. They trusted not in themselves but in God, who is able to make even our blundering work and planning serve ultimately life-preserving purposes.

But work and planning we must nevertheless do, blunderers though we be. For we are stewards! God has entrusted into our hands, as Pharoah entrusted to the prisoner Joseph, as much of God's economy as we are able reasonably well to handle. Better than our immediate forebears, we know that we are not really qualified for such responsibility. Even with all of the machinery and science and futurology that we have at our disposal, we could fail. But if ever we can get over the illusion of mastery, which is a species of the cardinal sin of pride, we may also overcome our disillusionment at finding ourselves so ill-equipped for responsibility—which disillusionment is a species of the antithetical sin, sloth. Having in the nineteenth and early twentieth centuries indulged pride to the hilt, and having since experienced a good deal of its antithesis—sloth, withdrawal, and apathy—we are perhaps ready to attempt the alternative to both. This alternative does not hold out the prospect of perfection for us. Stewards are still sinners. Even if they have done their very best, they are required to confess at the end of the day (because it will always be true), "We are unworthy servants" (Luke 17:10). But renouncing both the excesses of pride and of sloth, we may be able as stewards of "God's varied grace" to achieve certain "proximate goals" (Reinhold Niebuhr) that will at least ensure that our "children's children" will not inherit an ash heap!

## 7. An Invitation

In the foregoing discussion, I have used five rather awkward terms to try, at least in an initial way, to sketch the kind of spiritual, cultural, and physical revolution that could come to pass if once Christians permitted the radical character of the biblical metaphor of the steward, reconsidered in the light of our present civilization, to invade our imaginations and our consciences. The idea of stewardship, for reasons that may finally be more mysterious than we can know, has been kept alive in our ecclesiastical life, and has now been picked up by others amongst us who are employing it in ways that ought to stimulate our Christian thinking on the subject. If, I have proposed, we can sufficiently globalize, communalize, ecologize, politicize, and futurize our appropriation of this biblical metaphor, we shall enlarge our vision, not only of the meaning of stewardship, but of the gospel and of our mission. I have argued that the biblical metaphor itself will bear such principles as these, and without forcing them upon it. I have argued as well that the historical moment demands the application of these principles to our stewardship thinking.

But what if we really did apply them? What if we allowed ourselves really to become open to the magnificent inclusiveness of this ancient metaphor of our tradition that has become a contemporary symbol? I suspect that we should then find ourselves as Christians and Christian churches more and more at loggerheads with the dominant social forces of our First World societies. For with every one of these five principles of expansion there is an implicit criticism of and threat to the status quo:

> *globalization* can occur only against the entrenched spirit of a narrow nationalism, provincialism, and localism;
> *communalization* can take place only by confronting head-on the persistent individualism of both society and religion;
> *ecologization* runs headlong into the spirit of a rampant technology and the continuing bid for absolute sovereignty over nature;

*politicization* along any lines but those of the market economy immediately creates enemies in our society, and amongst influencial segments within all of our churches as well;

*futurization* flies in the face of every private and institutional desire to secure "the good life" here and now *and* the fatalized sense that in any case we can do nothing to alter the prospect of catastrophe.

In other words, a church that took stewardship seriously today might well find itself in an ostracized, shut-out, counter-cultural situation—disestablished far beyond the mild limits that it may till now have entertained for itself!

In other words, a church that took its stewardship of life quite literally might find itself amongst the poor and marginalized elements of its world rather than in the company of the rich and powerful; and amongst the protesting element more often than that of the powers-that-be; and amongst the defenders of nonhuman species more frequently than those who concerned themselves solely with the human "quality of life."

In other words, a church that explored the depths of the stewardship calling of Homo sapiens might have to suffer for its revolution.

In other words, a church!

# CHAPTER VI

# STEWARDSHIP AND "THE WORLDS"— A MATTER OF JUSTICE

## 1. Our Problem

Discussions entitled "The Problems of the Third World" or "The Plight of Developing Societies" and the like should probably be implicitly distrusted. Such titles frequently betray a fundamental error in their authors' thought. The "problem of the Third World" is first the problem of *our* world, that is, of this so-called First World. The poor are poor, and becoming yet poorer, because we are inordinately rich. It is our riches, and our need to maintain and increase our riches, that is largely responsible for the situation of the "Two-Thirds World." It is our problem!

As we have noted in the Preface to this revised and rewritten version of *The Steward*, the Sixth General Assembly of the World Council of Churches, meeting in Vancouver in 1983, adopted as the central theme of the Council's work and witness over the ensuing decade the motto, "Justice, Peace, and the Integrity of Creation" (JPIC). Chapters VI, VII, and VIII of this book in its original form did not incorporate insights and materials from the JPIC program because, while they covered precisely the same three themes, these chapters were written almost two years prior to the Vancouver Assembly. In this revision, as announced earlier, I intend to include references to some of the literature that has emerged from the Vancouver and subsequent deliberations on these themes. On the question of justice, there has been a great deal of thought and work both in the World Council, the World Alliance of Reformed Churches, and all the denominations associated with these ecumenical organizations, as well as by the Roman Catholic Church and many independent Christian agencies.

On the matter of First World accountability for Third World economic and other forms of oppression, the Vancouver Assembly of the World Council stated:

> The world economic order has institutionalized domination by Northern economies of trade, finance, manufacturing, food processing and knowledge. . . . The machine of the prevailing economic order starves millions of people, and increases the number of unemployed every year. . . . We interpret this development as idolatry, stemming from human sin, a product of satanic forces. We are in a situation where we must go beyond the normal prophetic and intercessory action of the churches. . . . The church is thus challenged not only in what it does, but in its very faith and being.[1]

1. Quoted in *Towards an Affirmation on Justice, Peace and the Integrity of Creation: Working Paper for the World Convocation on Justice, Peace and the Integrity of Creation* (Geneva: World Council of Churches, 1989), 6.

NOTE: In order to ensure that references to the JPIC program of the World Council of Churches are as up-to-date as I can make them for this publication, I shall quote frequently from this document. It is to be recognized that this is a working document, some version of which is planned to be presented to the World Convocation on Justice, Peace and the Integrity of Creation, which will meet in Seoul, Korea, in 1990. While therefore it cannot be assumed either that the Convocation will receive exactly the statements that I shall quote from the working document or that the Convocation in its actual meeting will approve any of these statements, it *can* be assumed that these statements (and the whole document from which they are extracted) represent quite fairly the findings of consultations, councils, theological deliberations, and research which have been taking place since Vancouver, that is, for the past nearly six years, and on a worldwide scale, with representation from all three "worlds" and all three major Christian groupings—Protestant, Orthodox, and Roman

Statements of this nature, challenging as they are, need to be supplemented and (as it were) interpreted by more immediate testimonies coming from the voices of the poor themselves. The same World Council document in which this pronouncement of the Vancouver meetings as well as many similar statements are contained includes the poem of a twelve-year-old Korean girl who lives in a slum of Seoul:

> My mother's name is worry,
> In summer, my mother worries about water,
> In winter, she worries about coal briquets,
> And all the year long, she worries about rice.
>
> In daytime, my mother worries about living,
> At night, she worries for children,
> And all day long, she worries and worries.
>
> Then, my mother's name is worry,
> My father's name is drunken frenzy,
> And mine is tear and sigh.[2]

This simple poem's implicit accusation of those who do not have to worry, an accusation made explicit, though less poignant, in the above and numberless similar statements which abound in all the documents of the concerned, should not be heard as though it were directed in a straightforward way at individuals. It does not assume that we are all equally rich, we who live in these relatively affluent nations. Nor does it mean that all our riches are necessarily tainted and evil. There are cer-

Catholic. They thus bear the weight of the official thought of a considerable portion of the Christian church at work in the world today.

In November, 1989, a second draft of this document was prepared in the light of responses to the first. While the substance of the two drafts is alike, the language and paging are frequently different. Anyone wishing to consult the document I refer to should bear this in mind—I have quoted throughout from the first draft. The second, entitled "Between the Flood and the Rainbow: Covenanting for JPIC," was presented at the WCC meetings in Seoul, March 5-13, 1990. This draft is available from the World Council of Churches offices in Geneva, Switzerland.

2. *Ibid.*, 5-6

tainly pockets of conspicuous poverty and oppression within our own rich nations—a fact that is borne out by the aforementioned unemployment problem, as well as by much of the racial, sexual, and other types of unrest and violence in our midst. As far as our wealth being tainted, it is surely quite understandable if the average citizen of Canada, the United States, France, or Norway, for example, reminds the writers and transmitters of such critical statements that he or she only just manages, after all, to pay the monthly food bills, to meet the rent or mortgage costs, to educate the children, to make payments on the car, and to finance a modest vacation for the family. One can readily sympathize with the impatience, and occasionally the resentment, of ordinary people in the First World when they are addressed as if they were directly to blame for the abject poverty of multitudes. Robert Hempfling speaks for many middle-class church members when he writes: "I'm tired of feeling guilty about being middle class and being characterized as mediocre, superficial, and banal in my thinking and lifestyle. I contend that such stereotyping is neither fair nor accurate."[3]

Little is accomplished by the kind of preaching that engenders such reactions. It is no more effective for change, ultimately, than its medieval or Puritan equivalent, the hell-fire and damnation sermon. We are guilty, and we need very desperately to be brought to a deep awareness of our guilt. But this cannot be achieved by "laying guilt trips" on individual persons. The only sort of awareness of guilt that will lead to *metanoia* of a significant quality is one that comes through the patient and nonvindictive exposure of persons to the global realities. Above all, this must lead to a consciousness of the corporate character of our guilt.

It is hard to understand corporate guilt when one's whole ethos is steeped in the myth of individualism. Although genuine individuality (as distinct from individualism) is one of the most difficult paths to walk in our conformist, fad-prone society, we

3. Robert Hempfling, "The Liberation of the Middle Class," *Journal of Stewardship* 34 (1981): 51-52.

are all plagued from our youth up by the disease of individualism. As we have noted in the preceding chapter's discussion of the principle of communalization, it is very hard for most North Americans at the emotional level (and even intellectually) to escape the tentacles of this ideological octopus. From the outset we are urged on all sides to develop our personalities, to achieve our personal potential, to stand on our own two feet, or to make something of ourselves. If we succeed it is because we've personally "made it." If we fail we have somehow brought failure upon ourselves. How, in such a social environment, can persons avoid taking it personally if they are told (for example by some activist young clergyman) that they are responsible for the forty thousand children who die daily of hunger-related causes?[4]

Accordingly, the first step towards significant change may be the necessity of learning, as First World citizens and members of the great middle classes in particular, how to think corporately. The prophet Isaiah, in the presence of the Transcendent One, cried out—

> I am a man of unclean lips
> And I dwell in the midst of a people of unclean lips. (Isa. 6:5)

In order to achieve the right sort of awareness of our guilt and sin, we shall probably have to learn to reverse the order of Isaiah's confession: (a) I dwell in the midst of a people of unclean lips; (b) I am one of these people.

For that is surely the order of things. We are guilty; each one of us is guilty. But the whole character of the sinful state of our world is distorted if we regard it in a simplistic way, as if it were our individual sin or the sum total of the personal sins of First World people that were at issue here. Corporate sin and guilt is much more complicated than that. It has a different genesis and a different structure. Corporate sin and guilt has, besides, a life of its own. This is what Paul meant when he said that we are not wrestling with flesh and blood but with "principalities and

---

4. *Integrity of Creation*, 3.

powers" (Eph. 6:12). Corporate sin would not be conquered even if, through personal guilt trips and various forms of conditioning, the majority of us managed somehow to slough off our individual greed, lust, insecurity, and covetousness.

In claiming this, I have no intention of exonerating individuals (myself included). But we shall never rightly comprehend even our personal involvement in evil until we begin to sense something of the far-reaching suprapersonal dimensions of that corporate sin that is certainly reflected in our personal lives. We may embody or reflect the sin of our world; we may give our assent to it every time we make a purchase at the supermarket (a sensitive radio commentator recently remarked that she could not find "a politically acceptable cucumber"); we may foster and even further complicate our society's propensity to global injustice, but we neither cause it nor can we cure it all by ourselves. The first principle of sin in today's world is its corporateness: "I dwell in the midst of a people of unclean lips."

The problem of the poor—to come directly to the issue at hand—is our corporate problem. We, who taken together as a people must certainly in relation to approximately two-thirds of the earth's population be named "the rich," are guilty in relation to these poor—as guilty as rich Dives in relation to poor Lazarus (Luke 16:19ff.). This makes no assumptions whatsoever about the sinlessness of the poor, any more than it is assumed that the rich are wholly and irredeemably sinful. The Bible assumes that "all have sinned and fall short of the glory of God" (Rom. 3:23). Lazarus too is a sinner—that is assumed. But it is not necessary in the parable in question to comment on the sin of Lazarus, because Dives, the rich man at whose gate he begs to no avail, is the "efficient cause" (Aristotle) of Lazarus' sinful condition. Dives could, if he would, alter that condition. Were he to do so, it would not erase the fact that Lazarus too is a sinner. It would however alter the spiritual as well as the physical condition of Lazarus, whose present circumstances are so constrained as to make it virtually impossible for him to exercise sufficient freedom even to sin! And, what is perhaps more explicitly the point of this parable, it would indicate that a significant change had taken place in the soul of Dives—a transformation without which he will be, and already is, damned.

At the level of efficient causation, the have-nations of earth are the cause of the poverty of the have-not peoples. As with Dives and Lazarus, it is not a case of the guilty versus the guiltless, or the impure the pure. All have sinned. But scripturally as well as practically, the sin of the rich is the thing that must be dealt with first and most stringently because it is both the source of the oppressive conditions under which the poor exist and the reality which, if it is confronted and changed, could alter the situation of the oppressed as well. In matters of justice, in other words, those who are closer to the causes of injustice are those on whom the gospel of God's judging and transforming Word must concentrate. The point is not to chastise the rich as if they alone were sinful human beings, but through the transformation of attitudes and practices within rich societies to alter the circumstances of both rich and poor.

This is why programs of aid to developing nations, laudable as they are by comparison with pure national selfishness, and necessary as they are for the alleviation of immediate problems, are neither long-range solutions to the great disparities between the have- and have-not peoples of the planet, nor programs to which Christians can devote their greatest energies. Through these necessary measures we may save some of earth's poor from today's worst human degradations, and that is commendable; but through them we shall do very little to modify the source of the problem—the spirit of Dives. As Jürgen Moltmann has put it, "The question is not what we can give them, but whether and when we are going to stop taking things from them. The poor nations are not our 'problem.' It is we—the rich, industrial nations—who are *their* problem."[5]

We can glimpse something of the character of the prob-

5. Jürgen Moltmann, *Experiences of God* (Philadelphia: Fortress Press, 1980), 26.

lem that we are for them, if we consider a number of items that bear upon the facts of injustice in today's global situation:

(i) Item: "North Americans throw away enough solid waste *each year* to build a wall 75 feet wide and 200 feet high along the Canada-U.S. border."[6]

The spectre of such a wall raises innumerable questions. If it were explored with sufficient imagination, it would probably contain all the questions that there are! But one of them will suffice for now: By what spiritual forces must a society be driven if it amasses such a quantity of waste? Whole populations could, if they had access to such waste, easily survive on it, just as the homeless poor in our larger cities survive on what they find in our garbage cans. What impels a people that must throw away once-used bottles, tins, and cartons; half-eaten steaks, fruit, and vegetables; packaging that was unnecessary in the first place; cars that had lost their fashionable lines or a few spare parts; furniture, appliances, toys, and machinery that had become slightly outmoded, soiled, less convenient, or efficient? In my city, very modest experiments have begun here and there in salvaging recyclable waste. Even among the university and college professors, public school teachers, lawyers, and business people who live in my quarter, one can hear complaints about the inconvenience of such a measure; and they are not even asked, as in West Germany people do on a regular basis, to separate different types of waste into different lots. The separation is to be done at special depots—at civic expense, of course. What is the explanation of such waste, and of such resentment over Band-Aid measures to control it?

The answer, at least in part, is implied in the statement I have chosen as the second item in the analysis of our corporate culpability.

(ii) Item: "In 1974, advertising in Canada cost about $1.4 billion, a per-capita expenditure of about sixty-four dollars. This [in a country with a universal public medical health program!]

6. Senator M. Lamontagne, "A Science Policy for Canada," *Consumer Notes* 1 (December 1975).

is about equal to the total federal and provincial government expenditures on medical, hospital, and health services combined."[7]

What this statistic tells us is that the needs of a society that wastes so much of its (that is, of earth's!) resources are comprehensible only on the assumption that a very high proportion of those needs are artificially created by competitive agencies which have high vested interests in making desires appear veritable requirements of daily existence—"daily bread." Even persons from the relatively well-off countries of the Second World, taken into a department or grocery store in North America or Western Europe, are overwhelmed by the quantity and variety of available goods. For Third World citizens, except the very few rich, such stores are beyond the reach of earthly imagination.

But we may ask this: Is it really necessary that there should be 250 varieties of breakfast cereals in one place at one time?

Every year druggists must throw out large quantities of unpurchased prescription medicines whose expiration date has been reached. For this reason, the medicines must be sold in most cases at prices far exceeding their inherent worth. The reason? Competing drug manufacturers produce variations of the same basic medicine and, since most medical practitioners prescribe by brand names, the druggist must stock all available brands. To pay for one sale, these businesses must include in their prices all the items that will not be sold. Who is responsible? The doctors? The druggists? The manufacturers? The purchasers? The advertisers? Yes, all of them! And with some imagination this kind of absurdity can be challenged and changed![8]

7. Donald Thompson, *Conserver Society Notes* 1 (December 1975): 17.

8. In the city of Saskatoon, Saskatchewan, I was a member of the lay board of a Community Health Clinic (one of several in that Province.) The modern clinic facility and its very up-to-date equipment was owned by its membership. The doctors, almost twenty of them, were paid very adequate salaries. The medical care that my family and I received there was better *and more personal* than ever before or since.

In this clinic a prescription service was instituted during my tenure as

Will it require a crisis of grand proportions, however, to alter significantly the social and economic circumstances that support and demand such a system? That is the question. For it is an entrenched system, and so long as it serves the needs that it persuades people they have, the majority of them seem oblivious to the fact that the famous "invisible hand" that is supposed to be regulating this system must be busy most of the time collecting and disposing of the waste that the system itself necessitates.

Such indifference can be analyzed at many levels. At the most obvious level, it is a matter of our sheer ignorance. Most people appear to give little thought to the car graveyards they pass on the way to work or the insulting and the infantile TV advertisements that entice them to get new cars. They are even less aware of the conditions of the overwhelming majority of earth's human citizens, who cannot even count on *basic* needs being met, such as fresh water, let alone entertain in their mind's eye a thousand varieties of soft and hard drinks! "In the 38 lowest income countries, only 28 percent of the population on the average has access to safe water, according to World Bank estimates (1980); the number of countries that have not yet been able to reach 50 percent of the population with safe water is well over 55, and may exceed 75. The rest of the people depend for their water on lakes, rivers, streams, irrigation canals, stagnant ponds and hand-dug wells—generally contaminated and often at great distances from home."[9] The real needs of the world's poor beggars the imagination even of our well-educated and informed citizenry.

(iii) Item: "The misery of 2.5 billion persons is beyond the comprehension of the average American." So writes

---

board member. All of the doctors agreed to prescribe the same brands (chosen from a variety). A small drug outlet was established on the premises, and in spite of this cost *plus* the cost of employing pharmacists and assistants it was possible to sell members of the clinic their prescriptions *and* certain patent medicines (like aspirins, etc.) at vastly reduced prices to the customers.

9. Stuart J. Kingma, "Mere Survival or a More Abundant Life?" *The Ecumenical Review* 33 (July 1981): 259-60.

Robert L. Heilbroner in his book *The Great Ascent;* and to dramatize the point he creates a scenario designed to indicate what would happen to an American family if its living standard were to be reduced to that of the underprivileged people of the world:

> We begin by invading the house to strip it of its furniture. Everything goes: bed, chairs, tables, television set. We will leave the family with a few old blankets, a kitchen table, a wooden chair. . . . The box of matches may stay, a small bag of flour, some sugar and salt. A few moldy potatoes already in the garbage can be rescued, for they will provide much of tonight's meal.
>
> The bathroom dismantled, the running water shut off, the electric wires taken out. Next, we take away the house. The family can move to the toolshed. Communications must go next. No more newspapers, magazines, books. . . . Next, government services must go. No more postmen, no more firemen. There is a school but it is three miles away and consists of two rooms. They are not too overcrowded since only half the children in the neighborhood go to school.
>
> The nearest clinic is ten miles away and is tended by a midwife. It can be reached by bicycle provided the family has a bicycle, which is unlikely. . . . Finally, money. We will allow our family a cash hoard of $5.[10]

While ordinary ignorance and incomprehension partly account for our indifference to the realities of our own overabundance as well as the destitution of the many, it is naive to think that this is a sufficient explanation. There are strong vested interests in our society that are served by this ignorance. They are by no means ready to excite or alarm the populace through programs of education and information that could somewhat combat this ignorance. We North Americans like to pride ourselves on being an open society, where news is not manipulated and information is available to all. It is true that in certain areas of

10. Quoted by Don Fabun in *The Dynamics of Change* (Englewood Cliffs, N.J.: Prentice-Hall, 1968), 27; see also Harry Ferguson, UPI, *Oakland Tribune,* 14 December 1965.

information we are very open—sometimes to the detriment of individuals and groups. But as one who has lived for significant periods in Europe, and in nations reputed to be highly circumspect and even secretive, I am convinced that the European public on the whole is very much better informed about the real character of the world we live in than are North Americans. I am also convinced that part of the reason for this (a significant part) is that the primary medium of public information in major European countries (television) is not manipulated by private enterprise. There are, to be sure, a few provocative and critically informative programs on American and Canadian television networks (especially the CBC and public television in the U.S.A.); but what is for us the exception is more nearly the norm in West Germany, France, England, Scandanavia, and other West European nations. Companies that want you to buy their gasoline, oil, and soap may be very happy to bring you entertaining family programs, or even opera; but they are not likely to treat you to documentaries on the condition of peoples whose economies are in ruins partly on account of our inordinate consumption of the world's energy supplies and the interest they must pay on their debts to us. Or, if such firms do offer occasional tidbits of information about other lands, one can be reasonably sure that it will be laced with the rhetoric of the trickle-down theory: i.e., that the way to world prosperity is through the greater and greater prosperity of the developed nations. (John Kenneth Galbraith in an Oxford debate spoke of this as the "horse and sparrow theory": the more you feed the horse, the more "you know what" the sparrow has to eat!)

The pathology of oblivion within the rich nations is not, however, exhausted by economic and political analysis, important as such analysis is. We have invoked the biblical doctrine of sin in the foregoing pages, and while the Bible knows perfectly well the greed of capitalists who are ready to sell the widow and the orphan for "a pair of shoes" (Amos 2:6; 8:6), it also knows that the corporate structures of evil are more subtle than the scheming of capitalists and entrepreneurs. The sinful consciousness (for example, as it is profoundly depicted in Gen. 3) expresses itself first and most characteristically in a falsification of reality. It hides and it lies. It is not for nothing that Jesus calls Satan "the Father of lies" (John 8:44). The hiding and the lying that is the hallmark of sin should not be interpreted after the fashion of petty moralists. "Thou shalt not lie," does not refer simplistically to telling "fibs" or making up explanations. It means the habit of constructing images of the world—worldviews, ideologies, or images of the human—that skillfully omit whole segments of experience and substitute theory for reality. The lying and hiding which belong to the sinful state make much use of that psychic mechanism that Freud named repression: raw experience, including thought that is too painful, is suspended at the subconscious level, blocked altogether, or subtly transformed before it is permitted to reach the level of conscious knowledge.

Referring to the relation between justice and peace as it is treated in the prophet Ezekiel, Walter Brueggemann concludes:

> God promises peacemaking. That peacemaking by God only happens, however, when there is truth-telling—costly, urgent and subversive. That is the work of the church. The issue, since Ezekiel, is clear: When we lie, we die. When we speak truthfully about human reality, God sends us peace.[11]

And now let us remember: We are not speaking here only or simply of individual sin but of corporate sin. When it is said (as many of the world's own wise have been saying now for at least three decades) that ours is "a repressive society," that is what we should hear. Namely, that our corporate sin expresses itself most profoundly not in the fact that our various authority structures suppress or manipulate the truth, but that we ourselves as a whole society are caught up in a network of repression. Repression means lying to ourselves about ourselves—but without the benefit of consciousness; it happens at a subcon-

11. Walter Brueggemann, "Truth-Telling and Peacemaking: A Reflection on Ezekiel," *The Christian Century,* 30 November 1988, 1098.

167

scious level. It transcends our individual wills. It is built into our institutions, including our educational institutions. It is part of our total environment. It is so common as to seem entirely natural. To oppose or resist it is to swim against the stream, to be branded unnatural or devious or simply crazy. Few therefore are driven to buck the system. And this is not only because people fear isolation and criticism; it is because they are usually served very well by their conformity. Working within the system of a dominant culture that is still cushioned from the shock of events by relative affluence, most people are able to carry on as if no question had been raised about their personal pursuits, their values, assumptions, and goals. And this is a great boon to the human condition, because the majority of us need to repress our knowledge of the darkness, even at the best of times. But, as Ernest Becker states bluntly: "Somebody has to pay for it."[12] For his skillful services, the Father of Lies asks a very high price: souls. But he takes his toll in bodies, too. Those who pay bodily for the spiritual repression of the rich nations of the northern hemisphere are (who else?) the poor nations of the southern hemisphere. More particularly the women of these societies pay, according to the findings of the Asian Women's Consultation on Justice, Peace and the Integrity of Creation (JPIC), meeting in Bangkok, Thailand, in December of 1986.[13]

12. Ernest Becker, *The Denial of Death* (New York: Free Press, 1973), 187.

13. See *Women in a Changing World* (Geneva: WCC, Doc. 24, Nov. 1987).

Aruna Gnanadason writes in this publication: "Women are most often the direct victims of the violence of war and other crisis situations. They also bear the brunt of a crisis-ridden economic system which exploits their labour and sexuality. . . . Women are the poorest of the poor, no matter how poverty lines are drawn. Women are increasingly marginalized and exploited economically, pushed into low skilled, low paying jobs. Women are the cheap labour in the transnational corporations and particularly in the free trade zones. Unorganized and ununionized, they are victims of occupational hazards. (The after effects of Bhopal are only now coming out. And there are Bhopals happening again and again, in smaller intensity, in different parts of India.)" *Ibid.*, 3.

"I dwell in the midst of a people of unclean lips." I, the average person, am caught up in structures of conformity and deceit that automatically necessitate the suffering of other persons, most of whom are far enough removed from the sphere of my life that I shall never have to look in their faces and see the "worry" in their eyes. Sometimes I am gripped by the appalling nature of all this. But I find in myself neither the wisdom, the courage, nor—alas!—the will to resist these structures. I am their victim. And yet I am also (I know it!) served by them. So, yes, "*I* am a man [a woman] of unclean lips."

(iv) Item:

> We have to ask who this average man is. He may avoid the psychiatric clinic, but somebody around has to pay for it. We are reminded of those Roman portrait-busts that stuff our museums: to live in this tight-lipped style as an average good citizen must have created some daily hell. Of course we are not talking only about the daily pettiness and the small sadisms that are practiced on family and friends. Even if the average man lives in a kind of obliviousness of anxiety, it is because he has erected a massive wall of repression to hide the problem of life and death. His anality may protect him, but all through history it is the 'normal, average men' who, like locusts, have laid waste to the world in order to forget themselves.[14]

The great weakness of repression (not to be confused with suppression) as a defense mechanism against reality is that it is effective only up to a point, namely, the point where the repressed truth asserts itself forcefully and refuses to be silenced or metamorphized by theory. (To illustrate by the lyrics of a favourite American folksong: it was one thing for the "old lady" to "swallow a fly" and not notice it; but by the time it came to swallowing a dog she could hardly sustain her characteristic nonchalance, and when she was obliged to swallow a horse . . . "she died, of course.") The rich nations have been remarkably adept at repressing their own evil and the plight of their victims. This

14. Becker, *Denial of Death*, 187.

has worked, after a fashion, so long as the victims have been willing to endure the status quo and so long as the earth has been able to sustain our own exorbitant expectations of it. But the victims have grown restive (e.g., Central America) and newly conscious of their oppressed state, and as for the earth it groans ever more perceptibly under the curse of a burgeoning population that makes ever more absurd demands upon its limited resources. What our grandparents in North America were still able to repress, our grandchildren (perhaps our children) will have to face in the most open, unsettling, and perhaps even tragic way.

(v) Item: "The cost of a ten-year program to provide for essential food and health needs in developing countries is less than half of one year's military spending." [Taken from the Brandt Commission Report, 1980]

"The cost of one jet fighter plane could set up 40,000 village pharmacies."[15]

As has long been recognized in Christian as well as in secular circles, justice and peace concerns are inseparable. Ostensibly, the incredible buildup of arms in the world is a matter between chiefly First and Second Worlds, notably the U.S.A. and the U.S.S.R. But if one asks who is being excluded, both by the economic greed and the military hardware protecting that greed, one comes face-to-face with a deeper truth: neither of those two armed worlds is prepared to lower its expectations so that the majority of earth's peoples can be brought to more humane levels of existence. The noise and the drama of saber rattling between the two empires, which on the surface of it is less nerve-racking today than it was five years ago, ought not to distract our attention from the stealthy dealings being undertaken by the "left arms" of both empires in the Third World. The arms race is a race between two empires, both of which are impoverished, physically and spiritually, by this preoccupation

---

15. Kingma, *Mere Survival*, 259.

("Every minute the nations of the world spend 1.8 million U.S. dollars on military armaments." *Integrity of Creation*, 3.)

with their security; but the greatest victim of their struggle is the Third World—the Lazarus at their gates—whose condition cannot be a priority for them except when and as its vulnerability can serve their purposes. Dorothee Sölle's 1982 conclusion, therefore, is still pertinent: "Our historical task [as First World Christians]," she wrote, "is the fight for peace and against militarism. *That* is how we may participate in the liberation struggles of the Third World."[16]

## 2. Their Problem

The problem of the Third World peoples, to speak now of the fact rather than of its efficient cause, is simply their abysmal poverty. Only, poverty is never simple. It is a complex amalgam of physical and spiritual pain, which robs the person and the community of dignity and meaning as much as it deprives the body of nourishment, shelter, and beauty.

> For a good two-thirds of the human family there is no such thing as "life in all its fulness" because they are impoverished, living on the edge of death in stark, economically conditioned poverty. They are hungry, they have no shelter, no shoes, no medicine for their children, no clean water to drink, no work—and they see no way of getting their oppressors off their backs. Trade agreement and international relations are dictated by the rich first world and imposed on the poor, plunging them daily deeper into destitution. The mere struggle for survival destroys the fulness of life, the shalom of God, of which the Bible speaks.[17]

It is of course too simple to speak of the Third World as if we were treating a sociogeographic monolith. Poverty of the most abject nature—the kind of poverty that cannot even be

---

16. Dorothee Sölle, *The Arms Race Kills: Even without War* (Philadelphia: Fortress Press, 1982), 54. (Italics added.)

17. Dorothee Sölle, "Life in Its Fulness," address, the Sixth Assembly of the World Council of Churches, August 1983; Document TH3-1.

imagined by us, not even by most of the oppressed minorities in our own midst—is to be found in what is sometimes called "the Fourth World." This term refers to almost one-fourth of earth's human population.

> Some 800 million people in the world are destitute and live in conditions of absolute poverty. Their lives are characterized by malnutrition, undernutrition, disease, illiteracy, unemployment, low income, inadequate shelter and high fertility. Some 40% of the population of developing countries fall into this category, and most of these are to be found in the rural sectors.[18]

These are the ones who suffer most from the catastrophic debt of Third World countries. This debt

> now totals over 1,250 billion U.S. dollars. [It] is primarily the consequence of an unjust world economic order, which keeps the South in economic bondage, enables unfair trade advantages to Northern economies, and guarantees a net flow of money from South to North, from debtor countries to creditor countries. This system also provides a mechanism by which the North can continue to impose its political and economic agendas on the indebted nations. Although the debt crisis is affecting the North through unemployment, it has become a matter of life or death for poor people in Third World countries.[19]

Those areas of the Third World which are not in the state of servile poverty designated "fourth" run the gamut from underdevelopment to semidevelopment. But just at this point we encounter the more subtle side of their problem. It is suggested both by the nomenclature of "development" and by the fact that development (i.e., the established models of life in the rich countries) is seen by the poor as well as by most of their Western advisers as the solution to their problem. In other words, the problem of the poor nations is not only a poverty that is caused or sustained by our prosperity but the import of a men-

---

18. Kingma, *Mere Survival*, 257-58.
19. *Integrity of Creation*, 5.

tality that encourages them to desire to emulate us. Thus, as William Ophuls points out, semideveloped nations like Mexico and Brazil

> have followed a basically American path, so that Mexico City has a smog problem rivaling that of Los Angeles, and Brazil's treatment of its underdeveloped wealth, especially such fragile and irreplaceable resources as the Amazon rain forest, epitomizes frontier economics at its most heedless. On the other hand, Taiwan and South Korea have proceeded more or less along the lines laid down by Japan and are beginning to encounter many of the same problems. In the same way, the countries (now mostly beyond the stage of semi-development) that have travelled the Soviet path experience the same kinds of environmental problems and suffer from similar political liabilities in coping with them.[20]

No doubt it is understandable that human communities that are poor should look upon the rich peoples—whose lifestyle their raw materials enhance, whose music and machinery they admire from afar, and whose well-dressed and overfed tourists they encounter—as models to be imitated. What is less understandable is that the rich nations themselves should have produced so little depth of self-knowledge that their Third World "experts" could assume the same sentiment. But this has in fact been the case:

> The ruling philosophy of development over the last twenty years has been: "What is best for the rich must be best for the poor." This belief has been carried to truly astonishing lengths, as can be seen by inspecting the list of developing countries in which the Americans and their allies and in some cases also the Russians have found it necessary and wise to establish "peaceful" nuclear reactors—Taiwan, South Korea, Philippines, Vietnam, Thailand, Indonesia, Iran, Turkey, Portugul, Venezuela—all of them countries whose overwhelming problems are agriculture

20. William Ophuls, *Ecology and the Politics of Scarcity* (San Francisco: W. H. Freeman, 1977), 207.

173

and the rejuvenation of rural life, since the great majority of their poverty-stricken peoples live in rural areas.[21]

The question that this "problem of the worlds" poses for all of us, then, is a multidimensional one. It cannot be answered wisely simply by saying, "Bring them up to our standards," or "Let them too become developed," because the best minds among us know perfectly well that the earth cannot sustain even its present population if all its peoples began to clamour for our style of high living! More important, such wisdom is well aware that our vaunted development is scarcely a way of life guaranteed to bring (in Jesus' sense) abundance, let alone (in the idealistic rhetoric of our founding forebears) happiness. At the West German *Kirchentag* in Düsseldorf in 1973, some delegates were wearing tags that read: "*Hilfe! Wir sind entwickelt!*" ("Help! We're Developed!") And in her Vancouver address before the World Council Assembly, Dorothee Sölle similarly urged, "Dear sisters and brothers from the third and second worlds, I beg you: Do not follow our example! Claim back what we have stolen from you, but do not follow us."[22] Can anyone really believe that a world filled with our First World kind of living would be the best of all possible worlds?

How does Christian stewardship speak to this problem of the worlds?

21. E. F. Schumacher, *Small Is Beautiful: Economics as if People Mattered* (New York: Harper and Row, 1975), 167-68.

22. Sölle, "Life in Its Fulness," 5. *Kirchentag* (literally, Church Day) was instituted in Germany in 1949 as a means of renewing Christian life in the aftermath of WW II. The first *Kirchentag* was held in Essen in 1949. It has grown to be a major movement, with Christians from all over Germany and (to some extent) the world coming together every two years for Bible study and lectures on theological, political, ethical, and other subjects. The semi-annual meetings last for four or five days. 120,000 were present at the last Kirchentag held in Berlin in 1989. *Kirchentag* is regarded by some leading German intellectuals as one of the three or four most important influences in postwar Germany. In recent years similar meetings have been held in East Germany and have contributed conspicuously to the process of democratization there. *Kirchentag* in 1991 will be held simultaneously in several cities in the Ruhr, it being too large now for one city.

## 3. Stewardship in the Global Village

### (a) "The Earth Is the Lord's"

The first and most obvious point that must be made out of the faith tradition in which we stand is that the primary object of Christian endeavours to effect change must be our own society. It is we, not the masses of earth's poor, who are judged by the "theo-anthropology" of stewardship. This does not preclude the necessity of other types of activity in relation to the developing world, including direct aid. But one can only be pessimistic about the long-range results of aid programs unless they are accompanied by a massive self-examination on the part of the givers.

If we are at all serious about stewardship as a symbol of Christian and human existence, then the thing that has to come under direct attack in our prophetic witness within our own First World is our worldview of sovereignty and ownership. For North Americans in particular, the questioning of the right to possess and dispose of one's possessions in whatever way one chooses appears almost an act of treason. Somehow, the ideas of possession and control took root in our soil more tenaciously than elsewhere—perhaps because so many of our forebears had themselves been have-nots. Having had the benefits of rich natural resources, in whose bounty large numbers of people could have some personal share, we have grown accustomed to thinking of ourselves chiefly as possessors. (Consider the expression: "Mr. X is *worth* such-and-such an amount of money.") Having seems a veritable human right with us—having property, having material goods, having houses and cars and every imaginable appliance; having also less tangible things—health, the confidence of the well-fed, or power over others. And at the collective level—national, state, provincial, or municipal—this has translated into the possessing of forests, minerals, lakes and waterways, and coastal waters (a constant source of dispute between nations).

175

Moreover, the churches, minority voices notwithstanding, have never significantly challenged this kind of thinking. Their periodic outbursts over materialism have all the earmarks of corporate flagellation to ease the guilty conscience; for the churches themselves are possessors of large holdings. Instead of challenging the assumption of possession, our religion has undergirded and legitimized our cultural acquisitiveness, and many Christians reflect in their own outlooks the same propensity to judge worth by possessions. The truncated nature of stewardship in Christian practice shows up nowhere more conspicuously than in the budgets of churches, which regularly demonstrate the *self*-supporting priorities of local congregations.

But if we take with even some seriousness the criticism of "possession" that the biblical steward symbol implies, a judgment buttressed by many other aspects of biblical faith, then we must begin to register a prophetic critique against the institution of private property. I do not mean that such a critique ought to be carried to the lengths of doctrinaire communism. That would be the quickest way to render it ridiculous and untenable in a world whose great experiments in communal ownership have floundered. Obviously something in the human spirit (whether it belongs to creation or Fall is hard to say) craves ownership. Of something or other, even if it is only a token, I need to be able to say, "This is mine."

But there is a difference, surely, between the need to say that about a few books and pictures and perhaps even a house and its furnishings and, on the other hand, thousands of acres of land, vast holdings of timber and mineral rights, and dozens of houses in the slums of big cities! The symbolic necessity of having something that is "mine"—something that will give me a sense of continuity with my own past, or a sense of privacy, or a link with those I love—is not going to be taken from me if I am denied the right to own three city blocks!

The Hebraic side of our faith never questioned the first kind of ownership, because it knew (it still knows) that as physical beings we need to express our spiritual yearnings and joys physically. Jesus the Jewish teacher understood the human desire to treasure things. But he also spoke out strongly against "laying up treasures" (Matt. 6:19ff.). This was strictly in line with the Hebrew prophets of old, like Amos and Ezekiel, who railed out against the rich who found their spiritual worth in their riches. If we may borrow a leaf from the Marxist notebook (a fair exchange, since the Marxists borrowed a great many leaves from the tradition of Jerusalem), there is a point where a change in quantity introduces a qualitative change. This is called Engle's law. Given certain needs and obligations, it may be perfectly necessary for, say, Smith to maintain a bank account in six figures. But when Smith's account grows to seven or eight figures, take care! Something will probably have happened to Smith, and it will not be just the effects of inflation! From being a person who kept up his bank account for pragmatic reasons, Smith now likely believes his bank account is of special interest in its own right—and therefore it is a symbol of a sort very different from the one about which we have been thinking. Smith will have moved from treasuring to laying up treasures, and probably without even having noticed the fact. Like the rich fool of Jesus' parable (Luke 12:20), Smith will have become a victim of his own deception. For surely we must give the rich fool of the parable the benefit of the doubt, and assume that his decision to build yet greater barns was only considered by him at the time a matter of necessity, and quite in keeping with his previous mode of problem solving. He had lost the capacity to recognize the fine but absolutely decisive line between being and having. Called to give an account of his stewardship ("this night!"), he discovered to his horror what he should have known all along: that having is no substitute for being, and that what we seem to have guarantees nothing at all about our ultimate security or our worth.

"The earth is the Lord's and the fulness thereof." Possession is always strictly conditioned by that prior claim, and so it is illusory whenever that claim is set aside. As a way of life, in fact, the quest to acquire is usually little more than a pathetic bid for security, permanence, and a meaning that we sense we do not have.

Bringing this down to the concretes of our own present situation, it means that the Christian community, to be true to its own roots, will increasingly have to be found on the side of those who argue that the basic resources of the earth belong neither to individuals, nor corporations, nor nations, but are global treasures, given perpetually by a gracious God for the use of all the families of the earth—including those not yet born. The preservation and distribution of these treasures must not be allowed therefore to fall into the hands of a few who, through such control, ensure their own brief moment of prosperity at the expense of the survival and welfare of earth's human and extrahuman creatures for generations to come. The globalization principle applies here, obviously enough; but so do the principles of politicization, ecologization, communalization, and futurization. If we have made these principles our own, having first taken to heart that as Christians the well-being of this world really is our business, then we are led to very explicit conclusions, such as this one about the institution of property in the context of the global village.

Let us recognize immediately that this probably implies that an obedient Christian community today will often find itself associated with persons and groups whose ideas are presently highly suspect so far as the dominant culture of the First World is concerned. For both the economics of capitalism and the sociology of nationalism (to be distinguished from patriotism) must be questioned by a stewardship theology that reckons globally. The frequent criticism of the World Council of Churches and other Christian bodies which support liberation movements in Third World and other settings where a few powerful and rich dominate many poor is perhaps a foretaste of things to come.

I reiterate: It is not implied that Christians must embrace either an ideological socialism or the sort of transcendental internationalism that has no room for patriotism or the love of "one's own." The collective greed of allegedly international communism is no answer to the competitive individualistic greed of capitalism. But I do not see how a serious stewardship praxis today can avoid seeking more just forms for the preservation and distribution of earth's resources, for a more truly global expression of the love of God for all earth's creatures, and for a future that lasts well beyond the next election year.

No doubt some readers will recoil if I illustrate my meaning by quoting from the Confession of Faith of the Presbyterian-Reformed Church of Cuba; but let these readers remember, first, that the denomination in question is a member in good standing of the World Alliance of Reformed Churches, and second, that nothing in the quotation could not have been said six hundred years ago by John Wyclif. It is to my knowledge the only contemporary confession of faith that employs extensively the symbol of the steward.

> The Scriptures teach us that the human being is characterized by being an "econome" [*oikonomos*] of all things, God's steward. All goods, material and spiritual, that we obtain as persons and as nations, cannot be considered in the final analysis as "individual" or "national" property in an exclusive way. . . . To make human spirituality essentially dependent on the exercising of the so-called right to private property constitutes one of the most tragic aberrations . . . that human spirituality has suffered to this day.[23]

### (b) "He Hath Filled the Hungry"

It is self-evident that the work of transforming an acquisitive and imperialistic society into one that is capable of proximate forms of economic justice is a long-range goal of Christian stewardship. But to all who continue to jab at the idealism of such a goal, the future is on the side of this ideal and against all the allegedly practical people. For it is no longer either practical

---

23. *The Confession of Faith* (Havana: Editorial Orbe, 1978), 6-7.

or practicable to assume that such grossly unequal distribution of the planet's limited resources can continue to be the norm. The First World will either learn some measure of sharing or it will be taught; and the lessons, in the latter case, will not likely be gentle ones. After generations of observing the laws of competition, we ought to have realized that those who play that game are first only temporarily!

But of course the plight of the poor cannot wait for the transformation of the rich. The second strategy of Christian stewardship must therefore be the steward's care of earth's greatest victims. There is never any excuse for leaving the one who has fallen amongst thieves lying in the ditch to die. Not even for the excuse of converting the thieves! Aid must be given, and it must be given regardless of the identity, color, or political persuasion of the victims.

Most important, the aid must be appropriate to the need; that is to say, it is the actual condition of the victim that determines what aid should mean. If the victim says, "I am hungry," it is not for the steward to determine that this of course means spiritual hunger and proceed to offer "food for the spirit." I shall reserve until the final chapter my answer to those who are afraid that when the church involves itself in the provision of material aid it will forget its spiritual mission. In his parable defining both the neighbor and our obedience in relation to the neighbor, Jesus at no point commanded his followers to use the occasion of the other's physical need to engage in a program of Christian indoctrination! Not even when the Samaritan took his leave of the victim, whose life was now out of danger and who was presumably rather comfortably set up in the inn—not even then did the Samaritan exact spiritual payment from the one who had fallen amongst thieves by making him listen to a sermon. We are not even told that he left a tract, discretely, with the innkeeper, to be given to the patient when he was a little stronger. At least with the 25 percent of the world's poor who are desperately poor (the "Fourth World"), direct assistance is needed. And it should be given, both by churches and governments whom Christians might vote for and otherwise influence, without strings attached.

As we have already insisted, direct assistance is no profound or permanently valid answer to injustice amongst the worlds. It can offer interim relief only for their part of the problem. But of course it must be given, and in far greater quantities and with much greater sensitivity to the real needs of the victimized peoples, than is presently the case. Persons and nations who do not act out of Christian motivation may think otherwise, but at least for Christians the thing has already been decided: Christian stewardship, servanthood under the banner of the Suffering Servant, means "filling the hungry with good things."

### (c) The Stewardship of Experience and Wisdom

Without in any way minimizing the importance of such aid, however, it must be considered little more than Band-Aid treatment without the stewardship revolution applied at home, and without sharing something else that in the long run is more important than bread. Here I should like to combine my own thought with that of a Christian thinker for whom I have the greatest respect, and who in my opinion has shown us the way of Christian stewardship as it applies to the rich in a manner more imaginative and more practical than most: the late E. F. Schumacher.

It was Schumacher's conviction, as we have already noted, that what bedevils our approach to the Third World is our assumption that they should emulate us: "what is good for the rich must also be good for the poor." This, he said, is the thinking of people (economists and others) who think about problems and populations and gross national products and the like, but not about people.

The question that must first be asked, in Schumacher's view, is this: Who are the people who constitute the Third World? The answer is they are poor people. They are the people (as he says in the title of a chapter of one of his books) of "Two Million Villages." Thus,

> the new thinking that is required for aid and development will be different from the old because it will take poverty seriously. It will not go on mechanically, saying, "What is good for the rich must also be good for the poor." It will care for people—from a severely practical point of view. Why care for people? Because people are the primary and ultimate source of any wealth whatsoever. If they are left out, if they are pushed around by self-styled experts and high-handed planners, then nothing can ever yield real fruit.[24]

If development means developing the potential of the human beings who constitute the have-not nations, then the primary emphasis must be not upon goods, but upon the "education, organization, and discipline" of the people:

> Without these three, all resources remain latent, untapped, potential. There are prosperous societies with but the scantiest basis of natural wealth, and we have had plenty of opportunity to observe the primacy of invisible factors after the war. Every country, no matter how devastated, which had a high level of education, organization and discipline produced an "economic miracle." In fact these were miracles only for people whose attention was focused on the tip of the iceberg. The tip had been mashed to pieces, but the base, which is education, organization and discipline, was still there.[25]

Development in this sense cannot be created by feeding society better food or providing it with nuclear reactors! Such development requires a process of education. But this does not mean that it requires centuries—centuries that we do not have. In the course of their own, slow evolution, the peoples of the West have learned some things that can be passed on rather quickly—provided it is remembered that these lessons are to be geared to the real situation of the people, and not simply to

24. Schumacher, *Small Is Beautiful*, 169-70.
25. *Ibid.*, 168.

satisfy the theoretical presuppositions of the modern Western technocrat.

Here I should like to supplement Schumacher's admirable proposals. For very understandable reasons, he concentrates on the positive side of what we First World people could pass on to our sisters and brothers of the Third World. In a word, it is the kind of practical know-how that can assist poor people in two million villages to develop the intermediate technology ("small" or appropriate technology) that would enable them to live with relative prosperity and dignity in their villages, instead of taking their poverty from the village to the city (as they do now), where it becomes many times more horrendous. As Dr. Schumacher puts it—

> Give a man a fish . . . and you are helping him a little bit for a short while; teach him the art of fishing and he can help himself all his life. On a higher level: supply him with fishing tackle; this will cost you a good deal of money, and the result remains doubtful; but even if fruitful, the man's continuing livelihood will still be dependent on you for replacements. But teach him how to make his own fishing tackle and you have helped him to become not only self-supporting but also self-reliant and independent.[26]

The logic of this, and of the whole approach of intermediate or "small" technology, seems to me above reproach. But there is one condition that I think Schumacher did not adequately meet. He neglected the fact that for the First World citizens (experts or otherwise) to transmit such knowledge, they must themselves have come to a high degree of self-knowledge concerning the limits, dangers, and undesirable side effects of their own high technocracies. And they must be able imaginatively and passionately to transmit that knowledge to the Third World, whose peoples naturally suppose that big technology alone brings human beings success, and who are very apt to suspect First World citizens who would withhold the great bless-

26. *Ibid.*, 197.

ings of technocracy of wanting to hoard those blessings for themselves.

I am thus in total agreement with Dr. Schumacher that "the best aid to give is intellectual aid, a gift of useful knowledge."[27] But a very significant part of that knowledge must be the knowledge of ourselves as a less than happy, less than egalitarian, less than free, and perhaps even less than fully human civilization. Such knowledge will be heard as real wisdom, perhaps, if it is given by people who know that our civilization is a problematic one, perhaps even a doomed one, because we have pursued so uncritically the modern vision.

This is the negative (but is it really negative?) lesson that must accompany our positive gifts of know-how if our gifts are to be in any sense honest, authentic, and sincere. For the problem of the Third World, as we have observed, is not only that it does not have, but that it is pathetically driven by unseen but powerful forces to imitate those who do have—and who, in the getting, may have gained the whole world and lost their soul.

In short, along with our knowledge, we must strive to comprehend our unique experience as rich and technically advanced peoples to the point of acquiring greater wisdom about the essential vanity of these achievements (Ecclesiastes). Knowledge *(scientia)* cradled in such wisdom *(sapientia)* could be a fitting posture for those who want to stand in the succession of the prophets and apostles.

---

27. "A gift of knowledge is infinitely preferable to a gift of material things. There are many reasons for this. Nothing becomes 'one's own' except on the basis of some genuine effort or sacrifice. A gift of material goods can be appropriated by the recipient without effort or sacrifice; it therefore rarely becomes 'his own' and is all too frequently and easily treated as a mere windfall. A gift of intellectual goods, a gift of knowledge, is a very different matter. Without a genuine effort of appropriation on the part of the recipient there is no gift. To appropriate the gift and make it one's own is the same thing, and 'neither moth nor rust doth corrupt.' The gift of material goods makes people dependent, but the gift of knowledge makes them free—if it is the right kind of knowledge, of course." *Ibid.*, 197.

# CHAPTER VII

# STEWARDSHIP AS KEY TO A THEOLOGY OF NATURE

## 1. The Integrity of Creation

Perhaps the most obvious application of the symbol of the steward in our time is its pertinence to our relation to the other creatures of God. Wisely, in view of the growing threat to the natural order, the World Council of Churches at Vancouver in 1983 added to the two existing concerns (justice and peace) on which most of the member churches had been working for years, a third: "the integrity of creation." The term is new.[1] In explaining it, Dr. Premen Niles, secretary of the JPIC process, draws the connection with stewardship:

> The term includes ecological and environmental issues, but goes beyond them. Its central thrust is on a caring attitude towards nature—an emphasis that is more evident in the German "*Bewahrung die Schöpfung*" and in the French "*sauvegarde de la création.*" The English "integrity of creation" says more. It tries to bring together the issues of justice, peace and the environment

---

1. For a discussion of the theological and biblical connotation of the term as well as the topic in general, see *Reintegrating God's Creation: A Paper for Discussion* (Geneva: WCC, Church and Society Documents, no. 3, Sept. 1987).

by stressing the fact that there is an integrity or unity that is given in God's creation. What this means will become clearer as we continue in the various struggles for life, and realize more fully that we live in an interdependent world of complex relationships and delicate balances. To realize, for instance, that justice for the poor and the hungry is tied up with the issue of justice for the land. To ignore the integrity of creation is finally to destroy all that sustains us. *In essence, it is a call for a new life-style that is based on stewardship and compassion rather than on mastery and exploitation.*[2]

Similarly, Professor Charles Birch, noting that "the phrase Justice, Peace and the Integrity of Creation recognizes three momentous instabilities of our time," writes:

Integrity has to do with wholeness, completeness, the notion of organic unity which is more than an aggregate, and the reciprocal relation of the individual elements to the ensemble. We may understand the meaning of integrity better if we think of its opposite: fragmentation, separation, alienation, estrangement.[3]

The most recent document available to me at the time of writing (one from which I have quoted several times in the preceding text) makes the following observation about stewardship in its connection with the integrity of creation:

In this term ["integrity of creation"], we hear that the human species is called to employ its wisdom and creative skills in all fields of endeavour—industry, economics, politics, science, art—under the impulse of a strong sense of stewardship. According to the Scriptures, stewardship, far from being a merely utilitarian and managerial metaphor, assumes as its basis a solidar-

2. *A Conversation with Dr Premen Niles: Answers to Questions that are often asked about the JPIC process or the Conciliar Process of Mutual Commitment (Covenant) for Justice, Peace, and the Integrity of Creation* (Geneva: WCC, n.d.).

3. Charles Birch, "Peace, Justice and the Integrity of Creation: Some Central Issues for the Churches," in *Report and Background Papers of the Meeting of the Working Group, Potsdam, GDR, July 1986* (Geneva: WCC, Church and Society, n.d.), 40ff.

ity with all for which the steward is responsible and answerable, and it issues in a life of service and sacrifice. In all that we do and are, we are to offer ourselves sacramentally to God, to one another, and to the world God loves.[4]

While Christians have absorbed the concerns expressed openly by scientists as early as 1960, we are not permitted quickly to leap in with our solutions; for we have a good deal of internal housecleaning to do before we may legitimately claim to be keepers of ancient wisdom that may be useful to the world at this critical juncture. If our theology of stewardship is to be credible in the face of dire crises like "the greenhouse effect" and the depletion of species ("every hour a score of nonhuman species becomes extinct"),[5] we have first to take seriously the criticism that is levelled against our religious tradition. As John Carmody writes,

> Ecologists now call upon Christian theologians to change the old image of "subdue the earth." The history of the various religions' attitudes towards nature shows that no tradition has been a simon-pure friend of the earth, but it is Western technology that has set in motion the forces of modern pollution, and behind Western technology one finds an anthropocentrism that sees nature more exploitatively than Eastern systems do. Perhaps biblical religion need not view nature so exploitatively. Perhaps it can expand its sense of stewardship into an equivalent of a Taoist reverence for nature's Way, a Buddhist reverence for nature's Dharma. Until it starts along this path, however, many ecologists will consider biblical religion a foe of the earth, a blind guide that has helped bring spaceship earth close to ditching.[6]

Not only do most Christians, like other citizens of the postindustrial societies, "tend for the most part still to see nature as nothing more than the stage on which the drama of

4. *Integrity of Creation*, 22.
5. *Ibid.*, 3.
6. John Carmody, *Ecology and Religion: Toward a New Christian Theology of Nature* (New York: Paulist Press, 1983), 6-7. See also David Spring and Eileen Spring, eds., *Ecology and Religion in History* (New York: Harper & Row, 1974).

human life is performed,"[7] but the Christian faith, the official "cult" of the majority of those societies, stands accused of being the primary spiritual sponsor of technocratic humanity's plunder of the earth. It benefits us therefore, first, to come to terms with our own culpability.

## 2. Christian Culpability

"Nature is the enemy! She must be brought to her knees!" Such were the triumphant words of the narrator of an unforgettable documentary film that I saw in the early 1970s. The screen pictures to which these words corresponded as a kind of litany depicted a vast upheaval, an explosion caused (one supposes) by tons of dynamite: rocks and trees and water and (in all likelihood) several thousands of little animals went rushing pell-mell heavenwards. And when the dust settled the earth movers and the heavy machinery moved in, ready to turn the wilderness of the north into one of the great hydroelectric projects of our continent. This undertaking, the actual need and worth of which has been seriously challenged by many scientists, economists, and politicians, is a monument to the technocratic mentality.

But what was so vexing to me as I viewed this promotional film was that the same script, in which nature was identified straightforwardly as "the enemy" (a thing that not even big industry would dare to do today), was studded with quotations from the Bible. I do not remember all of them, but some of the following texts were certainly used in this carefully written film script:

> And God said to them, "Be fruitful and multiply, and fill the earth and subdue it; and have dominion over the fish of the sea and over the birds of the air and over every living thing that moves upon the earth." (Gen. 1:28)

7. Birch, *Issues for the Church*, 45.

And God blessed Noah and his sons, and said to them, "Be fruitful and multiply, and fill the earth. The fear of you and the dread of you shall be upon every beast of the earth, and upon every bird of the air, upon everything that creeps on the ground and all the fish of the sea; into your hands they are delivered. Every moving thing that lives shall be food for you. . . . I give you everything." (Gen. 9:1-3)

> What is man that thou art mindful of him? . . .
> Yet thou hast made him little less than God,
> and dost crown him with glory and honor.
> Thou hast given him dominion over the works of thy hands;
> thou has put all things under his feet. (Ps. 8:4-6)

Look at the birds of the air. . . . Are you not of more value than they? (Matt. 6:26)

But these, like irrational animals, creatures of instinct, born to be caught and killed . . . will be destroyed in the same destruction with them. (2 Pet. 2:12)

Some time later, when colleagues in the life sciences at the University of Saskatchewan began to demand of me why we Christians have such a deplorable view of nature, I understood something of their meaning. They showed me the then newly-published essay of the historian, Lynn White, Jr., entitled "The Historical Roots of our Ecologic Crisis."[8]

Professor White's article, which has since become a kind of encyclical amongst the friends of nature and has been reprinted in many places, makes a clear-cut case: Behind the modern pillage of planet earth there stands the Hebraic-Christian religion with its too lofty estimate of the human species, its frank denigration of the animal and vegetable kingdoms, and its insistence that humanity has both the right and the duty to rule. Have dominion! Subdue! These two words (as Loren Wilkinson reminds us) are in Hebrew very strong ones: *Kabash*

---

8. Lynn White, Jr., "The Historical Roots of our Ecologic Crisis," *Science*, 10 March 1967, 27ff.

---

(subdue) "comes from a Hebrew root meaning to tread down; it conveys the image of a heavy-footed man making a path by smashing everything in his way." The connotation of *radah* (dominion), Wilkinson continues, "is no less harsh: it also conveys a picture of 'treading' or 'trampling' and suggests the image of a conqueror placing his foot on the neck of a slave."[9] Technology, Lynn White, Jr., contended in his provocative article about the historical roots of the crisis of environment,

> is at least partly to be explained as an Occidental voluntarist realization of the Christian dogma of man's transcendence of, and rightful mastery over, nature. . . . Our science and technology have grown out of Christian attitudes towards man's relation to nature which are almost universally held not only by Christians and neo-Christians but also by those who fondly regard themselves as post-Christians.[10]

What are we to make of this? Is biblical faith especially culpable in connection with the industrial oppression of the natural world? How can we reconcile (or can we?) the apparent contradictions of a religion that on the one hand clearly makes the world—God's good creation—the very object of the divine *agape*, and on the other seems to give to greedy *anthropos* all the justification needed for turning the beautiful place God made into a pig sty?

One thing is certain: The technocratic approach to existence has evolved within a civilization whose most influential religious background has been one that called itself Christian. This connection we cannot deny. It is in particular the anthropology of our Christian West that E. B. White had in mind when he wrote:

> I am pessimistic about the human race because it is too ingenious for its own good. Our approach to nature is to beat it into sub-

9. Loren Wilkinson, "Global Housekeeping: Lords or Servants?" *Christianity Today*, 27 June 1980, 27.

10. White, *Historical Roots*, 27ff.

mission. We would stand a better chance of survival if we accommodated ourselves to this planet and viewed it appreciatively, instead of skeptically and dictatorially.[11]

Does beating nature into submission actually express the meaning of "dominion"? Are skepticism and dictatorship authentically Christian attitudes towards the planet? Or does Christianity somehow, even unwittingly perhaps, encourage such attitudes? How, in the face of much ecological bitterness directed at the Judeo-Christian worldview, can Christians describe the relation between humanity and extrahuman creation—if not to exonerate ourselves from past guilt, at least to contribute something better to the future?

In my response to these questions, I shall consider three possible (as well as actual, historical) ways of formulating the relation between humankind and otherkind: (1) Humanity above Nature; (2) Humanity in Nature; and (3) Humanity with Nature.

## 3. Humanity above Nature

One way of conceiving this relation is to place Homo sapiens on a very high rung of the ladder of being, and to insist that nature is simply there for human usage. At the outset of the modern period, Western philosophic literature was crammed full of this sentiment. Indeed, the sentiment is of the essence of modernity, the very cornerstone of the religion of progress. One of its most straightforward statements comes from the pen of the English philosopher Thomas Hobbes, who over against the Medieval propensity to regard nature cautiously, as a realm of immense mystery, wrote—

She is no mystery, for she worketh by motion and geometry. . . . [We] can chart these motions. Feel then as if you lived in a world

---

11. Quoted in Rachel Carson, *Silent Spring* (Boston: Houghton Mifflin, 1962), vii.

which can be measured, weighed and mastered and confront it *with audacity.*[12]

Another architect of modernity, René Descartes, put the matter in somewhat gentler terms, but his claim for humanity is if anything even more extravagant than Hobbes':

> I perceived it to be possible to arrive at a knowledge highly useful in life, and in room of that speculative philosophy usually taught in the schools, to discover a practical [philosophy], by means of which, knowing the force and action of fire, water, the stars, the heavens, and all other bodies that surround us, as distinctly as we know the various crafts of our artisans, we might also apply them in the same way to all the uses to which they are adapted, and thus render ourselves *lords and possessors of nature.*[13]

*Maître et possesseur de la nature!* Francis Bacon reduced the sentiment to a slogan: *Scientia est potestas* ["science is power"].[14] We achieve knowledge *(scientia)* of our world, not for the beauty of knowing, not for the joy of discovering truth (that was the aim of the ancients), but for power *(potestas).*

This has been the dominant attitude of modern Western civilization into our own time. You can hear it still, chanted on every television advertisement, inserted openly or implicitly into nearly every election speech. Knowledge, not wisdom *(sapientia),* is the goal of human reason and (the sacred word of the modern university) research. Science is power. "Modern technique," wrote Bertrand Russell in the late 1940s,

> has given man a sense of power which is rapidly altering his whole mentality. Until recent times, the physical environment was something which had to be accepted and made the best of. . . . To the modern man his physical environment is merely

---

12. Quoted in Basil Willey, *The Seventeenth Century Background* (Garden City, N.Y.: Doubleday-Anchor, 1953), 95-96.

13. René Descartes, *Discourse on Method*, trans. Laurence J. Lafleur (New York: Liberal Arts Press, 1950), 40.

14. See also Moltmann's discussion of this in *God in Creation*, 27ff.

raw material, an opportunity for manipulation. It may be that God made the world, but that is no reason why we should not make it over.[15]

It is interesting to note that the same Bertrand Russell, near the end of his long life, confided in a BBC radio interview that he was pessimistic whether we would see the end of the present century.

However we may feel personally about the "humanity above nature" worldview, we are part of a society that has been built upon that premise. The idea that humanity is nature's lord and possessor, capable of making over what God rather thoughtlessly put together in the first place, is an almost exact description of the North American attitude towards the natural universe. It is our very birthright. We are, as the late George Grant, Canadian philosopher and theologian, so ably stated, the children of the modern epoch; we have no other past than the modern past:

> It is hard indeed to overrate the importance of faith in progress through technology to those brought up in the mainstream of North American life. It is the very ground of their being. The loss of this faith for a North American is equivalent to the loss of himself and the knowledge of how to live. The ferocious events of the twentieth century may batter the outposts of that faith, dim intuitions of the eternal order may put some of its consequences into question, but its central core is not easily surrendered.[16]

It is ingrained in our most rudimentary thinking as a people that nature, which has been exceptionally bounteous in our case, if not precisely the enemy, is at least there for the taking, the making, and the breaking. The ironic poem of Lewis Carroll might have been written with North Americans in mind:

15. Bertrand Russell, *The Scientific Outlook* (New York: W. W. Norton & Co., 1931), 151-52.

16. George Grant, *Philosophy in the Mass Age* (Toronto: Copp Clark Pitman, 1959), vi.

> The Walrus and the Carpenter
> Were walking close at hand;
> They wept like anything to see
> Such quantities of sand;
> If this were only swept away,
> They said, it would be grand.
> If seven maids with seven mops
> Swept it for half a year,
> Do you suppose, the Walrus said,
> That they could get it clear?
> I doubt it, said the Carpenter,
> And shed a bitter tear.

We have swept and mopped and cleared the natural world until it is hard to find traces of it in our more urbanized areas. As Ogden Nash lamented—

> I think that I shall never see
> A billboard lovely as a tree;
> Indeed, unless the billboards fall,
> I'll never see a tree at all!          (from *Song of the Open Road*)

Our vaunted way of life has spread ecological ruin to other parts of the globe. "Every year an area of tropical forests three-quarters the size of South Korea is destroyed and lost."[17] And in the planning sectors of our technocracies there are still people who "shed bitter tears" because we cannot yet control quite everything.

There are also those who rejoice over our increasing capacities for controlling life processes at their most basic—in the field of genetic engineering. The case of the turkey is symptomatic of far more subtle changes that are in the offing:

When Audubon painted it, it was a sleek, beautiful, though odd-headed bird, capable of flying 65 miles per hour. Benjamim Franklin said that it should be adopted as America's national bird, thinking it a "more respectable bird" than the "poor and often lousy" Bald Eagle. Today, the turkey is an obese, immobile thing,

---

17. *Integrity of Creation*, 3.

---

hardly able to stand, much less fly. As for respectability, the big bird is so stupid that it must be taught to eat, and so large in the breast that in order to breed, a saddle must be strapped to the hen to offer the turkey cock a claw-hold. The modern bird is not so much a turkey as it is a mutation, a commodity manufactured rather than a bird hatched. . . . [It sports] 60% of its flesh in the breast and wings. Americans like white meat, and the American poulty industry, using methods that may harm you, is happy to remodel its birds in order to comply.[18]

By comparison with what is now envisaged, the case of the turkey is primitive indeed. The new approach is "to engineer the entire temporal life span of living things."

Bioengineering is the manipulation of the becoming process of living organisms in advance. For the first time, it is possible to envision the "engineering" of the internal biology of an organism at conception so as to control its entire future development. When scientists engineer changes in the genetic code, they are programming the life cycle of the organism before it unfolds. . . . We are engineering organisms to make them compatible with an environment *we have created*. . . . We have managed to construct a concept of nature that is remarkably sympathetic to the way we happen to be managing nature.[19]

Is all of this really the product, by-product, or end-product of the Judeo-Christian tradition? Is "the nihilism practised in our dealings with nature"[20] finally to be laid at the doorstep of biblical faith?

The accusation must at very least be clarified. In its typical form (including the historian White's essay) it represents a rather naive understanding of the Scriptures of Israel and the church, however it may be justified in other respects. There are in fact many things in the biblical tradition that go straight against

18. In *Conserver Society Notes* 1 (December 1975): 15.

19. Jeremy Rifkin, *Algeny* (New York: Viking Press, 1983), 219. (Italics added)

20. Moltmann, *God in Creation*, xi.

the grain of a manipulative approach to nature. Amongst them—
a subject to which we shall presently return—is the Bible's way
of associating the human bid for mastery not with the positive
will of God, but precisely with disobedience in the human creature. Nature suffers, not when human beings are willing and
doing what, in God's intention, they are meant to do, but when
they sin! The following passage from Isaiah could be taken as a
text for the sermons of the most ardent of nature's friends:

> The earth mourns and withers,
> the world languishes and withers;
> the heavens languish together with the earth.
> The earth lies polluted
> under its inhabitants;
> for they have transgressed the laws,
> violated the statutes,
> broken the everlasting covenant.
> Therefore a curse devours the earth,
> and its inhabitants suffer for their guilt;
> therefore the inhabitants of the earth are scorched,
> and few men are left.
> The wine mourns,
> the vine languishes,
> all the merry-hearted sigh. . . .
> The city of chaos is broken down,
> every house is shut up so that none can enter.
> There is an outcry in the streets for lack of wine;
> all joy has reached its eventide;
> the gladness of the earth is banished. (24:4-11)

Even on strictly historical grounds, it is simplistic to trace
the idea of humanity above nature in an undialectical way to the
biblical tradition. If it were the essence of that tradition, then
why did not the early Christians and the great church of the
Middle Ages already institute such a concept of the human species? Why did it have to wait for a thousand years and more for
this allegedly Christian conception to flower? Leonardo da Vinci
at the close of the Middle Ages already knew about the sub-

marine; but he refused to pass along the idea to his aristocratic patrons because he believed humanity too diabolical to have that secret. Like the Greeks of old, medieval Christians were for limiting human power. They did not look upon *scientia* as *potestas* but as *veritas* (truth). They wanted wisdom, not control.

The real roots of the humanity above nature complex of Western civilization lie much closer to the origins of modernity than most scientists, being themselves children of modernity, either can recognize or care to recognize. The coincidence of the Reformation (and particularly of Reformed Christianity) with the advent of humanism, in whose traditions both Zwingli and Calvin were educated, means that there are some links between Protestantism and the modern vision. These links seem all the more significant because Protestantism of a sort was taken up by the social class, the *bourgeoisie*, which capitalized most on the emerging modern vision. But even here it is easy to exaggerate the "Christian connection." Not only is it necessary to distinguish serious Protestantism from the culture religion that it quickly became in the hands of dominant classes of northern Europe, but specific points of doctrine must be born in mind by any who wish to pursue this interpretive thesis. With his commanding sense of the sole sovereignty of God and his equally strong emphasis upon the total depravity of the human creature—a depravity most in evidence in the sin of pride!—John Calvin is hardly a candidate for the title Architect of Modernity! As for Luther, he remained essentially a medieval man— and particularly in his continuing reverence for the natural order and his deep commitment to the principle *finitum capax infiniti* ("the finite has a capacity for the infinite"), a commitment which deeply influenced his theology of the sacraments and his "Christ-mysticism."

What is obvious enough is that with the sixteenth century a new feeling for human autonomy and potential arose within the soul of European humanity. Perhaps it was the consequence of the preceding apocalyptic age, with the ravages of the bubonic plague, the breakdown of institutions, and the general demise of the medieval vision. Perhaps in the darkness of that age the idea began to dawn upon the sensitive that human beings need not wait passively for death and destruction, but might take their destiny into their own hands— "change the world," to use the famous dictum of Karl Marx. With such a spirit *(Zeitgeist)* brooding over the face of history, men and women will make use of whatever is at hand to construct the image of humanity that is required for the articulation and employment of that spirit: humanism, Protestantism, nominalism, empiricism—whatever can contribute to the ascent towards an imagined light. And who, whether from a sacred or a secular perspective, will dare to blame them for that? All the same, it meant that something had begun to be lost—something that belonged to both the tradition of Jerusalem and the tradition of Athens, namely, the sense of our essential smallness before "the Real."

Alistair Cooke's description of the man Christopher Columbus, who seems to have appropriated much of the new quest earlier than most persons of comparable station, fits rather well the image of the human that was being fashioned on this forge. This "giant of a redhead, six feet tall at a time when the average virile male was about five feet four [was] a fast-talking, obsessive egomaniac who combined in curiosity, romantic stubbornness, and sense of mission something of a Galileo, Don Quixote, and John the Baptist," writes Cooke. He was also (picking up strands of Christian triumphalism) "a Christian of almost maniacal devoutness [who] longed for the secular trappings of pomp and power, and, beginning with the Indies, he would convert every prince and pauper he encountered and have himself proclaimed governor of every land and island he discovered."[21]

As the Columbus character and achievement indicates, the new conception of human nature and destiny that emerged from this crucible contained many elements of Constantinian

21. Alistair Cooke, *America* (New York: Alfred A. Knopf, 1977), 30.

Christianity. But it also left something out: the darker side of the medieval analysis, which in spite of both theological triumphalism and ecclesiastical imperialism bore the ancient insight of the prophets and apostles that humanity's use of power is frequently if not habitually directed towards ambiguous or straightforwardly evil ends. In addition, as we have said above, modernity left out the medieval Christian respect for nature, exemplified in a highly positive and spiritual manner in the mysticism of Tauler and Eckhardt and others, and in a no doubt more primitive and superstitious way in the popular fear of nature's grandeur and unpredictability.

While both biblical and historical analysis necessitates locating the historical roots of our ecologic crisis at the beginning of the modern epoch, however, this does not exonerate the Christian church. For one must ask why the Christians at the turn of the modern epoch and beyond it permitted their faith and their sacred texts to be used in this way. Why were they not more diligent (why are we still not more consistently diligent) in saying to the Bacons and Descartes and Eric Hoffers and B. F. Skinners of this world that the name our religious tradition has given to the human quest for power without love is *sin?*

Instead of maintaining a prophetic vigilance against being co-opted by modernity, Christianity on the whole (with a few glorious exceptions!) courted and fawned upon the makers of the modern world. It aided and abetted the whole process, in fact, by openly supporting the notion of human mastery, or by indulging in the kinds of theological pronouncements and emphases that were naive and therefore impractical. Charitably, we may suppose that the latter—i.e., the lack of sensitivity towards the context—has been the more characteristic reason for Christian lack of prophetic insights. For it is only rarely during the course of these almost two thousand years that Christianity has manifested such sensitivity. For the most part, Christians, including Christian intellectuals, have announced "Christian truth" with very little regard for the manner in which it could be heard and used. Thus, for example, much of the theology of the *imago Dei* concept ("so God created man in his own image") has readily supported an anthropology of humanity above nature.

The following statement is typical: "Man is a creature divinely endowed with gifts which set him above all other creatures: he is made in the image of God."[22] A more contextually aware theology would think twice before making such a statement. To affirm the radical distinction between humanity and all other creatures in an age which was already in the grip of a Promethean image of the human is to be wholly innocent of prophetic vigilance. A theology in dialogue with the whole of the tradition would, in such a cultural context, feel the need at least for a more nuanced definition of the image of God.

Of course, what is really at fault in this whole approach to the relation between human and extrahuman being is signalled by just this kind of definition. If one thinks of the human creature as a possessor of superior endowments such as intellect and will, and locates the relationship between this creature and the others on a scale or hierarchy of being which is determined by such gifts, one is bound to end up with the humanity above nature alternative. But if the image of God does not refer to a quality that we possess (making us superior to other creatures), but to a relationship in which we stand vis-à-vis our Creator, and a vocation to which we are called within the creation, a very different conception of the humankind/otherkind relation follows. The symbol of the steward assumes the latter arrangement. We shall discuss it further under the subheading "Humanity With Nature."[23]

22. J. S. Whale, *Christian Doctrine* (Cambridge: Cambridge University Press, 1941), 44.
23. For an extensive discussion of this point, see my *Imaging God: Dominion as Stewardship.*

## 4. Humanity in Nature

The second theoretical and historical possibility for conceiving of the relation between human beings and the natural world is to think of Homo sapiens as one of the myriad of creatures. One species amongst others, mortal as they, dependent as they, having no more to offer than they, and no more right to life either—this is humanity *in* nature.

This conception of the place of the human species is also, so far as its historical application is concerned, a modern one. It is possible to find hints of it here and there in earlier civilizations and religions—for example in Epicureanism. One can discover such hints also in the Scriptures of Israel and the church. Amongst these, none is more significant than that picture of Adam provided in the second (and older) of the two creation sagas of Genesis: *Adam* is taken from *adamah*, the man from the ground, or, as Loren Wilkinson translates the Hebrew pun, "God made humans out of humus."[24] In this connection, too, we could consider the many scriptural references where the character and destiny of the human creature is compared to that of all other creatures—

> All flesh is grass,
> and all its beauty is like the flower of the field.
> The grass withers, the flower fades,
> when the breath of the Lord blows upon it;
> surely the people is grass.
> The grass withers, the flower fades;
> but the word of our God will stand for ever. (Isa. 40:6-8)

Yet in the literature of the Bible, as in other ancient sources, humanity is hardly ever just grass. There is a mystery about this being—the mystery of mind, of *Geist* (ghost, spirit). This mystery prevents the ancients both of Jerusalem and of Athens from regarding *anthropos* as "just another animal." To

---

24. Wilkinson, "Global Housekeeping," 27.

be sure, the creature is animal. But it is a thinking animal, a "rational animal" (Greece), a "speaking animal" (Jerusalem). Its thinking and speaking are not always good for it. Thinking does not make it happy most of the time. Evil flows from its tongue. And "no human being can tame the tongue—a restless evil, full of deadly poison" (James 3:9). Imagination regularly begets evil, and human ambition is "vanity" (Ecclesiastes). Yet thought and the articulation of thought do render this creature somehow transcendent. The ancients are nearly unanimous on this point, though they accentuate different aspects of the matter.

The tendency to naturalize humanity and to make a program of it belongs rather exclusively to our own historical epoch—as does the placing of humanity above nature. Naturalizing the human species must in fact be regarded as a clear reaction to placing it above nature. It is the reaction of a protesting element against the spirit of the Enlightenment and the industrialization and technicalization of existence that flowed from the Enlightenment mentality. It is the romantic reaction. Against the elevation of the human species along the lines of an almost divine rationality, the romantics rebelled on the side of the heart—on the side of nature. From Rousseau onwards, they fought against the modern world's rationalistic reduction of humanity. For they saw quite rightly that this supposed elevation of the human species above nature was at the same time a denigration of the species. Turning humanity into nothing but mind could lead to a situation in which everything about Homo sapiens itself that is not mind (feeling, love, emotion, the body, sex, suffering, etc.) would have to be repressed or, if possible, eliminated.

The romantic critics of Enlightenment rationality did not err in their judgment here. The technocrats and managers of the twentieth century provide us with foolproof methods for dispensing with all the unpredictable, messy elements that are present in the life of the human creature. "Science is power," and it does not stop with the altering of turkeys! If you start out (as did Hobbes, Descartes, and Bacon) to dominate nature, you must come at last to the domination of human nature. This is the

Catch 22 of the humanity above nature syndrome. You cannot have a world that is fully controlled and possessed in the hands of creatures who themselves are not in command of their allegedly lower natures—their emotions, their whims and moods, and their physical drives. The ironic thing about humanity being above nature is that it has to eliminate all that is natural in human beings themselves, finally, in order to seem plausible. So by now, as Abraham Heschel has reminded us, the efficient machine is a more acceptable model for human beings in the modern image than is Aristotle's category, the "rational animal."[25]

The "Romantic Rebellion" (Sir Kenneth Clark) was a necessary protest on behalf of what is natural in humanity against the industrial-technical society's reduction of humanity to mere rationality. The need for this protest is by no means over!

Sometimes, however, when the pendulum of history swings, it goes too far. Extremes beget extremes, and we find ourselves caught between one absurd reduction and a polarity that is equally absurd. Thus in the past few decades, and in the face of a technocracy that has gone much farther than ever Bacon or Descartes envisaged, a countercultural movement in the Western world and especially in North America has happened that carries the idea of humanity being in nature to sometimes ridiculous conclusions. It is now possible to hear even Christians speaking as if the only way of saving the planet were for the human species to plan itself out of existence. To become, so to speak, as "natural" as the dinosaurs!

To illustrate: During the late 1960s, the deplorable state of the natural world had just begun to come to the attention of minorities in every university town, like the one in which I lived. In our university, as I indicated in passing earlier, this new awareness inspired an interdisciplinary course entitled "Man and the Biosphere" (in a time prior to the awareness of sexist language). During the first several weeks of this course, representatives of one academic discipline after another paraded

25. Heschel, *Who Is Man?* 30.

---

before the large student assembly and told of the devastations wrought upon the natural world by technocratic man.

Then one night there was a panel discussion, and from the student audience this question emerged ("emerged" is the appropriate verb, because the young woman who articulated it did so very slowly, and as though she were making a discovery in the very act of pronouncing the words): "If man is the *problem* of the biosphere," she asked, "wouldn't the world be better off without him?"

My scientific colleagues on the panel did not know what to make of that, so they turned spontaneously to me (I am proud to record that as the one consistent defender of God on the teaching staff of "Man and the Biosphere" I was also perceived as "Man's" defender—frequently "Man's" *only* defender. Obviously someone had to respond, because the student's question was not just one student's question; it was *the* question. It hung in the atmosphere of the class from the outset, waiting to find an amanuensis—some Cassandra or other who would actually ask it! Every lecturer had begged it, and now it could no longer be avoided.

I do not remember exactly what I said, but what I should like to think of myself as having said on the occasion is something like this: What would it mean, after the disappearance of the thinking animal, to use a term like "better off"? Would the elephants hold a congress and announce in position papers that now, certainly, the world was better off than during the reign of Homo sapiens? Would the cockroaches organize a service of praise, and would all the creatures be given photocopied handouts of a newly composed *Te Deum:* "Now O Lord of Hosts we are better off! Praise God for the extinction of the creature Adam, bless God O ye stars and hails for Eve's demise"?

No doubt the human species has created more trouble in the world than any other creature. Christians affirmed this long ago when they made the fall of creation consequent upon the fall of Adam and Eve. Christians who have kept in touch with their own tradition will not be as surprised by the reports of human wretchedness that surface in these days as are humanists and others who, such a little while ago, assumed a very high destiny for the rational animal. But is the "mending of creation" (Fackenheim) to be achieved through the extinction of the troublesome human component? Not as I read the story of our redemption.

Besides, Yahweh already thought of *that* solution, as the story of the great flood mythically tells us.

Is the only way of saving the world, then, to circumscribe and chain down and control the allegedly "free" creature—condition this creature from birth, perhaps, so that it could do neither evil nor good, but simply *be!* Place it, so to speak, so unambiguously in nature that it could have no hand in the destroying *or the keeping* of the natural order? Must the human priest be so totally defrocked?

It is not only a counsel of despair but patent nonsense, in my opinion, to assume either that humanity is or that it ought to be simply "in" nature. Even the limiting of our powers, even the entire sacrifice of our powers, presupposes that we are after all unique creatures, who do not *simply* do "what comes naturally." As a corrective to the pretention of humanity above nature, this second approach is necessary and true. But as a permanently valid approach it is without foundation in reality, and under certain conditions—especially in contexts where there is already a propensity towards apathy and irresponsibility on the part of whole segments of human society—it can be positively dangerous. Many would argue that ours is precisely such a context.

## 5. Humanity with Nature

Using the two previous approaches for purposes of contrast and definition, we are led to a third possible way of conceiving of the relation between humanity and the natural order. It is probable that this must be regarded more as a possibility than as an approach that has actually been given a chance in history. It has certainly been envisaged, however, even if it has not been consistently enacted. For it is without doubt the approach that belongs in our religious tradition. Here humanity is neither superior to the rest of creation (above) nor simply identical with it (in), but the human creature exists alongside the others, in solidarity with them, yet also distinct.

Those who read the Bible with any frequency will have noticed the prominence of the preposition "with" in this literature. Husbands are with their wives, wives with their husbands. Friends are with one another—as Jesus' disciples are described as being "with" him in this or that place. Even God is depicted in these terms: Emmanuel—"God *with* us."

This predominance of the preposition "with" is not accidental. Language seldom is. The language of the Bible is determined by its ontology, that is, its assumption concerning the nature of what "is."And in the tradition of Jerusalem we have to do with a quite distinctive understanding of reality. Here there is on the one hand a strong sense of the interconnectedness of everything that "is."[26] This is present both in the creation theology of the Genesis writers, where all creatures share a common origin and life principle, and in the New Testament's redemption theology, where the unity and reunification of all informs both the doctrine of the church and of the consummation of all things.

At the same time, this feeling for the interconnectedness of everything is held in creative tension with an equally important emphasis upon the uniqueness of each creature. This is true of God, who despite being the "Ground" (Tillich) of all that is, is nevertheless distinct—not to be confused with creation. Likewise the human individuals who make their appearance in

26. Christianity shares this sense of the integrity of all that is with some other religions of the world, especially Buddhism. When I asked the renowned Buddhist scholar Masao Abe what as a Buddhist he felt it most important to preserve, he answered immediately, "the interconnectedness of all that is." See his *Zen and Western Thought,* ed. William R. LaFleur (Honolulu: U. of Hawaii Press, 1985).

this long story are, each one, unique. Jacob and Esau are brothers—but very different from each other. Peter is a human being like John, but he is not just a carbon copy of John, and he has to be told in no uncertain terms that John's destiny is not to be confused with his own (John 21:21-22). Eve is not Adam—and is not *Adam's!* So close are they ontically that Adam is inspired to name her "bone of my bones, flesh of my flesh." But already this ancient saga of creation and Fall gives distinctive characters to the two who are at the centre of it. So also with the animals. According to Genesis 2 (the Jahwist's account of creation) they are all created out of the same "dust" as the "earth creature" (Phyllis Trible) Adam. But they differ markedly from Adam, and will not do as his partner. They differ also from one another, as the flood story demonstrates in a subtle way.

Given this dialectical tension between participation and individuality, commonality and uniqueness, "with" is the only preposition that will serve with any accuracy. The underlying theory of reality, which with Joseph Sittler I should like to call Jerusalem's "ontology of communion,"[27] requires a language that will do justice to the nuanced combination of seemingly antithetical characteristics found in biblical thought. "With" is perhaps the only preposition that will serve this purpose, for it contains both the idea of sameness and the idea of difference, both being together and being apart, both participation and particularity.

Or, to put the matter more succinctly still, "with" is the preposition that belongs to the language of love. And love, to state the biblical ontology in its most direct and untechnical form, is the reality that the Bible wants to describe.

Love means difference: I am not you, you are not me. If we love each other, it does not mean (what it means in some ancient and also modern types of mysticism) that we simply merge into an ontic unity (John and Mary when they are married

27. Joseph Sittler, "Ecological Commitment as Theological Responsibility," *Zygon: Journal of Religion and Science* 5 (1970): 558. See my discussion of "The Ontology of Communion" in *Imaging God*, 113ff.

and are pronounced one flesh do not become a hybrid "Jarry"). Love means that I am *with* you and you are *with* me in a special sense. We evoke and support each other's individuality even as we discover our fundamental solidarity. We do not disappear into each other's being (love of this variety has usually meant that the weaker—invariably the woman!—disappears into the stronger). Rather, we become all the more present, real, and solid as persons, individuals, in the process of our being united with one another. What is forfeited in our relatedness is not our individual "thou-ness" (on the contrary, that is what is gained!), but the hostility, the suspicion, the bid for self-sufficiency that belong to the distortion of our personalities in their separation from the other, the counterpart.

Love, as the fundamental ontology of the tradition of Jerusalem, an ontology which incorporates even this tradition's doctrine of God (for "God *is* love"), positively needs something like the preposition "with"—as, of course, it also needs other forms of speech. If this preposition did not exist, love as it is understood in this tradition would have to invent it. For neither "beside," nor "within," nor "in," nor "to," nor even "between"— and certainly not "above"—is suitable for delineating what is intended in this most basic category of being.

In fact, the term "being" as such is misleading. The tradition of Athens could employ the language of being *(ontos)* honestly enough; but Hebraic thought has a different preconception of the nature of being. Everything of which it may be said that it "is" stands in relationship with everything else that is. The whole of reality, in other words, presupposes this dialectical interaction of sameness and difference, identity and distinction. Being itself is relational—or, to employ an awkward term, but one which nevertheless conveys something of what is intended: *being* for this tradition itself implies *with-being, being-with.*

What this implies about the relation between theology and ethics is very important. It means that the Christian's ethic, whose summation is the commandment "to love," is absolutely grounded in the basic Christian assumption about reality itself, which is what theology tries to describe. The ethic (love) is nothing more nor less than the theology (God loves) stated in the imperative mood. The ethic is not derived from the theology, as a second step; it is already present in the theology, and the only reason why it has even to be made explicit as commandment (love your neighbour!) is that our hearts are hard and our wills bound to patterns of behaviour that resist the gospel of divine love.

Both the theory and the practice of faith, both theology and ethics, presuppose this ontology of communion. All that *is* exists under the mandate of its Creator that it should seek out and dwell "with" (that is, and love) everything else that *is*. Our very being as human beings, as God intends it, is a being-with. The distortion of our being (sin) is nothing more nor less than our alienation from all that we are created to be with. Sin, we could say, is a resolute "being-alone," which implies also "being against."

Now, in their better expressions, Christian theology and ethics have known how to express all this with respect to two of the dimensions of our human relatedness: God, and our human partners (the neighbour). But Christian theology has rarely explored the meaning of this fundamental ontological assumption for the third major dimension of our threefold relatedness as creatures, namely, our relation to the extrahuman world, the inarticulate creation. This is now what must be explored—under the subheading "Humanity with Nature."

As the "being-with" of the ontology of communion applies to our human relation to the extrahuman world, it contains the same two polar movements that are found in the other dimensions of our relatedness. One pole of this dialectic contains the thought of human difference from the other creatures. We cannot escape this, no matter how romantically attached we may be to the idea of humankind's being simply part of nature. According to the biblical witness at least, we are different.

Difference, contrary to a kind of sentimentalistic spirituality which always wants to eliminate every barrier and distinction, does not mean superiority. In the case of this particular relation, it does mean that we human beings are more complex, more versatile, and also more vulnerable than most other creatures. But why? That is the important question! Not, certainly, in order that we can lord it over them! Rather, so that we can exercise a unique responsibility towards them, a unique answerability for them. We are—yes, why should we not use this word?—to "have dominion."

But what does that mean precisely in the full perspective of biblical religion? Does it only mean what the word literally connotes? Trampling and being heavy-handed and dominating? Why should it mean this, in its full context? Why should we be satisfied with such literalism? Words are not determined only by their etymology; in fact, as the history of language easily demonstrates at every point, the original meaning of a large proportion of the words we use every day has very little to do with how we now use them. Meanings change, and they change because of association with other words, events, and concepts.

With what does biblical faith associate the word "dominion"? What are the patterns that the Bible itself supplies for the interpretation of this term? When we hear the words "have dominion!", what or whom should we think of—if we were thinking biblically? Not, surely, of Caesar, or Pharoah, or Herod. Not even of Cyrus, the divinely approved king. Surely dominion as it is exegeted by the biblical story itself is to be interpreted on the model supplied by the Bible's description of the one, the only one, who really is Lord: "Hear O Israel, I am the Lord thy God."

And for Christians what is already implicit in that "I am" is made explicit in the one who is sent. The whole biblical testimony to God is our only legitimate model for conceiving of the meaning of dominion. And Jesus Christ "is God's exegesis."[28] If we want to understand the meaning of the dominion that we are to have within the sphere of creation, we should not take the word at its face value, a value determined largely by the fact that so many exemplars of this same dominion have been tyrants; rather, we should look to the one example, to him whom the early church

28. Sölle, "Life In Its Fulness," 1.

in the Latin West called *Dominus*. "Jesus Christ is *Dominus*," whispered the early Christians to one another; and Paul added, "—*and him crucified*" (1 Cor. 1:23; 2:2). *This* dominion, far from being a trampling over everybody and everything, seems to have involved his being trampled upon—a point so poignantly made in the beautiful story by Shusaku Endo, entitled *Silence*.[29]

We are different, then, from the beasts of the field and the birds of the air. Let us not be naive and imagine that we can just melt into nature. We have a reflective side that the other creatures do not have. It is harder for us to die than it is for them. We have always to choose, or to be victims of our lack of choice. But the purpose of all this is that we should "have dominion": that is, that we should be servants, keepers, and priests in relation to the others. That we should represent them before their Maker, and represent to them their Maker's tender care. We are the place where the creation becomes reflective about itself, the point at which it speaks, even sings! Homo sapiens? Perhaps. But more importantly, *Homo loquens*, the speaking creature.

But we do not speak for ourselves only (using the phrase in both its literal and its figurative sense). When we are true to our own essence, to the ontology of communion and community, we speak for all our fellow creatures, for the totality. And when we really do speak for them, and not just to hear ourselves talk, what we say—what we shall perhaps one day say without reservation or qualification—is simply "thank you." *Eucharistia!*

That is to say: gratitude alone authenticates any human claim to dominion. Until that gratitude has wholly and unambiguously permeated our being, "the whole creation groaneth" (Rom. 8:22, KJV).

But the other side of this dialectic of our being with nature must also be well remembered. We can be the keepers and priests of the others only if we are in some sense also the same

29. Shusaku Endo, *Silence*, trans. William Johnston (Rutland, Vt.: C. E.Tuttle, 1969). I have written an article on this work, entitled, "Rethinking Christ: Theological Reflections on Shusaku Endo's *Silence*," *Interpretation* 33 (July 1979).

as they. Of course, we do in fact share their being: their mortality, their limitations of power, their finitude, their reproductive capacities and incapacities, their need for air and food and water, their subjection to the laws of gravity, thermodynamics, and all the rest. We are the same as they in the rudiments of our creaturehood. But our temptation and possibility are to deny our solidarity with them, to exaggerate our difference from them, to seek to be above; and so (like the Prodigal envying even the swine he fed) regularly we fall into a degraded *contradiction* of our creaturely reality that animals never know.

Therefore we have to discover and rediscover, affirm and reaffirm our real identity with nature. It must become again and again for us, not only fact, but gladly accepted fact. Indeed, what is redemption in this tradition if it is not precisely that grace-given transformation in us, that *metanoia*, which gives us the courage to affirm our own creaturehood, and therefore our co-creaturehood, our communion with all the other creatures? Not the overcoming of our creaturehood, but its joyful acceptance: this is salvation!

And this is the only condition under which we may represent the other creatures. We can represent them because we participate in the same creatureliness as they. We may represent them because (and if!) we have ceased to resent our own and their creatureliness. Accepting our rudimentary solidarity with them, our difference from them is not a boast; it is only a means to the end of our serving both God and them. Our so-called endowments—thought and will and speech, for instance—are not ends, but necessary means to our peculiar service within the general creaturely sphere. If we are different, it is so we may perceive and speak out of what we perceive to be both their and our condition. "We perceive in order to participate, not in order to dominate."[30] Our representation of the unspeaking creation depends upon perception, thought, reflection, and imagination. But it also depends upon participation. One side demands the other.

30. Moltmann, *Experiences of God,* 59.

And this brings us back at last to that symbol we have hardly named in this discussion of the relation between humanity and nature. We have not named it, though it has been the very presence around which the whole discussion has been woven—as the chapter heading suggests: the steward. There is no other symbol in biblical faith—perhaps there is no other symbol in all of human literature—that so appropriately catches the two sides of this dialectical tension about which we have been thinking. The steward symbol is in the realm of the metaphoric what the preposition "with" is in the realm of the linguistic. One does not have to go outside the symbol itself to do justice to the two dimensions in question and their complex interrelatedness.

On the one hand, the steward is singled out for special responsibility. The steward is different. Unlike the other servants, the steward is truly answerable for what happens in the household. All the same, the steward is one of the others, by no means superior to them, having no absolute rights over them, but liable to judgment because of his treatment of them. The steward is different, but the steward is also the same. Like all the others, the steward is recipient of that which can never be his or hers to own.

It is no wonder then that an increasing number of persons, many of whom have no personal relation to the Christian faith, find in this Judeo-Christian symbol a profound metaphor for expressing a viable Western alternative to the status quo in our relation with nature. One of these observers writes:

Although much in Christianity has rightly been found by critics to be ecologically objectionable (in that nature is almost completely desacralized and man given quasi-total dominion over creation), others point out with equal correctness that stewardship and other Christian virtues could easily form *the basis of an ecological ethic*.[31]

31. Ophuls, *Politics of Society*, 242-43.

This could happen. The condition for its actually doing so has a good deal to do with how we Christians now handle our own tradition. In the foregoing chapters, we have seen something of our neglect and misuse of this symbol. Our first responsibility as Christian stewards today may be to become better stewards of the stewardship motif itself!

### 6. From Symbol to Political Necessity

When we speak about stewardship as the key to the relation between humanity and nature, we are speaking of a vision. Under the conditions of history, this vision is never fully realized. It is an eschatological vision, the vision of a state of final reconciliation, in which the enmity between creature and Creator, creature and creature, and creature and creation will have given way to true mutuality and unconditional love: "being-with."

It was this visionary aspect of our stewardship that the great American painter Edward Hicks (1780-1849) tried to express in his work, "Peaceable Kingdom." As James Thomas Flexner writes, Hicks

> painted many Peaceable Kingdoms illustrating the biblical prophecy that the lion and the lamb shall lie down together. Not the lax sermons of conventional moralists, these pictures do not ignore the problem of evil. Hicks, who fought daily engagements with his own passions, knew that it would not be easy for the lion and the lamb to lie down together.[32]

And, we might add, it would be even more difficult for the child of Adam and Eve to lead them.

But while this is and remains an eschatological vision, it is not merely (in the usual, easily dismissible sense) an ideal—

---

32. James Thomas Flexner, *The Pocket History of American Painting* (New York: Washington Square Press, 1962), 34.

an impossible dream. Today it has become the only real and practicable alternative. To continue trying to be nature's lords and possessors can only mean the premature end of the experiment, for our lording and possessing has become increasingly bellicose and vengeful. There is, in fact, much revenge in it.

On the other hand, to adopt the solution of the bourgeois romantics and disappear into nature (while ensconced in the comforts of a California bungalo by the sea or a New England classroom) may, if it could be brought off, solve some of the problems of the cockroaches; but what about the future Mozarts?

The only way left, surely, is to search our hearts, our pasts, and our present for clues as to how we might be in the world without simply being of it; how we might think, and make, and do, without through our thinking and making and doing ruining the very fragile craft that is our home. Stewardship is no longer just a nice ideal. It has become a social and political necessity.

That is why such statements as the following, which could once perhaps be received as ecclesiastical rhetoric, ought now to be heard by serious Christians as aspirations that challenge us to approximate the divine love that we have said, these many centuries, saves and surrounds us:

> Through the One who loved "the world" (John 3:16), we are called and enabled to love and to embrace with compassion the whole creation. Like the love of God by which it is enabled, love also involves suffering for "the other"—and "the other" understood, now, as inclusive of other species, not only of our own kind. In this solidarity with the whole, in the love of Christ, we shall find our own human fulfilment as well.[33]

---

33. *Integrity of Creation*, 22.

# CHAPTER VIII

# STEWARDSHIP AND THE QUEST FOR WORLD PEACE

## 1. The Primacy and Intricacy of this Issue

The three issues treated in this concluding part of our discussion on Christian stewardship are today of course not three separate or separable issues but parts of a whole—an unwelcome seamless robe that has been cast over the shoulders of late twentieth-century civilization. To quote the working paper preparatory to the World Convocation of Churches in Seoul, Korea, scheduled for March of 1990:

> While these three issues may be separated out, they in fact belong together in one indivisible whole. Indeed, justice cannot be realized concretely except where peace pertains and creation is not violated. So too peace cannot be realized except where justice and the integrity of creation pertain. Finally, human beings make a deadly mistake if they assume that peace and justice can be obtained at the expense of other species and even of the biosphere itself. The moving wings of a single butterfly eventually change the air surrounding the most distant mountain or institution. So too each human action eventually helps to build up or to destroy the whole creation. Future

generations will live the consequences of this building or destroying.[1]

The indivisibility of the three aspects of this theme constitutes perhaps the greatest difficulty in comprehending them. Quite apart from trying to act responsibly in relation to the "instabilities" (Charles Birch) that they represent, their intricate and complex interwovenness baffles the minds of most of us. Thus it is tempting to become preoccupied with one of them to the exclusion or near exclusion of the other two. For instance, persons who are concerned primarily for the issue discussed in Chapter VI (justice) may be less vigilant with respect to environmental problems—such as the use of pesticides or the threat to other species—that may be necessary, if unwelcome, by-products of programs designed to secure more equitable forms of justice. Conversely, ecologists and others whose primary *entree* into the world problem is the natural universe and humankind's desecration of nature tend to hold out for the preservation of nature at the expense of human survival, sometimes ending in a pessimism about the human race equalled only by the Augustinian-Calvinist tradition of total depravity.

In a similar act of reductionism, those most preoccupied with the struggle for world peace sometimes manifest a naivety respecting both human and natural issues, and in their zeal for the tactics of peace seem willing to sacrifice centuries of hard-won values.

What this complexity of analysis and vantage point signifies, beyond the fact that all simple solutions are implicitly to be distrusted, is the prodigious need today for a forum of analysis, reflection, and action, where the expertise of many disciplines can be in constant dialogue, and where enlightened research can temper the passion of the many and often disparate groupings who are committed to the healing of this world. In theory, the

1. *Integrity of Creation*, 3.

university is the place where this both could and should occur. The university, as the name implies, came into being for something like this very purpose. And there are noble efforts in many universities and colleges to serve society in just this way.

But for the most part our great contemporary "multiversities" have too much in common with the biblical Babel to function effectively as such forums. It should no longer be taken for granted even that dialogue of an interdisciplinary nature will occur in the universities, let alone that they will promote action designed to preserve and enhance the life of the world. Increasingly, the forum springs into existence outside or alongside established institutions, either in response to some specific need, or spontaneously. One can only be grateful for this. At the same time, without an ongoing identity (which must usually be supplied by institutions sufficiently anchored in society and broad enough to include considerable variety of motivation and approach), ad hoc movements and networks are frequently blown about by every wind of doctrine, and many do not survive their own internal turmoil.

For Christians this ought to raise the question (which I have already broached in Chapter V) whether the Christian church could not do more to foster such dialogue and mutual action. After all, what prevents it more than anything else (as anyone who lives and works in the university setting today knows perfectly well) is lack of trust and fear of involvement. People who are competent to inform their neighbors about the physical properties of modern weaponry and warfare, complex environmental data such as the causes of acid rain or the greenhouse effect, details concerning various cultures, resources, demography, and the like, feel an inherent alienation within their communities of learning, government, or business. The message given off by the very atmosphere of our institutions is, "Don't tell us sad stories. We are comfortable, well-paid, well-adjusted people. You can't expect us to solve the problems of the world."

Consequently, the passionate amongst the experts (often they are individuals who have become passionate about the state of the world in spite of themselves) are regularly driven outside the established institutions into communities of like-minded persons, with the result that interdisciplinary dialogue is again thwarted and the world again interpreted through the focus of one particular discipline, issue, or moral commitment.

In this setting, the Christian community—the church—is called to be, and *can* be, a place of reconciliation, where trust between persons is being learned, where those who are "many" may begin nonetheless to act as "one body."[2] Making good this identity of the body of Christ today could mean, quite concretely, the creation of "zones of trust" for precisely these world issues whose interrelatedness is so vexing. What more explicit application of the stewardship vocation of the Christian community could we wish for? Despite its own dividedness, the Christian church has some experience of the overcoming of alienation and the establishment of trust between persons of many differing conditions, traits, and concerns. The principle of communalization can at least be understood and fostered within the parameters of this experience and tradition.[3]

The quest for world peace, then, is one of a whole spectrum of struggles, in which the solution to each entails a continuing alertness to its effect upon all the others. Nothing is more to be feared today than the solutions of those who do not know what the problem is—that is, those who naively identify

2. The role of the church in Eastern Europe today, and particularly of the Protestant *(Evangelische)* church in the German Democratic Republic, graphically illustrates this point. In an atmosphere of repression and distrust it was the church that both provided the "forum" for a new conception of society and ensured that public demonstrations to that end would not erupt into violence.

3. I am of course speaking here only to one side of the necessity for dialogue. The other side is the need that comes from inside the Christian community itself. It must have dialogue with the world in order to discover the appropriate expressions of its message within its historical context. Today it is no longer possible for the *koinonia* to rely upon one discipline for this dialogue (philosophy was the traditional dialogue-partner of theology). Even to do its own "proper work" in the world (i.e., to engage in its mission), the church today must have interdisciplinary dialogue. (I have discussed this at length in my first volume of contextual theology, *Thinking the Faith*, Part I.)

the problem with this or that aspect of the problem, as if the hydra could be killed by cutting off one of its heads!

Many persons, not more than two years ago, would have agreed with the insistence of the first edition of this book that, even considering the inseparability of the three issues we are considering, the quest for world peace requires our primary attention. In the short time that has elapsed since then, attitudes have changed. Largely, I think, because of the leadership of the *Second World*, and more particularly that of Mikhail Gorbachev, the pulse of world opinion has become steadier where war and preparation for war is concerned. There is today even a kind of relaxation over the whole issue. Is it perhaps really possible, people ask or want to ask, that the peace which hopeful persons assured us could "break out" has in fact now broken out? Can we now breathe more easily, and devote our public energies to other concerns?

Or is precisely such a sense of security more dangerous than the former state?

Many observers feel that the latter question may be the more pertinent. Having noted the "hopeful changes in the geopolitical situation in recent years, including especially the improved relations between the two superpowers, the elimination of one category of nuclear weapons, and some positive steps towards peace in various regional conflicts," the aforementioned working paper for Seoul goes on to warn that

> despite these and other similar developments, however, in general our present situation is more unstable and more dangerous than at any time in history. Humanity and all creation continue to live under the shadow of the Bomb and the spectre of the "Final Event." A world with 55,000 nuclear weapons whose combined destructive force is 16,000 megatons (16 billion tons of TNT equivalent) is still a world on the brink of self-extermination. In addition, since 1983 the two super-powers have increased their already enormous stockpile of nuclear weapons, and even now are aggressively continuing their testing and development of first-strike weapons. Other nuclear weapons states are also adding new weapons to their arsenals. Nuclear war by inad-

vertance—by human miscalculation or technical malfunction—remains an ever present possibility. Nor can nuclear war by design be ruled out. Any nuclear war would be a terminal event.[4]

The quest for world peace is not, and must not seem to be, limited to the prevention of nuclear warfare, however. In addition to the fact that any war could become nuclear war, the existence of open hostilities of any type in itself constitutes a sufficient cause for those who care about the implementation of God's *shalom* in the earth. And the truth is that there are "more wars currently raging than at any other moment in recorded history."

Most of these conflicts are racial, ethnic, tribal, religious, or ideological, and they are proliferating both within nation states and regionally, causing incredible suffering and loss. Eighty percent of those who have died in these wars are civilians; modern war has become essentially indiscriminate. Thus in general our present situation has become more unstable and more dangerous than ever before. No dwelling place is outside the orbit of conflict, no human being is secure from the possibility of random annihilation. This atmosphere of insecurity is the result of policies pursued by nations in the name of security.[5]

Both the existence of widespread regional conflicts of this nature and the continuing devotion of money, energy, and human inventiveness to the preparation for worldwide conflagration ("a staggering 1.8 million U.S. dollars is spent *every minute* throughout the world on armaments")[6] remind us that working for the peace of the world is in fact a never-ending vocation. While welcoming instead of being cynical about any achievements in the realm of peaceful negotiations between mutually distrustful nations and peoples, we must still recognize that momentary lulls in open hostility and suspicion occur within a larger framework of time. As long as the horrendous machines of mass destruction exist (and who can suppose that

4. *Integrity of Creation*, 7.
5. *Ibid.*, 8.
6. *Ibid.*

they will magically cease to exist one fine day?), all who care about "the fate of the earth" (J. Schell) will have to maintain a constant surveillance for peace.

One of the principles that we established in Chapter V was that of futurization. Our stewardship of earth is not only for today, nor until the next election, nor even the next generation; it is for a future stretching out for an indeterminate period—hopefully a very long one! For all practical purposes, it is forever. Because without some unforeseen transformation on a grand scale, humanity for the rest of time must live with the possibility of annihilation; and it taxes the imagination to ponder whether the human race will find the wisdom, endurance, and courage needed to stave off that possibility even for the next century. In a provocatively titled article Gerald Barnes gave voice to the fear that lurks in the hearts of us all. "We have incontravertible and growing evidence," he wrote, "that Homo sapiens is too profit-motivated, too ignorant, too irresponsible, too fallible to handle plutonium without eventual—and repeated—catastrophe."[7] As the statement implies, it is not only nuclear warfare that threatens this destruction but the whole thirst for power and security that surrounds nuclear experimentation, including its allegedly good and peaceful uses.

The annihilation that is contemplated is no longer a divinely ordained apocalypse, which could fire the imagination of past ages because it somehow confirmed the race's presupposition of ultimate meaning and righteous judgment. The annihilation with whose prospect we live today is just a dreadful halt, a screaming termination, a million Hiroshimas.

> The atom bomb is today the greatest of all menaces to the future of mankind. In the past there have been imaginative notions of the world's end; its imminent expectation for their generation was the ethically and religiously effective error of John the Baptist, Jesus, and the first Christians. But now we face the real possibility of such

7. Gerald Barnes, "Nuclear Nemesis: Are There Enough Good People to Avoid Destruction?" *The Churchman* 190 (Oct. 1976): 9.

an end. The possible reality which we must henceforth reckon with . . . is no longer a fictitious end of the world. It is no world's end at all, but the extinction of life on the surface of the planet.[8]

Perhaps one reason why so many of us have "stopped worrying and learned to love the Bomb" is the sheer incapacity of the average mind to grasp the dimensions of such an ending, or even the scientific data and the technology of its genesis. Even highly trained minds boggle at the thing; for not only does C. P. Snow's "Two Cultures" syndrome pertain here,[9] but, since we are virtually being asked to contemplate nothingness, we are reminded of our inherent incapacity for such contemplation. We cannot even imagine the death of individuals, especially our own. How then could we place before our mind's eye the spectre of a lifeless planet?

The *skandalon* inherent in the nuclear issue is its sheer ungraspability, its abstractness. We live in a time when "what is most *real* is most abstract."[10] The abstract has always presented grave, and perhaps finally insurmountable problems to the human intelligence. How much more is this the case in a society like our own, which for centuries now has given itself to empiricism in observation and functionalism in thought!

## 2. The Question at the Core of the Enigma

While we may be incapable of contemplating nothingness (the *Nihil*), however, we are perhaps not incapable of contemplating the question that is put to us by the prospect of worldly annihi-

---

8. Karl Jaspers, *The Future of Mankind* (Chicago: University of Chicago Press, 1967), 4.

9. In his important work, *The Two Cultures: And a Second Look—An Expanded Version of the Two Cultures and the Scientific Revolution* (Mentor MP 557, 1964), Snow identifies as one of the salient problems of our age the non-communication between the "literary" culture and the "scientific" culture. Not only do the two cultures fail to understand each other's language and orientation, but their fracture constitutes a grave *social* threat.

10. I am indebted to my colleague, Principal Pierre Goldberger, for this insight.

lation. Christians at least ought still to possess a certain aptitude for this question, for it is the question that belongs to the core of our gospel, the question to which the cross of Jesus Christ speaks directly and decisively. In the cross God offers us an unambiguous and final response to the question (for it is a question with which the biblical God too has wrestled!), and this answer is entirely positive. For the cross means that *God loves this world*. Despite its existential unloveliness, despite its wickedness, despite its penchant for apostasy and its drive towards death—and therefore despite the *cost* of loving it, God loves this world. That, at its most basic, is the message of the gospel of "Jesus Christ and him crucified."

But unfortunately the followers of the Crucified One have never been so unambiguous. We have vacillated, hesitated, and hovered between love and hate. And we have taken refuge in sophisticated dialectics: "on the one hand . . . on the other hand." This is no doubt understandable enough. It is a terribly costly thing to love this world. It is not simple, either; because love must never mean mere acceptance! Much, very much, about this world should not be accepted. Injustice, we have been insisting, must be uncompromisingly rejected, as must the despoilation of the environment, and as must all forms of war. Yet even to struggle against these realities one must have determined, at some profound level of one's soul, that the world as such, life as such, is eminently worth saving. And that is where the cross of Christ speaks for God's determination. And that is also the level at which we Christians have wavered.

But now the question of questions is put to us again. The threat of the kind of ending implicit in the gravest of the environmental and injustice problems and explicit in the nuclear madness, poses to Christian faith perhaps its greatest historical challenge. For in the face of such an ending we are under obligation as never before to declare clearly and without reservation whether this world matters to us, and matters ultimately. The whole course of 2,000 years gathers itself in this single issue and puts to the hesitating, ambiguous, and covertly Docetic faith that we too frequently still represent the question: Do you or do you not care about this world?

The Bomb is thus not only a real (i.e., physical) threat to our future; it is also a symbolic threat to all who have been less than affirmative in their relation to creaturely existence. Since the means are now at hand to implement human resentment, hatred, revenge, and lovelessness in the world, nothing can prevent this implementation from being deployed except a change of heart on the part of the world's human inhabitants.

What we are being asked, if I may again try to articulate this outrageous question, is not merely whether we are against the destruction of the world, but whether we love the world. Only a few bold egos have ever been found who are ready to destroy the world, who would actually name themselves haters of life, or even nihilists. The problem is not the few "overt nihilists" (Helmut Thielicke) in our midst, it is the covert nihilism of those who hover on the edge of life, enjoying its erstwhile benefits but refusing actually to commit themselves. Or, to use the category Friedrich Nietzsche himself put opposite his term "nihilists," the problem today is "the last men," that is, the many who pursue their own personal pleasures.

> Alas, the time is coming when man will no longer give birth to a star. Alas, the time of the most despicable man is coming, he that is no longer able to despise himself. Behold, I show you the *last man*.
>
> 'What is love? What is creation? What is longing? What is a star?' thus asks the last man, and he blinks.
>
> The earth has become small, and on it hops the last man, who makes everything small. His race is as ineradicable as the flea-beetle; the last man lives longest.
>
> 'We have invented happiness,' say the last men, and they blink. They have left the regions where it is hard to live, for one needs warmth. One still loves one's neighbor and rubs against him, for one needs warmth.
>
> Becoming sick and harboring suspicion are sinful to them: one proceeds carefully. A fool, whoever still stumbles over stones or human beings! A little poison now and then: that makes for

225

agreeable dreams. And much poison in the end, for an agreeable death.

One still works, for work is a form of entertainment. But one is careful lest the entertainment be too harrowing. . . .

Everybody wants the same, everybody is the same: whoever feels different goes voluntarily into a madhouse. . . .

One has one's little pleasure for the day and one's little pleasure for the night: but one has a regard for health.

'We have invented happiness,' say the last men, and they blink.[11]

The problem is in other words a phenomenon which is known by periodically changing names (the latest is "yuppie"). It is the emergence of whole classes of persons who in their hearts have really abandoned this world, though they reap from its decline everything they can salvage for their own enjoyment.

Alas, there are such persons also in and around the churches. Moreover, they conceive the very purpose of the church to be to assist them in their quest for personal happiness. The whole liturgical, moral, historical, biblical, and theological equipage of Christianity exists to protect them from the gnawings of negative thought and to enhance their daily lives with a vague aura of divinity. They certainly do not wish the world destroyed! No, but neither will they dare to expose themselves long enough to its pain to give a thought to its healing! They may like it, but they do not love it. Perhaps they do not love anything, though the idea of love charms them.

Christian stewardship is not about lovely ideas. Its basis in reality is not a sentiment but an event: "Jesus Christ and him crucified." It is into this event that we are baptized—into this stewardship that we are being incorporated. The Bomb is a symbolic form of the question that Christ has always been putting to his would-be disciples: Will you be baptized with my baptism? Will you take up your cross? Will you also love? Simon Peter, do you love me more than these—these ideas and ideals,

11. Kaufmann, *Portable Nietzsche*, 128ff.

these vows of friendship, these momentary transfigurations, or these cosy little times of fellowship? Will you cease using your connection with me to enhance your self-esteem and save your own skin? Will you follow me back into burning Rome?

We Christians come to the decisive question with a very shaky past. For not only fringe Christianity but in one way or another almost all the historical forms of our faith have manifested a strange hesitancy about "burning Rome,"—indeed, a strange fascination for the End. This latter stems partly from the belief, which seems to have informed the earliest congregations, that the coming kingdom necessitates the destruction of earth and the cessation of history. It is also in part of course born of that distaste for matter coming to us from our Hellenistic past and expressing itself (as we noted in the Bonhoeffer reference)[12] in the displacement of the biblical theology of resurrection by a non-Hebraic religion of immortality of the soul. Only Christian Liberalism of the nineteenth and early twentieth centuries tried to translate into historical, earthly terms the biblical symbol of the heavenly kingdom or reign of God. But as we have seen, Liberalism tied its expectations so uncritically to the aspirations of modern Western society that when that society faltered and the religion of progress gave way to the quest for sheer survival, the Liberal version of "the kingdom of God in this generation" was widely rejected as naive and utopian.

Ever since World War I, Christian theology has tended, in reaction to a failed Liberal optimism, to remove the reign of God further and further away from anything that could ever be realized in time and space. The numerical victory in North America today of those forms of Christianity most characterized by otherworldly apocalypticism (neo-apocalypticism) is only a stage—perhaps not the last one—in this evolution of nonworldly spiritualism. Neo-apocalyptic sectarianism is the visible tip of an ecclesiastical iceberg. Will Christians find again the confidence, not only to love the world, but to show the world that God loves it too?

12. Bonhoeffer, *Letters and Papers*, 336-37.

### 3. "Thy Kingdom Come, Thy Will Be Done on Earth"

There is no doubt truth in the insistence of post-Liberal Christianity that the reign of God must remain a vision and a symbol, and not become a blueprint for political experiments. The history of Christendom is strewn with the wrecks of "heavenly kingdoms"—including the one that began in New England! Certainly some of the most intolerant and intolerable states in history have been produced by persons who imagined their ideology to be not the product of mere human dreaming and scheming, but the very model of the heavenly Jerusalem. However much we may admire from afar the theocratic state Calvin and his colleagues tried to set up in sixteenth-century Geneva, no one who lives in contemporary North America, not even the most ardent Calvinist, would have found that city blessed!

Yet there is an opposite danger, and it is perhaps the one most tempting for those who will read these pages. I mean the danger of regarding the symbol of the divine reign in such poetic terms that in the end one is drawn into that same Docetism and spiritualism that we have chastised here, namely, the kind of de-historicizing tendency that is the undoing of genuine Christian stewardship. If we are to struggle against our own Christian otherworldly past, as well as against the narcissistic inner-worldliness of our present post-secular society, then we must learn again for our time how to let this unattainable vision of God's righteous reign shape our thinking and acting within this world. "Thy Kingdom come, thy will be done on earth as it is in heaven." So long as we are prepared to continue praying that prayer, we are making ourselves responsible as earth's stewards for the blessedness, the *shalom*, of this world. The rejection of Liberalism, which is still rather unaccountably too fashionable in some circles, ought at last to give way to a respect for what the Liberals in general and the Social Gospel movement in particular were attempting. They wanted to make the gospel concretely applicable to the life of the world. It was perhaps their peculiar sin to be somewhat naive about the

world's receptivity to God's Word and plan. It is our sin, I suspect, that we are too skeptical about God's capacity to overcome
the world's lack of receptivity.

Translating the stewardship of the kingdom into the
terms of our own context means, certainly, that we must be more
critical of worldly ideologies than our Liberal forebears were. In
relation to all the ideologies we should maintain a certain distance—without indulging in self-righteousness! On the question
of peace, this distance is particularly important; for there are
many who preach peace where there is no peace—where peace
only covers gross economic, racial, and other forms of injustice.

But when we distance the gospel from ideological solutions to historical problems, we shall also have to be careful not
to fall into the world-weariness of the cynical, the world-forget-
fulness of the apathetic, or the inner- and otherworldliness of
the religious. All three of these responses end by making straight
in the desert the way of the oppressors. Of the visionaries and
idealists it may at least be said that they did not accept the status quo. Christians are stewards of a gospel that assumes the
possibility of significant change. The message we bear speaks
not only of the "serenity" of acceptance but also of the "courage"
to seek change.[13]

"Humankind," wrote C. F. von Weizsäcker, "is currently
in a state of manifold crisis, the catastrophic conclusion of
which probably still lies in the future."[14] In a world that is
threatened by terrible realties that, without constant vigilance
(stewarding) can only become still more terrible, acceptance of
the status quo means nothing less than the acceptance of death,
the meaningless and agonizing death of worlds.

13. The reference here is to Reinhold Niebuhr's not only beautiful, but
also theologically sophisticated, prayer: "Give us the serenity to accept what
cannot be changed, the courage to change what can be changed, and the wisdom to distinguish the one from the other."
14. Weizsäcker, Die Zeit drängt, 25. ("Die Menschheit befindet sich
heute in einer Krise, deren katastrophaler Höhepunkt wahrscheinlich noch vor
uns liegt.")

**Status Quo**
Wer will dass die Welt
soll bleib wie sie ist,
der will dass die Welt
nicht bleibt.[15]

## 4. The Divine Imperative: An End to Docetism!

"Nothing in our time is more dubious, it seems to me," wrote Hannah Arendt in her essay on Lessing, "than our attitude towards the world, nothing less to be taken for granted than that concord with what appears in public which an honor imposes on us, and the existence of which it affirms." She continued:

> In our century even genius has been able to develop only in conflict with the world and the public realm, although it naturally finds, as it always has done, its own peculiar concord with its audience. But the world and the people who inhabit it are not the same. The world lies between people, and this in-between . . . is today the object of the greatest concern and the most obvious upheaval in almost all the countries of the globe. Even where the world is still halfway in order, or is kept halfway in order, the public realm has lost the power of *illunionation* which was originally part of its very nature. More and more people in the countries of the Western world, which since the decline of the ancient world has regarded freedom from politics as one of the basic freedoms, make use of this freedom and have retreated from the world and their obligations within it. This withdrawal from the world need not harm an individual; he may even cultivate great talents to the point of genius and so by a detour be useful to the world again. But with each such retreat an almost demonstrable loss to the world takes place; what is lost is the specific and usually irreplaceable in-between which should have formed between this individual and his fellow men.[16]

The specific thoughts and deeds that make for the world's *shalom* cannot be set forth in a program. The stewarding of a

---

15. By the West German poet, Erich Fried. (Whoever wants the world / to stay as it is / doesn't really want the world / to stay.)
16. Arendt, *Men in Dark Times*, 4-5.

---

world on the brink of catastrophe, like the care of a patient in the crisis of a dread illness, must be moment-to-moment, a matter of intensive care. Moreover, to carry the metaphor of the hospital ward a little farther, as the tending of the critically ill patient requires the expertise and labor of a whole hospital staff, so the tending of a sick world must be a team effort. Christians can perhaps, as Christians, contribute little more than passionate dedication to the intricate task of keeping such a world alive.

Precisely that, however, is the point! We cannot as Christians dictate policies and engineer negotiations and make decisions concerning the technicalities of arms reduction and so on (though many of those who in their vocations and professions do such things are avowed Christians, and can presumably draw certain conclusions from that). But as Christians we can do something—can be something—far more significant in the long run; something which, if it is not done, will prevent all the other, practical things from happening. It is this: we can determine that we shall not any longer be amongst those who are ambiguous about the world, who withdraw from it, and whose withdrawal results in an almost demonstrable loss to the world. This kind of determination is the *sine qua non* of all activity directed towards world peace today. Even if we devote much time and energy to the peace movement; even if we march with the marchers and contribute our money to the right causes; even if we give our bodies to be burned, "but have not love," love for the world, it will be as "nothing."

An end to Christian Docetism—an end to our ambiguous attitude towards this world—is the divine imperative that is contained in the dread nuclear and other deadly data of our epoch. If that imperative were obeyed, even by a minority of the followers of Jesus Christ, there could be a demonstrable gain to the whole movement for peace. If as stewards of the mysteries of God we make this first and most rudimentary step towards tending God's garden-become-wilderness, by declaring our love for it, we shall have leapt over a chasm that has long separated us from those who lie in Abraham's bosom.

# CHAPTER IX

# ON BEING STEWARDS

## 1. A Manner of Speaking

"For too long we have emphasized the *doing*, with superficial, short-term results. We need to reverse our strategy and put the emphasis on *being*, for more authentic, long-term effects." So writes one of North America's most experienced and dedicated stewards of stewardship in the churches, Theodore S. Horvath.[1]

The cumulative effect of the foregoing chapters in this study will, I hope, have upheld Dr. Horvath's concern for being stewards. Stewardship does not describe any one dimension of the Christian life; it describes the whole posture called "Christian." Through this metaphor, the biblical authors with their genius for images found a single term that could point simultaneously to all three foci of Christian faith: its orientation to the one whose sovereignty the steward acknowledges; its orientation to humans, who participate in the universal stewardship

---

1. Horvath, *Identity As Stewards*, 9. Theodore Horvath was for many years Associate for Stewardship Education with the Stewardship Council of the United Church of Christ, and a very active member of the Commission on Stewardship of the National Council of Churches in the U.S.A.

of "the speaking animal"; and its orientation to otherkind and to the earth, our common home.

There is no need, of course, to make extraordinary claims for the metaphor. It is not the only way in which the first witnesses to the "grace in which we stand" articulated their conception of faith. It is not even the most important among them. In comparison with many other images, ideas, and terms that have made their impact upon historic Christianity ("body of Christ," "bride of Christ," "ambassadors for Christ," "witnesses," "kingdom of priests," or "people of the Way"), the metaphor of the steward is perhaps even of minor importance.

But images have their time and place. Symbols—as we have noticed from the outset—are not created, they occur. They are born and they die. Unlike signs and categories and systems, symbols cannot be arbitrarily chosen or dispensed with. For certain ages of the church, the terms referred to above, along with many others that could be named, were lively and immediate symbols: they were sufficiently related to the fundamental structures, beliefs, hopes, fears, and goals of the societies in which they functioned to make their use both meaningful to believers and comprehensible to unbelievers. Some of the terms to which I am referring still have currency today, and some of them belong so essentially to the story that Christians tell that they can never be given up, even when it is hard to find points of contact for them in ordinary discourse and public concern. Yet it is also true that a great many of the categories that historic Christianity has used to describe the being of Christians are less than accessible to our present-day understanding, and also are replaceable. They may sometimes be made meaningful, if they are sufficiently interpreted, illustrated, and explained by reference to other categories that twentieth-century people can grasp. But they do not speak to us directly, as they did to some of our forebearers.

One could think in this connection of a category like "priest" and "priesthood." The fact that the term "priest" is still used daily to describe an important office in the Church of

Rome, the Anglican/Episcopal communion, and Orthodox churches may or may not help to make it accessible as a way of depicting the being and calling of all Christians, corporately and individually. I suspect that today's use actually inhibits the concept of priest, since it seems all too obviously to designate a particular and unique person and office. But Protestants are hardly more blest when it comes to the modern communicative potential of this ancient and important biblical term. Some Protestants will tell you that the whole Reformation of the sixteenth century was fought over the issue of "the priesthood of all believers" (which is not true); but when they then proceed to define what precisely that means they are usually less than articulate and even more frequently wrong. Most casual Protestants think that the priesthood of all believers is a Protestant polemic against priests of any explicit variety, offered in the name of a faith which insists that we do not need any priests at all since we have direct access to God as individuals. The notion that we are priests to and for one another is hardly the average Protestant's work-a-day self-image! To be sure, it must in some way become our self-understanding if we are to approach Christian maturity. But few of our contemporaries, I suspect, will arrive at that maturity through the contemplation of the traditional category of priesthood, indispensable as this category is.

The term "steward" is also—as I have been at some pains to show already—not without its problems. As we have seen, it is far too narrowly associated with church finances and the general maintenance of a narrow conception of the house of God. In a word, it is too much associated with doing—and a confined sort of doing at that! In addition, it can be heard and used in a manner that is far too slanted towards the managerial mode. Some European, Asiatic, and other Christians think they detect behind this term a very American way of conceiving of the human and Christian life—almost, as one high ecclesiastic of East Asia told me, a sanctified version of the technocrat!

This criticism should certainly be taken seriously. North Americans rather easily slip into managerial language and role-playing. It is part of our inheritance from a pioneer past, where people had to manage things for themselves. They could not wait for experts or professionals or highly skilled craftsmen to do what needed to be done. So, unlike their counterparts in the older societies, they built their own houses and barns, damned up their own streams, tended their own sick animals, and painted and papered their own rooms. And who is to say that this was all wrong! It at least created generations of human beings who felt some sense of responsibility for their own lives, had enough confidence in their abilities to take initiative, and were skeptical enough about authority to resist the kinds of tyrannies that developed regularly in the older societies!

But this historical conditioning, which is cruelly countered and vitiated by other influences at work in our present context, has nevertheless produced in us a tendency to overestimate our managerial skills. It can be assumed, therefore, that generally we are tempted to exaggerate that side of the symbol of the steward, and that in consequence wisdom in the churches will require a certain critique of activism that is insufficiently grounded in thought, prayer, and study. We have seen in this discussion that the steward metaphor assumes two mutually informative poles: responsibility and accountability. The steward is not the master and owner (possessor) and therefore is accountable. The steward is given a vocation to fulfil and the wherewithal to fulfil it, and therefore is responsible. Probably it is the first of these lessons to which North American Christians should be particularly attentive.

Having said so, however, I am immediately mindful of the phenomenon to which I just alluded—how the earlier, activist tendencies fostered by the necessary as well as unnecessary forms of individualism characterized by our past are today vitiated by other influences. I am of course thinking of that same tendency to withdraw from the world, more particularly from public life, on which we commented in the previous chapter. In some ways, it seems to me, there needs to be a new emphasis upon human and Christian responsibility for and in the world.

While the criticism of managerial assumptions in the stewardship symbol must no doubt be taken seriously, it would be un-
wise to assume that the temptation to fall into a one-sided
managerial view of the Christian steward's calling is our only
danger.

There is, let us acknowledge at once, no safe theology or
theo-anthropology. Neither stewardship nor any other symbolic
term for the Christian life and calling can be employed un-
guardedly. Yet despite its dangers this symbol is eminently right
for our historical moment. Its truncation by narrow ecclesiastical usage does not present an ultimate problem of communication. In fact, it has been my experience over the past decade that
enlarging this term and giving it something like a holistic meaning is received by most serious members of the churches as a
liberating experience. For there is much dissatisfaction in the
churches themselves with the confined way in which stewardship has been understood; it seems to many thoughtful Christians a matter of putting the cart before the horse. If Christian
people feel themselves to be stewards in this larger sense, they
are much more likely to do stewardly deeds—both in the world
and in the church.

Another reason why this particular biblical metaphor has
symbolic significance today, as I have indicated in the foregoing, is that it is accessible to a much wider public than that represented by committed and articulate Christians alone. In fact
it is quite possible that the terms "steward" and "stewardship"
are used with greater frequency outside the churches than inside them. If one develops ears and eyes for it, one will see this
symbol employed everywhere today. Indeed, its symbolic
character is precisely bound up with its having achieved this
common coinage. The fact that the term also signifies common-
place work, such as that of the airline steward, should not worry
us in the least. Some of the most honored metaphors of the faith
(shepherd, teacher, disciple, bridegroom, judge, and friend) have
their origins in just such everyday offices. It will certainly not
hinder the communicability of the idea that airplane personnel

are normally good-natured people who look after other people! In some tangible, linguistic sense, then, as well as in terms of its deeper meaning, the metaphor of the steward has blossomed. It describes a way of being Christian that is apologetically "ripe" (Tillich). Looking about the world today, one can really think that "the coming age will be seen as the age of stewardship" (Skolimoski).

## 2. "The Stewardship of All Believers"

Not only is stewardship a word that our world uses and in some genuine way understands, it also has apologetic possibilities because it does (or can do) justice to important dimensions of the Christian message, including the Christian's *self*-understanding. There are two basic reasons for this: (1) It conveys what is essential in much of the tradition, including ideas that were conveyed in conventional terms whose coinage is questionable or diminished today; (2) it does this without carrying along with it some of the injurious or misleading connotations of older categories.

To consider the second aspect first: Some of the conventional language used to depict the life and work of Christians, when it is not simply mystifying even to Christians, often implies certain qualities that constitute barriers to both communication and community. Frequently, of course, these undesirable qualities have been put upon the term by centuries of ecclesiastical malpractice. By association they have become humorous, presumptuous, pretentious, or offensive. Theologians and preachers still use them (one has to, of course), but even in the act of stating them one often cringes inwardly, particularly if one is using them outside the "household of faith" (a case in point!). A phrase like "Christian witnesses," for example, has a slight but unmistakable tinge of self-righteousness about it, not to mention stereotypes of street-corner evangelism. To exchange it for "proclaimers of the Word" or even "people of the cross" is to jump from the frying pan into the fire. "Ambassadors for Christ" was excellent in the Pauline context, perhaps; but ambassadors nowadays have a high reputation for official stuffiness, when they are not perceived as mere functionaries of state. "People of the Way" and "the pilgrim people" are in my opinion better (because less triumphalistic and pompous); but they are all of them in-church phrases, as are so many of the New Testament's metaphors, even the most famous one, "body of Christ."

The most objectionable aspect of a number of the terms by which we conventionally designate ourselves as Christians is of course that (to the nonchurched at least) they smack of a false security, superiority, and authority. They conjure up what Reinhold Niebuhr called "the pretention to finality." Just try using what was one of the most common categories employed by our Puritan and other ancestors in North America ("the elect of God") at the next community meeting or Memorial Day observance! We all know Christians who persist in naming themselves "the saved," to the continuing consternation of "the damned"; but the offensive nature of Christian self-description is not limited to biblicistic and fundamentalist religion. Even our more bourgeois Christian appellations—not only the category "priesthood" but also the less definitive Protestant form, "ministry"—carry with them enough holier-than-thouness that they readily function as "false scandals" (Bultmann) to communication and community. In particular, they suggest a certain authority—or rather pretention to authority—that immediately puts the world on the defensive (including that world from which the priests and ministers so often distinguish themselves, the Christian laity!).

It is precisely the nonsacrosanct, nonauthoritarian character of "the steward" that commends it. As we have already acknowledged, any word—through bad practice—can become tainted. But while the steward metaphor has been truncated, it has not been badly tainted. In particular, it has not been made to serve the characteristically triumphalistic assumptions about ourselves that have informed our whole history, especially from Constantine onwards. Like the general nomenclature of servanthood, of which it is after all a specific application and nuance, the symbol of the steward militates against its co-optation by power. There is an implicit modesty in it, and this makes it much more compatible with the theology of the cross than many and perhaps most of the concepts by which Christians have identified themselves. Even priesthood, which is of course much better in this respect than "kingship"—a nomenclature which is not only imperialistic but also inescapably sexist—can without great difficulty be co-opted by the triumphalist urge. The prophets of Israel knew that long ago! Glory no doubt has its place in the Christian story; but given our particular history it is hard for the world to separate Christian glory from Christian power. It befits us therefore to explore what we mean by glory through the use of images (and of course deeds) that clearly locate power elsewhere than in ourselves!

It is for this reason that stewardship can be perceived even by secular observers as an alternative to the power pursuits of imperial Christianity. Insofar as the churches pursue the stewardship motif, one such observer insists, they convey an entirely new and different image, both of being Christian and of being human:

> Stewardship requires that human kind respect and conserve the "natural" workings of God's order. The natural order works on the principles of diversity, interdependence and decentralization. Maintenance replaces the notion of progress, stewardship replaces ownership, and nurturing replaces engineering. Biological limits to both production and consumption are acknowledged; the principle of balanced distribution is accepted; and the concept of wholeness becomes the essential guideline for measuring all relationships and phenomena.
>
> In reality, then, the new stewardship doctrine represents a fundamental shift in humanity's frame of reference. It establishes a new set of governing principles for how human beings should behave and act in the world. As a worldview, the steward-

ship doctrine demands of the faithful an uncompromising adherence. . . .

The new concept is that dominion is stewardship rather than ownership and conservation rather than exploitation. . . . *This new emphasis on stewardship is providing the foundation for the emergence of a second Protestant reformation and a new covenant vision for society.*[2]

The apologetic coinage of the stewardship symbol is due, however, to positive as well as negative considerations. Not only does it guard against injurious and misleading images of the Christian life; it also conveys the essential meaning of some (not all) of the important traditional categories by which Christians have identified themselves and their mission. Here I am thinking again especially of that biblically and traditionally important term, "priesthood." I for one would certainly not advocate dropping this category from the church's vocabulary. It will continue to be meaningful within all the great divisions of the ecumenical church. It is indeed for the sake of the meaning that priesthood implies that I would propose that it be supplemented by stewardship.

In the most provocative and even exciting ways, the steward metaphor can revive and preserve what is most precious and indispensable in the concept of priesthood. For like the latter concept, the symbol of the steward is at bottom a symbol of representation. Like the priest, the steward is a vicar, deputy, *Stellvertreter*. The authority that the steward bears is wholly bound up with the One whose creation she or he tends; and, like the shepherd (and unlike the "hireling") the steward's authority is valid only when it is an adequate representation of the Creator's love for what God will have tended. The steward not only represents the loving Creator to the other creatures (responsibility); she or he also answers to the Creator in behalf of the other creatures (accountability). In other words, a thoroughly representational conception of human calling is assumed, as in the concept of priesthood.

2. Rifkin, *Emerging Order*, 270-71. (Italics added.)

This is not to say that the two terms are simply interchangeable. There are indeed nuances in the priest image that are not contained in that of the steward—and vice versa. But the essence of the office is very similar. Both are mediatorial figures, both "re-present God" to the world and the world to God. Neither needs to be considered a replacement for the other. But a considerable advantage of the steward symbol is that it has apologetic potential for communicating the essential and concrete meaning of Christian (and human) representation (not substitution) without conveying at the same time the narrowly sacerdotal connotations that, unfortunately, adhere to the office and nomenclature of priesthood.

What then if we spoke about "the stewardship of all believers"? I am almost positive that for many Protestants at least this could redeem a concept that, when stated literally in the Reformation language of priesthood, is increasingly remote and perhaps meaningless. The very worldliness and concreteness of the stewardship of all believers puts flesh on the skeleton of a traditional idea. It brings the being and mission of Christians down to earth. Their business is not just with God, and certainly it is not just the very private traffic with the divine that is connoted by the common misappropriation of the Reformation teaching. Their business is the being of stewards in all phases of life—in their relationships with one another, in their everyday worldly existence, in their attitude towards nature, and in their conduct of individual and corporate public life. Through the symbol of the steward we might once again, we who are Protestants, find our way back to the real meaning of our corporate and personal priesthood.

## 3. A Way of *Being* Christian

We return to the point with which we began the considerations of this chapter and its chief thesis. It is essential in realizing the potential of this symbol that it connotes a manner not just of speaking but of being. It is perhaps here that the biblical concept of priesthood could help, in turn, to prevent stewardship from signifying only a function, a work. Without conjuring up the whole tangled history of the meaning of priesthood, complete with the notion of indelible orders and the like, we may certainly affirm that priesthood as it is conceived biblically refers to something that one *is* and not just something that one *does*. The main point that Protestants would insist upon here is that the "one" in question is not just the ordained minister or priest but the whole people, the *laos*. Ministry as office or function in the Protestant mode of ecclesiastical thought and practice refers to various types of ministry within the larger ministry of the whole people. Where the ministry of the whole is concerned, most Protestants are just as insistent as are Catholics, Anglicans, and Orthodox that priesthood is a matter of *being* and not just a function. The whole people of God as "a holy priesthood" (1 Pet. 2:5) is called, not merely to do this or that, but to be a representative people in the world.

Similarly, stewardship must be understood first as descriptive of the being—the very life—of God's people. Deeds of stewardship arise out of the being of the steward. It is no different here from what pertains elsewhere: the act is an expression and consequence of the life that enacts it. A mother does certain things with respect to her child because of the relationship in which the two stand. A musician must play or sing because the music is there, and will find its outlet one way or another. Jeremiah must prophesy because he has been grasped by divine truth; when he tries to squelch the prophetic utterance, it is as if his soul were on fire (Jer. 20). We are able to love and to perform deeds of love because we have been loved (1 John 4). No doubt human beings do many things that do not emerge out of the depths of their being. We even try, often, to perform loving acts ("make love") when there is no real love in us. The world is full of nonmusical children and adults who, to please parents or win approval, torture their souls and bodies in order to perform tolerably on instruments. And while we are on the theme, let us also admit that there are many would-be Jeremiahs who are not inspired by (afflicted with!) truth. All the same, the only authentic deeds, whether of love or art or truth, arise from spirits and minds that have been inspired and must give of what they have received.

Stewardship honors this same law: the deed springs from the gift—the gift of new life. It presupposes endowment by an abundance (John 10:10) that must be shared with others. Unfortunately, this has not been understood well in the churches; and therefore many of us are stewards in the same manner as the parent who loves the child out of a sense of duty, or the musician who hammers out a few boring pieces on the piano, though he has no music in his soul. We regard stewardship as something you do rather than someone you are. I do not discount the possibility that, through doing, some may learn the deeper lesson of being the steward—just as some people become fairly good musicians through sheer determination and practice. But while that may happen, it should not be translated into ecclesiastical method. Real and effective deeds of stewardship will occur only when persons hear that gospel and are moved by that Spirit that changes their *being*, lifting them from the sloth of irresponsibility or judging their pride of mastery and giving them new being—the being of stewards.

And so we come to the notorious "bottom line" of the bookkeepers: funding and filling the offices and handling the physical affairs of churches. This book is not intended to be an exercise in Christian bookkeeping, but what I say in it I intend to be entirely practical. If what I have claimed in this immediate context about the being of the steward is true, and if the whole direction of this study has any significance at all, then the place to begin our lessons in stewardship is not with some of the consequences of the life of the steward, such as the offering of time, talents, and treasures to the congregation, but with its genesis. Instead of periodic or regular efforts at conjuring up deeds of stewardship; instead of financial campaigns and bazaars and garage sales aimed at making temporary stewards out of essentially slothful or self-centered people; instead of ca-joling and harping and "bugging" people to become Sunday School teachers or parish visitors or members of the official board—we need to learn how to teach and preach the gospel and interpret the Christian life as stewardship. The world is cry-ing out for keepers and tenders of its wonderful, frail beauty, and God desires to send us out as stewards into this astonishing, unique creation. Until we have been grasped by that Word and deed of our God; until we have begun to *be* who we are, no amount of exhortation or works will alter greatly the image of the church or the course of the world.

### 4. Mission as a Function of Stewardship

Being the steward is not only the vocation of individual Chris-tians, it is the mission of the whole body. What I mean is that stewardship is the church's mission. Rightly to understand the depths of this old-metaphor-become-contemporary-symbol is to realize that when we speak about the stewardship of the church we are speaking about its mission.

This may seem a shocking and even heretical claim in the light of that conventional logic (about which we spoke at the outset of this study) which assumes that stewardship is the means ("only the means," as it is usually phrased) to the end of mission. But in view of the holistic understanding of steward-ship that I have attempted to explicate in these pages, such a claim could be received by many who have followed the argu-ment up until now as a logical and even necessary conclusion to all that so far has been said. It is, I think, precisely because stewardship has been placed in such a subservient relation to mission that we have ended up with a truncated view of steward-ship—and at a time in history when the world is ready to re-ceive from us something far more basic. But now, in conclud-ing this study, I want to suggest that our questionable prioritizing with respect to mission and stewardship has resulted in a truncated and questionable understanding of the church's mission too. Through a deeper comprehension of stewardship we can arrive at an understanding of Christian mission that is both more appropriate to the authentic roots of our faith and more prophetic in relation to the character of the context in which we find ourselves today.

### (a) Mission and Stewardship in the Imperial Church

In order to demonstrate this hypothesis, I must ask the reader to recollect some aspects of our historical reflections in Chapter II. There we noted, as a matter entirely pertinent to our topic of stewardship, that in the year 313 C.E. the Emperor Constantine issued an edict of toleration favouring the Christians, and that by the end of the same century only Christianity was legally permitted in the Western empire. From this point onwards, the characteristic forms of Christianity in the world have been established forms. That is to say, throughout approximately four-fifths of its history, Christianity has existed chiefly as the official or semi-official religion of empires, nations, and peoples. One empire after another has courted this faith and been courted by it. When therefore we speak about Christianity—historically, sociologically, or phenomenologically—we are speaking of an imperial religion.

Now in the "Constantinian situation," that is, wherever and however Christianity operates as the established cult of the dominant culture, mission is inextricably bound up with power. It is necessary to discuss this from two complementary angles. On the one hand, the link between mission and power in the imperial church refers to the church's particular orientation towards the institutional and economic sources of power within that empire. The church must pay court to these sources, for its continued existence and welfare depend upon its fundamental acceptability to them. It sustains its power by seeking and maintaining proximity to their power. Thus its mission, which is to say its total witness, consists in large measure in its appeal

245

to the dominant classes and the structures of authority operative in that particular society. It may indeed play a significant role in that society, as guardian of a higher morality, bearer of foundational traditions, and the place to which the human need for mystery, ritual, and pageantry may refer itself. Yet even at its best, cultic Christianity walks a delicate tightrope between challenging the society and confirming it. Its challenge must never be felt as a contradiction to the overt values and practices of the ruling social strata. Thus it may plead for a higher morality, but not for an order of justice altogether different from the regnant systems of social behaviour.

This has to be seen as part of what is meant by the mission of the church in the imperial situation, because the church not only requires the major portion of its energies to sustain such a *modus operandi* with power, but power is altogether determinative for the rest of what mission means. It is hardly likely that a church which aligns itself with the ruling classes of a society will preach to the rivals or potential enemies of those classes (including the lower classes within the same society) a gospel that might contradict the aspirations of the ruling element. To be sure, the gospel has sometimes foiled its own preachers and brought to the oppressed the very courage they needed to rise up against their oppressors. As the black community in the United States and South Africa learned; as some of the indigenous peoples of North America have learned; as women in the churches have learned within this past decade or so, it is hard to keep the revolutionary dimension out of the Christian story, even when it is passed along in platitudinous forms and as an opiate for anxious and bored souls. The emperor, hearing for years on end the intonation of the Magnificat—"He hath put down the mighty from their seats"—may one evening be roused from his stupor of simulated prayer by actually hearing what is being said! But imperial Christianity never intends this kind of spin-off! When it has happened, it has happened as a matter of sheer grace, and human embarrassment!

The second and more direct way in which mission is linked with the quest for power in the imperial church is that it is inevitably associated with the survival and expansion of the church. Without at all dramatizing the matter, we could at this juncture reflect upon the centuries-long involvement of all forms of Christianity in the acquisition (often enough through devious and sometimes criminal means) of properties, treasures, resources, and souls, all in the name of the Christian mission. But we should not permit our critical analysis of imperial Christianity to become too much bound up with its lower manifestations. It is too simple to depict imperial Christianity's quest for power as a thoroughly sinister thing. Even where sinister or devious methods have been employed, the motivation has often been high, sometimes even noble, given certain theological assumptions. Let us even admit that the imperial church is impelled by the desire not primarily to secure its own power but rather to establish the power of the gospel and the rule of Christ in the lives of persons and societies.

But in fact that does not make the power foundation of mission in the imperial church less questionable. Rather, it brings us to the heart of the more serious question. For what must be asked (what we must ask ourselves as Christians at this juncture in our historical sojourn) is whether it is in the first place Christ's will that we gain this kind of power and ascendency for him. The power foundation of mission in imperial Christianity is not to be questioned primarily because of the sinful use of power by the church, i.e., using it for its own direct aggrandizement. Rather, the question must be raised at the level of what has been our highest motivation. Imperial Christianity at its best and noblest has been impelled by the desire to "win the world for Christ."

*But does Christ want to win the world?* Is it not possible that that kind of winning is in fundamental conflict with the purposes of Jesus Christ? May it not be that what he himself said of individuals could apply equally to his church as a whole, namely, that it would be possible to gain the whole world and lose the very soul, the very essence of the thing? Mission understood as winning, as triumphing over all alternative forms of faith and unfaith, simply does not fit the picture of the one who said plainly that he had come to serve, not to be served. Even then when it is the mastery of the Christ that is intended and not (not directly, at any rate) sheer ecclesiastical mastery, it is still mastery and not servanthood that informs this whole, deeply influential tradition of Christian mission.

Given such a missionary presupposition, it was and is inevitable that stewardship could be present in imperial Christianity only in reductionist forms, as we have seen. It could never achieve the status of a basic orientation or even of a major dimension in the life and work of the Christian churches. It could exist only on the ethical level and, at that, only as a kind of optional or fringe ethic for the enthusiastic. It could only be the means, never the end.

This reductionist conception of stewardship is not accidental. Its presence amongst us still is not due to the fact that stewardship committees have failed to be enthusiastic enough in their educational and promotional campaigns. It is present as a direct consequence of our primary image of the church, including our missiology. So long as our understanding of the church and its task in the world is informed by magisterial assumptions, stewardship can enter the life of the churches only in minimal, functional, and usually trivial forms.

The fundamental assumptions of stewardship seriously conceived are inimical to the monarchical conception of the church and its mission. While mission under the conditions of Constantinian Christianity must mean the expansion of Christian influence, stewardship seriously conceived refers to the expansion of Christian service. While mission in the imperial church implies that the missionizing community is in possession of something not enjoyed by the others (truth, salvation, or righteousness), stewardship in its very essence, as we have seen, implies a polemic against the whole idea of possession, whether material or spiritual possession. While mission in Christendom has meant molding the wills and minds of persons and nations to preconceived states of spiritual and moral rectitude, stewardship implies the husbanding of the good wherever it is found, the midwifery of truth in all of its varied and unpredictable manifestations. With stewardship, conceived holistically and in depth, the one who is to be served takes precedence over the one who serves. Stewardship is not therefore the gaining of influence, power, property; not the winning of souls and tongues to the Christian confession; not even (as an end in itself) the extension of the manifest sovereignty of Christ in the world, but rather the care and nurture of life, the healing of the one who fell amongst thieves, the feeding of the hungry and freeing of the oppressed, the befriending of the friendless, the equitable distribution of earth's bounty, the passion for justice and peace, and dialogue with all who hunger and thirst for authenticity. That is the essential attitude of Christian stewardship. In this work is its peculiar *doxa* (glory). It does not seek its glory in power; it does not even seek to establish the omnipotence of the God who commissions and sustains it (God does not need us to establish God's sovereignty!). Rather, stewardship seeks to establish that which God also sought and seeks, in great humility, to establish: the peace, abundance, and glory of the creation. Like the God who sends us, who is *Emmanuel*, God *with* us—the Christian steward is anthropocentric and geocentric.

To state the same thing in other words: stewardship means our incorporation into the being and work of the One who came to serve and not to be served, the chief steward Jesus. In Protestant circles it should not have to be said that this incorporation is a matter of grace and not works. If in our new identity as members of the body of Christ we find that we are orientated towards humanity and the biosphere, it is not because we are altruistic people; it is because the grace by which we are being grasped pushes us towards the world and enables us to begin to act like true servants and not hirelings—and not dominating managers either! Let us not however mistake it: this same grace does not permit us to regard such service as an option, or merely one possible consequence of faith. It is at the centre. It is a total attitude and orientation, not just an ethical addendum. It is a matter of being.

As a total orientation, stewardship contains an implicit and radical polemic against imperial Christianity and the interpretation and practice of mission that has informed imperial Christianity in all of its historic expressions. Therefore stewardship as a serious, fundamental approach to the life of the Christian *koinonia* was never able to achieve a lasting foothood in the church throughout the greater share of its history. The imperial church did not and does not have great difficulty perceiving its own triumphant image and mode of being in some of the New Testament's more aggressive language and terminology concerning the role of the church. Just contemplate for a moment the fate of a text like the so-called "Great Commission" at the end of Matthew's Gospel (28:19-20). As soon as the sociological conditions of the church were altered from the status of an illicit religion to that of the official cult of empire, Matthew's exhortation to "make disciples of all nations, baptizing them in the name of the Father, and of the Son, and of the Holy Spirit," could seem a veritable licence for the whole Christendom enterprise, even its most militant aspects. But the biblical concept of stewardship could never be comfortably adapted to Constantinian religion. It could only be reduced and marginalized. For with the keen sense that power always has for sniffing out its own betrayal from within, imperial Christianity could easily recognize in the way of the steward, taken as a symbol for the whole behaviour of the church in the world, an altogether different route from the one to which it was committed.

### (b) Stewardship and Mission in the Post-Constantinian Church

It is just here, however, that we may begin to reflect upon the second, constructive aspect of this analysis of the relation between mission and stewardship. For as we have remarked in the

Introduction and at various points along the way, it is precisely that different route that opens up to the church today as its only authentic way into the future. Just at the point where imperial Christianity, embodying the way of religious mastery, has failed, this other route becomes available, viable, and full of practical meaning. Of course the alternative has always been there, and of course there have always been Christian minorities who knew of it and tried to follow it. But now it becomes for us the only way left. For the other way—the old, broad way of triumphalistic Christendom and the "theology of glory" (Luther)— is already closed to us, if only we realize it. More important, and on the positive side of this observation, the world itself, having meanwhile been humbled by time, is vastly in need of the friendship of the steward. For it has fallen amongst thieves.

Already at the outset of this study we introduced the theme of the death of Christendom. Christianity, having existed throughout most of its history as the religion of empire, finds itself being reduced to the status of one religious alternative amongst many others, and at a time when large numbers of earth's inhabitants doubt that any specifically religious alternative is either justifiable or, perhaps, necessary. Christianity is less influential at the end of this century that was supposed to have been "the Christian century" than it was at the beginning. In many parts of the formerly Christian world, the church has been notoriously decimated. Even in avowedly Christian societies like ours, the tenets of Christianity are no longer regarded as obvious or axiomatic, and in many parts of Africa and Asia where Christianity seems to be on the rise, there are admixtures of other influences which make it difficult for the leadership of indigenous churches to sustain vital links with both tradition and Scripture.

Not only numerically, but in terms of its presence and influence upon the dominant cultures of the West, the Christian faith has been "humiliated" (Albert H. van den Heuvel). The most basic dogmas, stories, and myths of the faith are now as unfamiliar to the young as the teachings of Confucius or

Norse mythology. We are indeed living in "the last days of the Constantinian Era" (Günther Jakob). This is not a new phenomenon; it is a process dating back to the breakdown of the Middle Ages and the dawning of the Age of Reason. But it has become a conspicuous phenomenon in the present century.

It is natural that this situation has produced a conservative reaction in the churches. As with all dying, one of the inevitable responses to the death of Christendom is denial. Not only are there many Christians who close their eyes to this sociological and historical phenomenon, being unable psychically to entertain the thought of an unsuccessful church; but there are many who, in the face of this ending, commit themselves with renewed vigour to the recovery of Christendom. Much contemporary evangelism, with its bid for world evangelization by the year 2000, is inspired by that sort of last-ditch effort. And in "the Age of Uncertainty" (Galbraith), any ideology that can offer certitudes of the kind offered by biblical literalism and doctrinal fundamentalism every day of the week will have no difficulty finding adherents.

But no matter what temporary gains this kind of "hard sell" is able to make, the end of the Constantinian era is a datum of modern history that undergirds all the fickle fluctuations of the spiritual pulse of Western (and especially American) civilization. From this point onwards, Christians who are earnest about their faith must live in a world where their faith represents one alternative, and with no external props or head starts. Being a Christian today and tomorrow becomes a matter of decision, and the decision will have to be made over and over again, always in the presence of alternatives and of much evidence to the contrary. It can no longer be assumed that generation after generation will be eased into the churches by the sheer force of social convention.

This can be regarded as a desperate or threatening situation only by those Christians who are committed to an a priori version of the Constantinian model of the church. Given the assumptions and goals of imperial Christianity, the death of

Christendom must of course be seen as a failure of the Christian faith. But if one tries to read the Bible without the dubious benefits of Constantinian assumptions, one may begin to believe that this "death" could be a highly provocative experience—as death regularly seems to be! This "end" could mark a new beginning, as endings often do! As I have put it elsewhere,[3] the end of Christendom could be the beginning—or a new beginning—of the church. This is conceivable just at this point in time, precisely because imperial Christianity has become impossible. That perennial way of "being the church," the constant temptation of faith already with ancient Israel, is and will become increasingly closed to us. Prophetic faith may have a better chance in the world precisely as and because that way is closed.

The positive implications of this ending are many. But for our present deliberations there is also an instructive negative or at least critical implication. For what the demise of Constantinian arrangements means is that the imperial missionizing assumptions of historic Christianity are no longer really pertinent or even realistic. They are strictly dated assumptions. Whatever one may say about the mass baptisms of Charlemagne or the nineteenth-century Christian blitzes on Asia and Africa, such activities were at least somehow credible in their historical contexts; for Christianity in those contexts could count on the backing of powerful empires. But when Christian denominations emerge in our own time with plans to take earth by storm, even when they can count on plenty of money to back their efforts, they strain our credulity. The ways of imperial Christendom, whether Protestant or Catholic, conservative biblicist or liberal cultural, simply do not work in a religiously pluralistic world where even avowedly Christian regimes can no longer afford politically to assume the stance of *defensor fidei* (defender of the faith). Christians who act along the lines of empire today simply do not know what time it is.

3. See my *Has the Church a Future?*

Not only is time denying us Christians our time-honoured role as cultic saviours and heroes, but simultaneously time (providence!) is offering us a new role—or rather an old one that we have never really tried out. We shall say no more about the reasons why that new/old role has become possible. Our cultural analysis in Chapter III must suffice for now. It is enough to remember that what could be entertained only by the most pessimistic observers in the past—people like Spengler who wrote of "the decline of the West"—is now the subject of nearly every Hollywood movie! The formerly buoyant industrial society limps uncertainly from one news broadcast to the next. Rationality, which was supposed to have redeemed us all, is no longer trusted, even by ordinary people. The institutions of democracy founder and are the prey of every little terrorist band. No one speaks any more about "Humanity" (certainly not of "Man"), or "History," or "Progress"—all the great words have a hollow ring after Auschwitz and in the shadow of "the future Hiroshima" (Wiesel).

And who cares? It is hard to find anyone who cares in this "age of diminishing expectations" (Christopher Lasch). Who really cares for the forests, the land, the sea, the human beings, the animals—for the future? Who cares enough for the world to rise above the pursuit of pleasure and escape and become the champion of justice, peace, and the integrity of creation?

## 5. Conclusion: Stewardship as Theological Possibility and Worldly Necessity

Christians have never really cared unconditionally. We have admitted that already. But neither have Christians been quite free to say openly that they *do not care*. We have been and continue to be "ambiguous" (Arendt) about the world, most of us; but so long as we have our eyes on the Suffering Servant we can hardly state openly that we do not care. We have hovered on the verge of it—and some may be found who in moments of extreme spirituality sound as if they had already left this paltry planet behind! But with that cross at the centre, we can hardly turn our backs altogether on the world.

What if now we cast aside our precious qualifications, our ambivalence, our Manichaean disdain, our Docetism, and declare in word and in deed (praxis!) that we care? What if this care became not just a sentiment, an official ethic, a duty, but a very way of being? What if, in the midst of a society of technocrats and pleasure-seekers, nihilists and "last men," Christians—instead of showing up as a well-known religious element pursuing its well-known attempt at saving the world, winning converts, winning arguments, influencing the powerful, or just trying to survive—began to be a community that cares for the world—for its welfare, its justice, its peace, and its integrity? What if, in place of thinking itself the dispenser of salvation which must turn as much "world" into "church" as possible, the Christian community began to act out of an avowed care for this world—a care which (it admits when asked) it has learned to have in its encounter with a God whose care for the world is infinite?

And so what if this community (not alone, certainly, but in company with all persons and groups and movements of good will) began to think and plan and act and suffer for the preservation and enhancement of that beloved world? What if a religion that had acted out of the motives of mastery for so long were to begin now—even so late in time!—to act out of the motives of service; not as yet another predator on the community of humankind, but as neighbour to a species that had fallen amongst thieves? What if stewardship became our very mode of operation, our characteristic stance, our way of being in the world, our means of expressing and confessing our faith—not an addendum, not a means to something else, not an evangelistic come-on, but the very heart of the matter?

Is it sheer idealism to think that the church of the Crucified One, crucified for the love of the world, is incapable of such depths of caring? Surely it is a matter of trust—not of course in ourselves—to believe that such care is really possible for those who themselves have been the recipients of a care they did not deserve! Surely we may hope for something different from such a community. It is a test of our earnestness to believe that such hope is founded on a firm foundation, of which Jesus Christ is the chief cornerstone.

That hope will not disappoint us. Stewardship is not just another ideal, commendable but impractical. It is a gift that we are given as those who by faith are being delivered from pride and sloth, and who find it in themselves to care for others in proportion to their liberation from neurotic care for self. Stewardship is a way into which we are being initiated by a Spirit stronger than our own bid for preeminence and also our own fear of involvement in the life of the world.

The Spirit is aided by the contextual possibilities and impossibilities by which we are met. There is no future for a Christian church that tries to behave like those who want to own the world. But there is a future for a church which owns the cross, and is prepared to be as rooted in the earth as was the cross of that one who is the prototype and the means of our solidarity with the broken world. There is a future for a Christian minority that can be truly centered in the world because it is centered in the world's Creator and Redeemer. There is a future for a disciple community that does not have an axe to grind or an ideology to guard or an ulterior motive for its services, but can simply be there for humanity, for the earth.

Christians who are committed to a militant form of Christian evangelism will no doubt find this a retreat from faith, an escape into Christian humanism, a loss of missionary zeal, and similar forms of apostasy. Certainly it does involve letting go of mission in the sense in which mission has been largely understood and practiced in Christendom. We could not legitimately play the part of the steward and have something besides caring as our ultimate aim—for instance the conversion of those for whom we cared. But does giving priority to stewardship as our way of being really mean the loss of our mission?

I should say instead that it means gaining it! The loss of a form of mission does not mean the loss of the Christian mission, any more than the loss of a form of the church means the loss of the church. I take it as the essence of Christian reasonableness today to think, in fact, that the only authentic form of mission in which, after such an imperious history as ours, Christians could engage and still be credible, would be a form of mission that emerged out of the kind of solidarity with earth and humankind implied—rather exactly—in this symbol of the steward. We should not fear going in that direction, or assuming that role. If we were able genuinely to establish our care in and for the world, the opportunities to tell about the reason for our care would certainly not diminish.

For real love of the world is a rare thing! And even at its most decadent and cynical, humanity is still made curious by such love. "See how these Christians love one another!" said some of the old pagans of Rome, waiting for the spectacles of the arena. And in a world where love is rare, and where especially unconditional love of the world is rare, is it not conceivable that some would remark, "See how these Christians love the world!"—which would be a much better remark than the one heard on the lips of the old pagans, much nearer to God's own rationale for suffering!

And then would it not happen, sometimes, that this worldly curiosity would pass beyond the casual remark and become a serious question—even perhaps on occasion a question of ultimate concern? "Why? Why, Christians, do you strive for the welfare of this second-rate planet? Why do you seek justice for these wretched oppressed people on the margins of the great world? Why do you give up your shares in profitable multinationals—why all this divesting? Why do you struggle against inequality, starvation, and despair? Why are you expending so much psychic energy in the pursuit of peace? What is peace? Why have you identified yourself with these disappearing species? Why have you put your life into such jeopardy, your mind into such turmoil, your body into such peril? Why do you not simply accept death? Why are you still trying to make hope work? Why, you Christians?"

And then—but mostly not until then—the Christians would tell their story, judiciously, and unpretentiously. Then they would give the reason for their hope. And sometimes, of course, their story would be smiled over, and the word "idealist" might well be whispered, and the polite ones of the world would repeat the line that was once heard on Mars Hill: "Perhaps we shall hear you again sometime on this matter" (Acts 17:32).

But sometimes the story, the reason, and the hope would be like a seed falling on fertile ground. And would this not be mission? And would it not be authentic mission, being the response to a question and not, as so much of what has called itself mission has been, answers to questions nobody asked. Being grounded in participation, in solidarity with the general human and earthly condition and not just another petty ideology vying for the souls of human beings; being attested by life and death and not just in pious words and gestures and rumours of miracles—would it not be mission?

Yes, it would be mission. It would not be enormously successful, probably. It would not conquer the world. It would certainly not convert, baptize, confirm, marry, and bury everybody!

But it would be enough.